The Politics of Staying Put

In the series *Urban Life, Landscape, and Policy*,
edited by Zane L. Miller, David Stradling, and Larry Bennett

Also in this series:

Evrick Brown and Timothy Shortell, eds., *Walking in Cities: Quotidian Mobility as Urban Theory, Method, and Practice*

Michael T. Maly and Heather Dalmage, *Vanishing Eden: White Construction of Memory, Meaning, and Identity in a Racially Changing City*

Harold L. Platt, *Building the Urban Environment: Visions of the Organic City in the United States, Europe, and Latin America*

Kristin M. Szylvian, *The Mutual Housing Experiment: New Deal Communities for the Urban Middle Class*

Kathryn Wilson, *Ethnic Renewal in Philadelphia's Chinatown: Space, Place, and Struggle*

Robert Gioielli, *Environmental Activism and the Urban Crisis: Baltimore, St. Louis, Chicago*

Robert B. Fairbanks, *The War on Slums in the Southwest: Public Housing and Slum Clearance in Texas, Arizona, and New Mexico, 1936–1965*

Carlton Wade Basmajian, *Atlanta Unbound: Enabling Sprawl through Policy and Planning*

Scott Larson, *"Building Like Moses with Jacobs in Mind": Contemporary Planning in New York City*

Gary Rivlin, *Fire on the Prairie: Harold Washington, Chicago Politics, and the Roots of the Obama Presidency*

William Issel, *Church and State in the City: Catholics and Politics in Twentieth-Century San Francisco*

Jerome Hodos, *Second Cities: Globalization and Local Politics in Manchester and Philadelphia*

Julia L. Foulkes, *To the City: Urban Photographs of the New Deal*

William Issel, *For Both Cross and Flag: Catholic Action, Anti-Catholicism, and National Security Politics in World War II San Francisco*

Lisa Hoffman, *Patriotic Professionalism in Urban China: Fostering Talent*

John D. Fairfield, *The Public and Its Possibilities: Triumphs and Tragedies in the American City*

Andrew Hurley, *Beyond Preservation: Using Public History to Revitalize Inner Cities*

Carolyn Gallaher

The Politics of Staying Put

Condo Conversion and Tenant Right-to-Buy in Washington, DC

TEMPLE UNIVERSITY PRESS
Philadelphia • Rome • Tokyo

TEMPLE UNIVERSITY PRESS
Philadelphia, Pennsylvania 19122
www.temple.edu/tempress

Copyright © 2016 by Temple University—Of The Commonwealth System
 of Higher Education
All rights reserved
Published 2016

Library of Congress Cataloging-in-Publication Data

Names: Gallaher, Carolyn, 1969–
Title: The politics of staying put : condo conversion and tenant right-to-
 buy in Washington, DC / Carolyn Gallaher.
Description: Philadelphia : Temple University Press, 2016. | Series: Urban
 life, landscape, and policy | Includes bibliographical references and
 index.
Identifiers: LCCN 2015021860| ISBN 9781439912645 (cloth : alk. paper) |
 ISBN 9781439912652 (pbk. : alk. paper) | ISBN 9781439912669 (e-book)
Subjects: LCSH: Condominiums—Washington (D.C.)—Conversion. | Con-
 dominiums—Conversion—Law and legislation—Washington (D.C.) |
 Landlord and tenant—Washington (D.C.) | Gentrification—Washington
 (D.C.) | Real estate development—Washington (D.C.)
Classification: LCC HD7287.67.U52 W343 2016 | DDC 333.33/8—dc23 LC
 record available at http://lccn.loc.gov/2015021860

♾ The paper used in this publication meets the requirements of the
American National Standard for Information Sciences—Permanence of
Paper for Printed Library Materials, ANSI Z39.48-1992

Printed in the United States of America

9 8 7 6 5 4 3 2 1

Contents

	Acknowledgments	vii
1	Staying Put in the New DC	1
2	From Bullets to Cocktails: A Capital Transformation	33
3	Gentrification and Its Discontents	67
4	The Rental Housing Conversion and Sale Act of 1980	90
5	Sample Conversions and Metrics of Analysis	106
6	Displacement Mitigation and Its Limits	120
7	Markets, Politics, and Other Obstacles to Low-Income Home Ownership	158
8	"95/5": The TOPA Sidestep	181
9	Is TOPA the Politics of Staying Put We Want?	209
	Appendix 1: Glossary of Terms	231
	Appendix 2: A Short Primer on Condominiums	233
	Appendix 3: Interviews	239
	References	241
	Index	259

Acknowledgments

This book wouldn't exist without the tenant leaders who have over the years made the Tenant Opportunity to Purchase Act (TOPA) a reality in Washington, DC. Specifically, I could not have written this book without the input of ten tenant leaders who helped me piece together how the TOPA process works, what it does and does not accomplish, and who it does and does not help. Afifa, Cajia, Cathy, David, Genevieve, "John," "Lawrence," Matthew, Shirley, and Stephen were generous with their time and more than patient with my sometimes obtuse questions.

I came away from my research with a deep appreciation for the hard work these and all tenant leaders do. Being a tenant leader is often a thankless job. Although the tenants in a building up for sale must collectively reject a contracted sale and purchase the building instead, most of the work is shouldered by a small group of people in each property—the tenants' association. All the tenant leaders I spoke to described the process as akin to having a second job, albeit one without pay *and* with substantial risks, including potential intimidation by landlords and threats of lawsuits.

Tenant leaders' work is also complicated by the various things that can divide the people who share a landlord and very little else. In DC, race and class divides are long-standing, and as the city becomes whiter and wealthier—as Chocolate City gives way to something else—these divides have been amplified. Demographic differences aren't as trenchant, but they can sow divisions as well. As tenants negotiate whether to convert to condo or remain rental, they often find that their elderly, middle-aged, and young residents want different things.

Anonymity is still another barrier. Neighbors in DC apartment buildings often don't know one another or never get past a polite hello in the hallway. During my second year in DC, I lived in an apartment without ever seeing my next-door neighbor. Our doors were literally inches apart, but I could not tell you whether my neighbor was male or female, let alone any of her or his identifying features. Getting dozens or even hundreds of strangers to make a collective decision is no mean feat.

I am also grateful to the experts I interviewed for this project—three attorneys who represent tenants going through the TOPA process (Eric Rome, Blake Biles, and Rick Eisen) and one nonprofit developer who has helped low-income tenants convert their buildings (George Rothman). They put me in touch with tenant leaders, explained complicated land deals, and clarified legal minutiae for me. I could not have done this book without them. And like the tenant leaders I interviewed, they were generous and patient with me.

Two local columnists/bloggers—Clinton Yates and Dan Silverman—were also exceptionally helpful and gracious with their time. Clinton, who grew up in DC, helped me understand what DC was like before gentrification arrived and how longtime residents interpret gentrification. Dan helped me understand how new arrivals to the city see its changes and their part in them.

I must also thank my DC reading group. Until I began research for this book, all my research had been on the politics of irregular armed forces. Luckily, just as I decided to study TOPA, a former student, Jamie Winders, put me in contact with one of her students, Katie Wells, who was moving to town and wanted to connect with other geographers in the area. When I contacted Katie, I discovered that she did research on DC and had recently started a DC reading group. Katie invited me to join, and I soon met a wonderful group of academics working on DC. Along with Katie, Amanda Huron, Brett Williams, Derek Musgrove, Johanna Bockman, Kathryn Howell, and Susan Bennett shared their work, gave me great feedback on mine, and happily debated the meaning and implications of DC's rapid gentrification with me. Most important, they never made me feel out of my depth or crazy for wanting to study a topic in which I had no background. In fact, quite the opposite was true. I felt immediately welcome, and I remain immensely grateful for it.

I also thank Temple University Press for giving me and my book a chance. Temple is a storied urban press, so I was over the moon when Aaron Javsicas told me he wanted to send my manuscript out for review. He has been unfailingly supportive through the entire process, and he selected two anonymous reviewers who gave me excellent feedback. The marketing and production people (Kate Nichols, Sara Jo Cohen, Gary Kramer, Rebecca Logan, and Cynthia Lindlof) have also been a joy to work with—everything an author could ask for from a press. I also thank Larry Bennett for agreeing to consider my book for the Urban Life, Landscape, and Policy series he edits at Temple. He gave my manuscript a thorough read (twice!) and pushed me to improve it, even when I was tired of working on it. As a midcareer academic, I've found that it is rare to get such detailed, thoughtful, and useful feedback on a manuscript. I can't thank him enough for taking the time and care that he did with my work. I know that he ultimately made this a much better book. I also owe gratitude to my student Juanita Taylor, who read my manuscript twice and gave me invaluable insider advice as the granddaughter of a DC native. Juanita also brought her place-based expertise to the index, which she put together in a thorough and timely manner.

Finally, I would be remiss if I didn't acknowledge that my decision to study TOPA was born of personal experience. In 2001, my landlord sold the property where I was living, and I soon found myself in the midst of a TOPA process. I had never lived in a tenant-friendly city before I moved to DC, so the idea that a city law would help me buy my apartment seemed like a stroke of extraordinary good fortune. Although I was not a tenant leader, I followed our two-year process closely, not only because I'm innately curious but also because I knew it was going to turn my life upside down (albeit for the good).

In fact, TOPA is the reason I am now fascinated with a city I once struggled to like or feel connected to. Intellectually, I knew DC was special. It had a European feel, a lot of free museums, and the federal government in my backyard. But it felt cold to me. I moved to DC for my first professional job, and though my colleagues were lovely, most of us were in different stages of life. They had young or even adult kids; I was single and on my own. I struggled to find a peer group.

After two years, I decided to get a dog. It took a while, but I finally found a dog-friendly apartment, and a year later I adopted a dog from the shelter on New York Avenue. I named him Coltrane. He was fluffy and manic and all mine. And he opened doors I could never have opened on my own. My landlord owned an empty lot behind the alley off our property, and he allowed his tenants to exercise their dogs there. We called it the dog park, even though there wasn't much that was parklike about it. I didn't care about the aesthetics, though, because I started feeling connected. Slowly, I learned the names of my neighbors' dogs. Eventually, I learned the owners' names as well. Then we got to know each other, to have dinner out, to go for a drink, to dog-sit for one another, or to shoot the breeze on the front stoop. The dog owners were a small portion of the total residents on the property, but it was heaven compared to my former building, where the only people I knew were my roommate, the super, and the building's maintenance guru.

Those connections in the dog park would prove useful when our landlord decided to sell the property to the National Cathedral, our neighbor across the street. Although the cathedral never shared its intentions publicly, rumor had it that it wanted to tear down our buildings and replace them with a visitors' center. Fortunately, three of the four tenants who formed our tenants' association knew each other because they were dog owners. As soon as they saw the sales notice, they reached out to one another. Soon after, they called a meeting. Then they started researching the TOPA statute and the rights it gave us. Two years later, our tenants' association bought the building and converted to condo. We saved our homes. And we did so just as the city's property market was taking off and fast becoming unaffordable.

If I'm honest, though, the best thing that TOPA gave me wasn't a one-bedroom condo but a sense of belonging. After I bought my unit, I felt like I lived in a small town (warts and all) that had the amenities of a big city. I'd found my place. It was the place I would meet my husband, Ever Guandique, and where I would have our son, Wesley. The three of us and Coltrane—it was home. TOPA helped me create that home.

TOPA doesn't work for everyone—a fact I document in detail throughout this book. But its promise—being able to stay put and forge community—is remarkable among cities in the United States. That promise is something we can and should improve on.

The Politics of Staying Put

1

Staying Put in the New DC

"We were very afraid." —Shirley Lawson, tenant leader at Mayfair Mansions, describing her reaction to the news her apartment building had been contracted for sale

A Unique Way to Stay Put

This book is about the effort to stay put in a fast-gentrifying city. There are, of course, different ways to stay put. Some people make compromises—they stay in apartments they have outgrown (through marriage or kids) because they are near public transportation or work. Others resort to the court system to fight intimidation from landlords trying to force them out. Still others rely on government intervention to stay put, using housing vouchers to afford out-of-reach rents or winning leases in units set aside by city ordinance for those with low incomes.

This book focuses on a formal, city-sponsored initiative to help people stay put, a law in the District of Columbia (DC) that allows tenants in apartment buildings contracted for sale the right to refuse the sale and purchase the building instead for the contracted sale price. The law, the District's Tenant Opportunity to Purchase Act (TOPA), was initially passed in 1980 in response to a spate of condo conversions then occurring in Washington's gentrifying inner core (Proscio 2012; R. Eisen 1993; Grim 2006a, 2006b). Its goal was to prevent displacement by allowing tenants to become owners in a two-step process—first, by having the tenants' association purchase the property and, second, by converting the property to a condominium or cooperative so tenants could buy their existing units (R. Eisen 1993).

Condos have long been a flash point in battles over gentrification. They are usually seen as gentrification's leading edge, the manifestation of public and private efforts to spur urban reinvestment (Kern 2010; Kern and Wekerle 2008; Gotham 2005). And because condos are often built for, and marketed to, well-paid professionals, they are seen as a harbinger of displacement to come (Fujitsuka 2005; Gotham 2005).

Opinions about condo conversion are less common but similar in tone where they exist (N. Smith 1996; Feagin and Parker 2002; Slater 2010). Scholars complain, for example, that condo conversion reduces the rental housing stock on which the poor and working class depend (Feagin and Parker 2002; Fine 1980). The late renowned geographer Neil Smith (1996) once identified condo conversion as a process elites employ to "take back" cities from the poor and working class so that they can be used by the wealthy for their own housing, leisure, and investment.

Given this context, TOPA is somewhat remarkable. It uses a process—condo conversion—to help those usually harmed by it. Perhaps not surprisingly, given the unusual marriage of who is helped (tenants) and how they are helped (condo conversion), TOPA presents all sorts of interesting contradictions. This book examines these incongruities empirically and theoretically.

Empirically, it examines the degree to which TOPA does what it is meant to do—mitigate displacement. It analyzes seven tenants' associations that attempted to purchase their buildings, tracking their level of success and, where applicable, highlighting practices surrounding the law that work at cross purposes to its stated goal. It also looks at a shadow case to put these results into wider relief. Specifically, the case follows the legal fallout that ensued after a local landlord sold eleven of his properties without alerting his tenants of their right to refuse the sale (these so-called TOPA notices are required under the statute[1]). This case highlights external constraints that can limit TOPA's effectiveness.

While these findings are specific to DC, they are relevant for other cities as well. A number of municipalities and states regulate condo conversions in tenant-friendly ways. In the late eighties Bernard Keenan (1987) estimated that nearly 50 percent of states regulated condo conversions to help tenants

---

1. The formal name for a TOPA notice is an "offer of sale notice." The city's Department of Housing and Community Development (DHCD) provides a standardized "offer of sale" form that may be customized by landlords to account for property-specific details (e.g., total number of units, contracted buyer, etc.).

subject to displacement. Some municipalities required landlords to pay the moving costs of affected tenants. Others placed caps on how many apartment buildings may convert to condominium per year. Since then, cities have continued to regulate conversions in tenant-friendly ways. In 2013, for example, the San Francisco City Council placed a ten-year moratorium on condo conversions in exchange for permitting a backlog of two thousand tenancy-in-common home owners the right to convert (Jones 2013).[2]

Unfortunately, the relative success or failure of most programs has never been evaluated. As a result, localities considering enacting or strengthening the regulation of condo conversion in tenant-friendly ways have few studies to consult as they consider their options. Moreover, though DC's TOPA program has been evaluated, most studies are dated (Lauber 1984; J. Eisen 1979; Harrison Institute for Public Law 2006) or focused on narrower elements of the program (Howell 2013; Huron 2012; Diamond 2013). Given that DC's program is routinely described as one of the most tenant-friendly laws in the country,[3] a comprehensive analysis of what does and does not work about it is in order. Such an analysis can also be of use to other, fast-gentrifying cities.

Theoretically, this book is meant to nuance how we understand the role of condo conversion in the gentrification process. Unfortunately, there is no cohesive literature on condo conversion. Most of the work is in the field of law and focuses on specific statutes and legal issues pertaining to condo conversions rather than how they fit into wider processes of urban change (Keenan 1987; Chabot 2008; Kahan, Leshem, and Sundaram 2012). Social scientists have examined condo conversion only sporadically (van Weesep 1984; Hamnett and Randolph 1988; Hamnett and Whitelegg 2007; Huron 2012; Diamond 2013). As a result, much of what we know about condo conversion is largely anecdotal or based on empirically untested theoretical assumptions. Condo conversion is often treated as a singular phenomenon where tenants are always on the losing end of the bargain (for exceptions, see Howell 2013 and Huron 2012). However, the presence of tenant-friendly conversion mechanisms demonstrates that condo conversion can unfold in various, sometimes unexpected ways. Indeed, the fact that TOPA was designed to protect in situ tenants suggests that tenants do not always have to be on the losing end of urban reinvestment.

Before highlighting these contributions in more detail, however, it is worth considering how DC came to need a displacement mitigation strategy.

---

2. San Francisco used to run a conversion lottery that permitted up to two hundred conversions per year. Given the pace of conversions prior to the 2013 law, the moratorium was seen as a clear win for tenants (Jones 2013).
3. Although they agree on little else, TOPA's advocates (Lazere and Pohlman 2008) and opponents (Gelman 2010) tend to agree that TOPA is one of the most pro-tenant laws in the country.

Although the city experienced a round of gentrification in the early 1980s, disinvestment was the norm for the two decades that followed. And though DC's changing fortunes are broadly consistent with those in other gentrifying cities, its story is (as every city's is) uniquely its own (for information on New York, see Osman 2012, DeSena 2009, and Freeman 2011; on San Francisco, see Beitel 2013; on New Orleans, see Crutcher 2010; on Chicago, see Bennett 2010 and Hyra 2008; and on Mexico City, see Walker 2008).

Urban Rock Bottom

In 1998, the year I moved to DC, the city was not far from rock bottom. Three years earlier Congress had enacted the District of Columbia Financial Responsibility and Management Assistance Act, which put the city under the control of a presidentially appointed panel called "the authority." Although most city residents referred to the panel with a more mundane moniker—"the control board"—the Orwellian-sounding name for the panel fit its scope of power (Barras 1998). The authority had ultimate power over the city's budget and legislative process. Though the mayor was still tasked with drawing up an annual budget, the control board had to give its final stamp of approval before it could be implemented. The control board also had the power to block any legislation it believed would negatively affect city finances.

The Orwellian nature of the bill notwithstanding, the city's finances were truly in shambles and had been for some time (Barras 1998). Like many U.S. cities at the time, the District had experienced decades of population loss, as middle-class citizens of all races headed for the suburbs. The city reached its population zenith in 1950, when 802,178 people resided within its borders; by 2000 the population had declined by nearly 29 percent to 572,059 (Gibson and Jung 2005; Benfield 2013). Not surprisingly, the city's tax base took a beating in the process.

Declining population and the flight of investment that followed were hard on the city. Poverty increased and so did crime (Gillette 2006). The city felt obligated to increase spending, especially on social programs. And to offset persistent unemployment, the city created thousands of jobs in its bureaucracy (Loeb 1998). The goal was to buttress the city's middle class,[4] although critics argued that the result was to make the city "an employer of last resort" (Fisher 2011, B1). The numbers bear out the trend. In 1980, the city payroll included just over forty-four thousand workers (Robinson 1981).

---

4. Although the idea of beefing up city bureaucracies to stave off middle-class flight is derided today, the idea had traction in academic and policy circles in the early and mid-seventies (see Harrison and Osterman 1974).

By 1990 that number had grown to nearly fifty thousand, even though the city's population had declined during the same period (Walters 2002).

By the late 1980s, the city's finances were in dire straits, and its bureaucracy seemed inept despite all the resources poured into it. City leaders appeared unable or unwilling to deal with the city's problems. Things came to a symbolic head in January 1987 during a pair of back-to-back snowstorms (Loeb 1998). Roads went unshoveled for days, and the city's subway—the Metro—had only sporadic service because its third rail was not properly weatherized. Residents and commuters from Virginia and Maryland struggled to get to work, with some journeys taking several hours. Complaints poured into city offices. Mayor Marion Barry, who was on a Super Bowl vacation in California at the time, offered a dismissive response, telling reporters that "it doesn't snow here very often" (McGrory 1987, A2).

More substantive signs of trouble were not far behind. A three-part series in the *Washington Post* two years later found that city leaders were dealing with cash shortages by illegally transferring funds between government agencies to meet immediate needs as well as purposefully underestimating spending (Abramowitz and Greene 1989). A U.S. Government Accountability Office (GAO) audit of the city in 1994 found a similar pattern under the mayorship of Sharon Pratt Kelly, accusing the city of using accounting gimmicks such as "deferrals" and "optimistic assumptions" to balance its budget (*Financial Status* 1994, 2). By the time the city approached Congress for help in 1995, it found an unsympathetic audience. The new Republican majority's response was the opposite of what the city had requested. Instead of granting a bailout, Congress imposed an austerity program on the city.

The city's bleak financial condition was mirrored on the streets. A crack epidemic had torn through the city in the mid- to late 1980s, shredding a social fabric already frayed by poverty and limited opportunity (Lusane 1999; Waller 2000). Addiction strained and eventually tore apart many families. Battles over turf for lucrative open-air drug markets across the city left residents feeling like they were living in a war zone. For five consecutive years (1989–1993) the city recorded annual homicide figures above four hundred. In 1990 and 1991, DC recorded more homicides per capita than any other city in the country, earning it the dubious title of the nation's murder capital (Weil and Escobar 1991).

Flash forward to the present. The control board, which wrapped up its work in 2001, is a distant memory. City finances are in good shape despite the 2008 recession. And for the first time in sixty years the city is growing again. In 2010 the city recorded a net increase of nearly thirty thousand residents (Morello and Keating 2010), and new residents keep pouring in. In the first twenty-seven months after the 2010 census was taken, the Census Bureau estimates an additional thirty thousand new residents moved to the city (DeBonis 2012a). Violent crime is down as well. In 2013 the city recorded 104 murders—a 75 percent reduction from the murder capital years (Metropolitan Police Department 2013).

Change on the Landscape

In DC there is no better place to see the changes that have swept the city than in the U Street and Columbia Heights neighborhoods.[5] In 1998 I took a day off from work to photograph these and other city neighborhoods. I was teaching an introduction to human geography course, and I thought it would be nice to use pictures from DC for an upcoming module on urban geography. My goal was to help students visualize the city's stark socioeconomic divide, and these neighborhoods provided a good contrast to the tony area where my university was located.

I started my journey on Wisconsin Avenue, near my university, traveling south toward the Georgetown neighborhood (Figure 1.1). Once there I parked and started taking pictures of its high-end boutiques and picturesque side streets. These photos, I thought, would help my students see what a fully gentrified neighborhood looked like. Although there was little obvious evidence left of it on the landscape, Georgetown had a sizable working-class black population (approximately 30 percent) as recently as the 1940s (Lesko, Babb, and Gibbs 1991).

I returned to my car and headed east on P Street. I crossed Rock Creek Park and found myself just north of downtown. In DC poverty tends to increase as you move from west to east, and historically, Rock Creek Park was a point of demarcation between the city's haves and have-nots. As I maneuvered through the southern end of Dupont Circle, tidy, compact row houses gave way to empty lots, liquor stores, and undefined buildings.

As I crossed 15th Street, I saw a run-down grocery store, the Food Rite Metro Supermarket (Figure 1.2), and parked the car. I was unsure Food Rite was actually a grocery store, but if it was, I wanted a picture. I remembered what an urban geography professor had told me years before. Inner-city neighborhoods often have a dearth of grocery stores, and the ones they do have are not much to look at. I suspected few of my students knew what an inner-city grocery store looked like, and Food Rite fit the bill. Despite the sign, the front of the building looked like a warehouse, with loading docks facing the street. I had to search for the entrance, tucked off to the side of the

---

5. U Street is technically the commercial strip of the Shaw neighborhood. However, the names "U Street corridor" and "Shaw" are often used interchangeably. I use the term "U Street" because it is more recognizable to people outside DC. However, my discussion of changes here refers to the Shaw neighborhood as a whole.

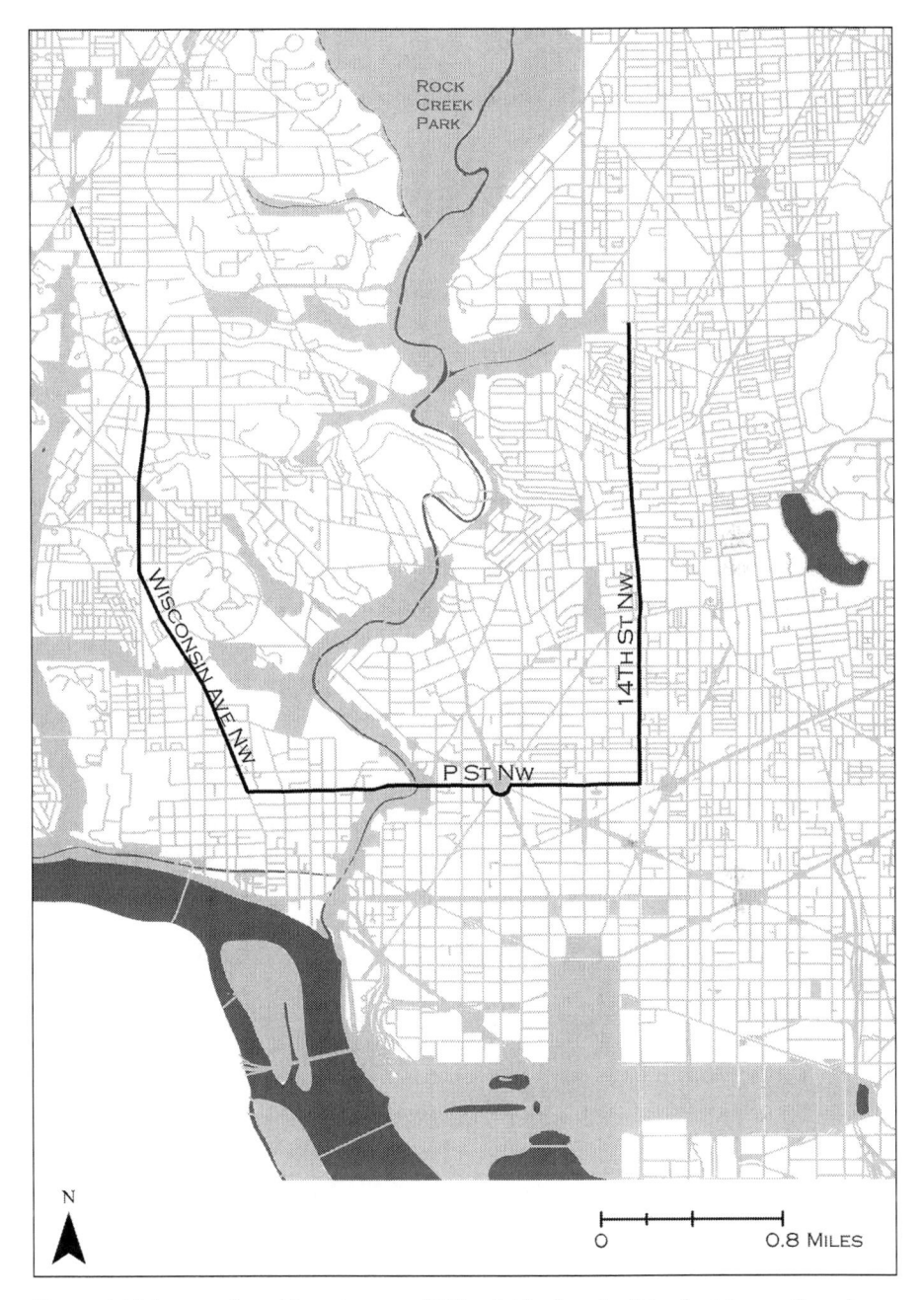

Figure 1.1 My route for taking pictures of DC neighborhoods. (Map by Meagan Snow.)

Figure 1.2 Food Rite Metro Supermarket, near the corner of 14th Street and P Street NW in Washington, DC, autumn 1998. (Photo by the author.)

building. Across the street stood a liquor store with black metal grating over the door. The sign above the door—"Liquor"—was no-nonsense (Figure 1.3).

After snapping a few shots, I got back in my car and turned left onto 14th Street. I saw the classic signs of what sociologists and geographers call the "zone in transition."[6] The term describes the area between downtown and the first residential neighborhood in most cities. Usually, these areas have an eclectic mix of low-rent activities. A beat-up storefront sign had a simple message: "Free Evangelistic Church, Founder, Pastor Theresa" (Figure 1.4). Farther up the street, on the east side, a used-car lot announced a sale. A few cars and a truck sat behind a fence with barbed wire along the top (Figure 1.5).

Soon, I reached the intersection of 14th and U. At the time I had no idea how important this intersection was in the city's history. During the Jim Crow era, the intersection was in the middle of the city's black downtown, a thriving retail and cultural center (Ruble 2012; Gillette 2006). The city's black middle class came here to shop, eat, and dance. Jazz greats like Duke Ellington and Cab Calloway used to play in the area's live-music venues, and

---

6. The zone in transition was first described by the so-called Chicago School of Urban Studies (see Park, Burgess, and McKenzie 1925).

Figure 1.3 Liquor store near the corner of 14th Street and P Street NW in Washington, DC, autumn 1998. (Photo by the author.)

go-go greats like Chuck Brown got their start there.[7] During the civil rights era it would become a flash point for social unrest. After Martin Luther King Jr. was assassinated in 1968, riots broke out in cities across the country. In DC, some of the worst rioting occurred at the intersection of 14th and U Streets. Things got so bad that President Lyndon B. Johnson called in National Guard troops to restore order (Figure 1.6).

When I got to the intersection that day in 1998, I did not know any of this history. Even if I had, it would have been easier to point to the legacy of rioting than to the rich heritage that preceded it. A modern-looking glass-fronted municipal building gleamed in the sun on the northwest corner, an effort, I later discovered, to spur rebuilding in the area, but the building on the opposite corner sat vacant, with strips of paper littering the windows. Vacant storefronts dominated the street I could see from my car.

---

7. Go-go is a musical genre born in DC that blends elements of funk, rhythm and blues, and soul. Go-go music is energetic, danceable, *and* political. Writer Natalie Hopkinson argues, for example, that go-go was not only "the beating heart of the Chocolate City" but also a "metaphor for the black urban experience in the second half of the twentieth century" (2012, 2). Although go-go music remains a largely local genre of music, some of its songs have received a national audience, including "Bustin' Loose" by Chuck Brown and the Soul Searchers (1978) and "Da Butt" by Experience Unlimited (E.U.; 1988).

Figure 1.4 An advertisement for a storefront church on 14th Street NW in Washington, DC, autumn 1998. (Photo by the author.)

Figure 1.5 Used-car lot on 14th Street NW in Washington, DC, autumn 1998. (Photo by the author.)

Figure 1.6 National Guard troops in DC after Martin Luther King assassination riots, 1968. (Photo by Warren K. Leffler. Courtesy of the Library of Congress Prints and Photographs Division.)

I kept driving, heading up a fairly steep hill. At the top I found myself in Columbia Heights. The street was wide, and I was clearly in a retail corridor, but things looked empty. On the east side of the street I saw an old theater with the sign still on top—Tivoli Theatre. From the looks of it, there had not been a production in Tivoli's hall for quite some time. The streetscape was just as bleak on the west side.

Since I first made my trek in 1998, the U Street and Columbia Heights neighborhoods have been radically transformed. The Food Rite Metro Supermarket has vanished. The block on which it sat has been turned into a mixed-used development with apartments and street-level retail (Figure 1.7). Across the street from its former location is a new Whole Foods Market, an upscale grocery chain (Figure 1.8). The liquor store across the street from Food Rite still remains, but the metal grating on the windows has disappeared and a yoga studio has moved in next door (Figure 1.9).

The corner of U and 14th is also thriving. The retail space across from the municipal center now has a tenant, as do many of the formerly empty buildings along the street. New apartment buildings line the main drag, and new condos and refurbished row houses grace side streets. Things are just as bright in Columbia Heights. A few years after I first drove along its business corridor, the city announced the arrival of big-box retailer Target

Figure 1.7 New mixed-use development on P Street NW between 15th Street and 14th Street NW in Washington, DC—the site of the old Food Rite Metro Supermarket—spring 2014. (Photo by the author.)

Figure 1.8 Whole Foods, an upscale grocery chain, opened on the same block of P Street NW as the Food Rite Metro Supermarket, spring 2014. (Photo by the author.)

Figure 1.9 The P Street liquor store post-gentrification, spring 2014. (Photo by the author.)

(Figure 1.10). The space, which includes several other retail chains, also sits across the street from a new mixed-use development. And a block north, the Tivoli Theatre was redeveloped with a small theater and several restaurants and bars.

Placing the Changes

Although this book is about displacement mitigation, it can be understood only in the wider context in which it becomes necessary—gentrification. There are often heated debates about how to define gentrification and, by extension, what does and does not count as an example of it, but I use a simple definition here. Gentrification is the process by which a working-class or poor neighborhood is converted into a middle- or even upper-class area (Hackworth 2002; Lees, Slater, and Wyly 2008; Slater 2010).

Figure 1.10 Big-box retailers come to Columbia Heights in Washington, DC, spring 2014. (Photo by the author.)

As the quick then-and-now photo tour here suggests, gentrification leaves a substantial visual trace—you can literally see it as you walk down the street. An old house gets a new roof and a fresh coat of paint. A vacant storefront finally gets a tenant. A red-light business disappears, and a higher-end one takes its place. A new building pops up with a sign announcing "luxury condominiums for sale." Streetlights are built, or repaired, and the local bus stop gets a covered waiting area. In isolation, none of these changes constitutes gentrification. However, when they occur near one another, and in roughly the same time frame, you have gentrification.

You can also feel the impact of gentrification on your wallet. Not only do rents and home prices rise; the costs of everyday items like groceries do as well. Before the Food Rite store on P Street closed down, the *Washington City Paper* asked its longtime customers what they thought about the new Whole Foods store across the street. One customer was shocked at how little she could buy there. "Me and my husband go to buy groceries over there and come out, easily—without meat included—and it's, like, $60" (Flores 2001).

Scholars usually see contemporary gentrification as part and parcel of a wider political-economic process known as neoliberalism, which began in the early 1970s. Neoliberalism is often described as an ideological rebuttal to Keynesianism (Harvey 2005).[8] Unlike Keynesians, who argued that the state should intervene in markets to ensure particular outcomes, neoliberals contend that societal needs are best met through a free market in which state involvement is minimal (Harvey 2005).[9] Indeed, neoliberal ideology rejects the idea that the state should intervene on behalf of groups on the losing end of capitalist competition, such as the urban poor, minorities, or even particular industries. Neoliberals believe that state intervention on behalf of such groups creates a dependency that in its own right amounts to a form of oppression (Hayek 1944).

To be fair (and clear), scholars do not believe that neoliberalism caused gentrification, at least in the first instance. Rather, they see gentrification as the eventual by-product of suburbanization, a process that began after World War II well before the advent of neoliberalism (N. Smith 1979; DeFilippis 2004). As James DeFilippis explains, "Long-term disinvestment in inner-city areas created the potential for profitable reinvestment in some of those very same disinvested areas" (2004, 88). However, most scholars agree that the advent of neoliberalism ushered in a set of economic and political practices that were ideal for gentrification to occur.

On the economic front, the rise of the so-called FIRE sector (Finance, Insurance, and Real Estate) during the 1980s facilitated the integration of property and financial markets. Housing stopped being a fixed asset with small, if steady gains and instead became something on which to speculate (Shiller 2008; Gramlich 2008). Financial deregulation in the mortgage industry, which began in the 1980s and accelerated in the 1990s, also meant that people formerly kept out of the housing market could now enter it (Holt 2009; Wyly and Hammel 2001). The influx of potential new customers provided an incentive for developers to build and banks to fund their projects. In this context, the disinvested inner city became ripe for redevelopment.

It is also worth noting that the postwar disinvestment in cities primed their leaders to accept neoliberalism in the 1990s. After years of population decline and shrinking tax bases, cities were desperate for reinvestment. Most knew they could no longer rely on the federal government to fill budget gaps caused by disinvestment. In the 1980s Ronald Reagan engineered a

---

8. Although neoliberal ideas were in circulation in the mid-1940s, the crisis of Keynesianism in the late 1970s afforded an opening for advocates of neoliberalism (Peck, Theodore, and Brenner 2009). The crisis of Keynesianism is often attributed to a declining rate of profit, which in turn put social spending into question (Lipietz 1992).
9. Most neoliberals believe that the state should confine itself to defending property rights and ensuring national security (see Harvey 2005 for an overview).

number of cuts to federal assistance for cities, and the drawdown continued under George H. W. Bush (a Republican) and Bill Clinton (a Democrat), a signal that cities could not wait for a party change to rebuild their budgets. In short, city governments were forced to adopt what David Harvey calls "urban entrepreneurialism," slashing social services they could not afford without federal assistance and actively courting developers by offering them tax incentives and agreeing to assume some of their risk (1989, 4).[10]

Although gentrification stems from macroeconomic processes, it could not have happened without the participation of individuals who decided to move into disinvested or transitioning urban neighborhoods. And though there is no such thing as a prototypical gentrifier, commentators often define them that way. In the 1980s, for example, it was common to hear gentrifiers referred to as "urban pioneers" (N. Smith 1996). The term is still in use today (Broadwater 2011; Gratz 2010). At times the "pioneer" label has been used with admiration. Urban pioneers are applauded for taking a chance on the city. Subjecting themselves to an unwelcome, difficult environment (high crime, hostility from longtime residents, incompetent city bureaucrats), urban pioneers are seen to risk their own comfort to bring life back to the city (Gratz 2010). In other tellings, urban pioneers are seen as interlopers and castigated for displacing existing residents. As Neil Smith explains, "The idea of urban pioneers is as insulting applied to contemporary cities as the original idea of 'pioneers' in the US West. Now as then, it implies that no one lives in the areas being pioneered—no one worthy of notice, at least" (1996, 30).

Individual gentrifiers have also been described as members of the so-called creative class. Richard Florida first coined this term in 2002 to describe what he deemed a "new social class." "If you are a scientist or an engineer, an architect or designer, a writer, artist, or musician, or if you use your creativity as a key factor in your work in business, education, health care, law, or some other profession, you are a member" (2002, ix). Florida argued that the creative class is flocking to cities, which should do everything in their power to encourage them. Unlike previous epochs, during which workers were expected to move where the jobs were, businesses now follow highly skilled workers. Cities that embrace the creative class will see urban reinvestment. Those that fail to embrace it face stagnation (for a critique of the "creative class" concept, see Peck 2005 and Leslie and Catungal 2012).

More recently, individual gentrifiers have been described in demographic terms. In DC, for example, the term "gentrifier" is often used synonymously with the word "millennial," the label given to people born in the 1980s and early 1990s. A recent article in the *Washington Post Magazine* about the

---

10. For an extended analysis, also see Peter Eisinger's (1988) book *The Rise of the Entrepreneurial State*.

city's changing fortunes notes that nearly all of the city's growth between 2000 and 2010 consisted of people in this age bracket, observing that this is "Washington's millennials moment" (Chang et al. 2013, 14).

Dealing with the Changes

Although no one likes urban disinvestment, especially those forced to live through it, the problem with urban reinvestment is that it often results in displacement (N. Smith 1996; Feagin and Parker 2002; DeFilippis 2004; Slater 2006, 2009). In DC displacement happens in multiple ways. A *Washington Post* series in 2008, for example, identified hundreds of cases of landlords trying to empty buildings so they could sell them to developers (Cenziper and Cohen 2008). They turned off the heat, refused to repair leaking pipes, and failed to treat vermin infestations. Some even tried to get tenants to leave by sending them threatening letters.

Displacement can also happen when property taxes go up (Fujitsuka 2005). New development often leads to increased property taxes, leaving home owners on fixed incomes struggling to make higher payments. In DC when home owners fall behind on their taxes, the city places liens on their properties and then sells the liens to debt collectors. A recent *Washington Post* investigation discovered that a majority of the city's tax liens were sold to one company, Aeon Financial, which aggressively pursued collection by charging exorbitant fees and threatening foreclosure to settle debts (Cenziper, Sallah, and Rich 2013). Between 2005 and 2010, nine hundred homes were threatened with foreclosure proceedings by Aeon.[11] Often targeted were elderly residents who owned their homes outright and whose original tax bills were usually less than $2,000 (Sallah and Cenziper 2013).

Displacement can also happen after a child is born. It is not unusual for renters with new children to look for larger apartments. In many cities, however, renting a two-bedroom apartment is out of reach for people in lower income brackets. In DC a family needs to earn at least $60,240 a year to afford a two-bedroom apartment at fair-market rent. According to the National Low Income Housing Coalition (2012), a low-income renter in DC would have to work 3.5 full-time, minimum-wage jobs to meet that threshold. Although some families stick it out in one-bedroom apartments—sleeping on the couch and filling every spare corner with storage—many move to suburban locations where rents per square foot are cheaper. In short, whether the

---

11. Since 2005, tax lien debt collectors have foreclosed on 509 homes. There are, however, 1,598 cases pending (Sallah, Cenziper, and Rich 2013). After the *Washington Post* investigation, the city canceled all tax lien sales for the year (2013), and the city council started working on legislation to curb such abuses (DeBonis, Sallah, and Cenziper 2013).

issue is an unscrupulous landlord, a property tax hike, or cramped sleeping quarters, many people living in fast-gentrifying cities find that their only option is to leave.

We also cannot look at displacement without acknowledging the cultural interpretations that surround it. As noted previously, DC is getting wealthier, which comes with a cost to minorities that is often downplayed if not outright ignored. When DC mayor Marion Barry pinched Parliament's 1985 album title *Chocolate City* and made it his own, he did so affectionately. For Barry's peers who came up during the civil rights era, the nickname suggested DC was a haven, a place where black people could control their destiny despite their minority status. It was also, at times, a rhetorical cudgel, a signal to DC's then-white political elite that their time at the helm had passed (Barras 1998). By 2011, however, Parliament's ode to DC no longer applied. That year, the census announced that African Americans accounted for less than 50 percent of city residents, down from a high of just over 70 percent in 1970 (Morello and Keating 2010; Tavernise 2011). That shift is painful for many of DC's black residents—a symbol that the safe spot, and the dream it afforded, is lost (Prince 2014; Crockett 2012a, 2012b).

In this context, staying put is often a political act. It is a process of staking a claim to the city, and a home within it, even if one does not own that home. It is a recognition that people have ties to the city that are more than economic—they are familial, cultural, and emotional—and that these connections should count for something when gentrification arrives. Chester Hartman argues, for example, that tenants should have a "right to stay put," that there should be "a kind of tenure guarantee for those who do not own their own homes" (1984, 306). Unfortunately, a right to stay put is easier to assert than achieve, especially in the context of gentrification. The sacrosanct nature of private property in the United States means that landlords of multifamily housing can usually convert their buildings to condominium with little concern for what existing tenants want.

DC is a notable exception. In 1980 the city created TOPA, a legal mechanism for tenants hoping to stay put. Although TOPA is the focus of this book, it is actually part of a wider statute, the Rental Housing Conversion and Sale Act (RHCSA). RHCSA contains two parts, both of which are designed to regulate condo conversion in tenant-friendly ways. The first part, the Conversion of Rental Housing to Condominium or Cooperative (CRHCC), allows landlords to convert their buildings to condo only if more than 50 percent of tenants vote for conversion in a city-administered election. The second, TOPA, gives tenants' associations in residential properties for sale the right to buy their buildings and, if contracted sales have already been arranged, the right to refuse the sales (the so-called right of first refusal) and purchase the properties instead for the same price.

The statute also allows tenants to assign their TOPA rights to a third party to assist with financing. Most tenants' associations cannot afford to purchase their buildings outright, and few banks will extend credit to groups with no business experience. As a result, most tenants' associations seek the assistance of developers (for- and nonprofit) to help with financing. Low-income tenants usually work with nonprofits and are eligible for city assistance, such as short-term loans to cover the cost of conversion or grants to help low-income tenants afford purchase. Middle-income tenants usually work with for-profit developers and engage in "horse trading" to win concessions. Tenants, for example, typically give a developer the right to offer buyouts to incumbent tenants in exchange for insider (i.e., below-market) prices for those staying put. Bought-out units are then usually sold at market rates (see Appendix 1 for a glossary of TOPA-related terms).

While TOPA is often viewed from the outside as a mechanism for fostering home ownership, the city's tenants have also used the right of first refusal to select third parties willing to buy their buildings and keep them rental. Buyouts are common in these cases as well. Indeed, tenants who want their buildings to stay rental still need something to entice developer assistance, and the right to offer buyouts usually suffices since DC law allows landlords to increase rents at slightly higher-than-allowed rates in units where leases are terminated early (Department of Housing and Community Development 2013).

The city council introduced TOPA in response to a boom in condo conversion in the city's inner core (J. Eisen 1979; Robinson 1981; Grim 2006a, 2006b). And its sponsors cited "discourag[ing] the displacement of tenants through conversion or sale of rental property" as the bill's primary objective (Rental Housing Conversion and Sale Act of 1980, D.C. Code §42-3401.02). Although TOPA was crafted in response to conditions in the late seventies, it would be a mistake to view it as a relic of another era. TOPA has actually taken on heightened importance in recent years. Between 2000 and 2007, for example, 1,147 buildings, with 26,645 apartments, were converted to condominium.[12] These units amount to nearly 10 percent of the District's occupied housing units and 18 percent of its rental units as of 2000.[13] These contemporary figures are greater than those used to justify the original bill, which found that 4.5 percent of the city's rental stock was deemed to have been lost to conversion between 1977 and 1980.

---

12. These data were provided to me by the Department of Consumer and Regulatory Affairs in the summer of 2007.
13. These figures were calculated by dividing the number of converted units by the number of occupied housing units (2000) and the number of renter-occupied housing units (2000), respectively. The census data used in these calculations were dynamically generated using the U.S. Census Bureau's American FactFinder website (http://factfinder2.census.gov).

Although the city does not record how many buildings have been converted to condo by tenants, their right to do so under TOPA is especially meaningful when we consider that contemporary gentrification in DC has gone into "overdrive," contributing to what one *Washington Post* reporter describes as DC's "gilded age," in which cocktails sell for $16, rents in gentrification hotspots average $2,700 per month, and two-bedroom condos sell for nearly $1 million (Shin 2013).

Analyzing TOPA

Although researchers are supposed to approach a topic analytically, my decision to study TOPA was prompted by personal circumstances. Until 2001 I had never heard of TOPA. That changed when my landlord signed a contract to sell the apartment complex where I was living. I first saw an announcement of the sale in the neighborhood newspaper, the *Northwest Current*. I was new to my building and had just adopted a dog. I did not want to move again and worried I would not be able to find another pet-friendly building near work. When a flyer went up in my hallway announcing a tenants' meeting, I made sure to attend.

We met in the informal dog run off the alley behind our property. The tenant who called the meeting told us that DC had tenant-friendly laws and that one of those laws permitted us to buy the property even if the landlord already had a contract of sale.[14] He also told us that once we bought the property, we could convert it to condominium. It seemed like a long shot to me and a lot of work to boot. However, four of my fellow tenants thought they were up to the task and worked what became second jobs to make it happen. In 2002 our property converted to condominium. In early 2003 I bought my unit and became a property owner in the District of Columbia.

Although my interest in TOPA began for personal reasons, it remained long after my apartment complex completed the conversion process. The real estate market took off just as we were converting. I recall watching with disbelief as the value of my apartment seemed to grow monthly, even though nothing had changed in its interior. It still had a whiff of 1980 about it—pink and gray wallpaper in the bathroom, ratty teal carpet in the living room, and a creaky stove with an unpredictable pilot light. The cosmetics were not particularly pleasing, but I did not care. I felt extraordinarily lucky.

---

14. Our property's initial buyer, the National Cathedral, did not publicly disclose what it wanted to do with the property, located directly across the street from the main entrance. However, the cathedral's public desire to build a visitors' center and parking lot left most residents fearful the buildings would be torn down.

Yet my social science background also told me that my experience—an "*n* of 1"—was not a large enough sample from which to judge TOPA. Though I did not know at the time how the process played out in other buildings, I sensed that there might be variation. Indeed, the city's formidable race and class divides suggested as much. Several of my fellow tenants, for example, were lawyers. When we received official notice that our building was contracted for sale, their first response was to "make some calls." They were not intimidated by the statute's legalese, the landlord's lawyers, or those of the contracted buyer. They spoke the same technical language. I wondered if the relative smoothness of my conversion process was the norm for properties in less affluent neighborhoods where tenants were not likely to have legal training, or even in some cases to speak English. I also wondered if low-income residents could afford the insider (i.e., below-market) prices that come with most TOPA conversions. At the time I did not know that tenants could use the process to remain rental, and I wondered if below-market prices might still be out of reach for many of them. TOPA felt like a topic ripe for analysis.

As I would discover in due time, however, neither TOPA nor condo conversion more broadly has been extensively researched. The research on TOPA is too small and temporally dispersed to have created any central canon on the program's impact on gentrification. Scholars were generally upbeat about TOPA in the years just after its passage. Daniel Lauber argued, for example, that the District's TOPA law was "perhaps the most effective" attempt by affordable-housing advocates to make condo conversion work for low-income residents (1984, 295). Likewise, Richard Eisen described TOPA as the "primary anchor" of the city's efforts to regulate its affordable housing supply (1993, 111).

Recent assessments, however, are mixed. Amanda Huron (2012) is largely positive. She focuses on tenants using the TOPA process to create limited equity cooperatives (LECs), a type of housing that preserves affordability by placing caps on the amount of equity a seller can retain. Although Huron notes that LECs can be hard to form and maintain, they have made a real difference in the city. Likewise, Kathryn Howell (2013) argues that low-income tenants and their advocates have used TOPA to keep parts of fast-gentrifying Columbia Heights affordable. In contrast, Sarah Comeau (2012) argues that judicial decisions on TOPA-related cases have effectively gutted the legislation's power, resulting in "judicial sponsored gentrification." These differences aside, none of these studies provide a comprehensive, citywide analysis of the TOPA process; nor do they cover the variation in how TOPA is used, especially for buildings working without city assistance and thus grappling more directly with market forces.

Similarly, though condo conversion is a well-established part of the gentrification landscape, there has been little written about the topic in academic circles. As noted previously, most of the work on condo conversion has been written by legal scholars (Fine 1980; Day and Fogel 1981; Keenan 1987; Chabot 2008; Kahan, Leshem, and Sundaram 2012). Much of this literature is dated and focuses narrowly on the legal issues surrounding the practice and its limits rather than wider, contextual issues such as the role of condo conversion in processes of gentrification (for exceptions, see Comeau 2012 and Huron 2012).

Urban affairs scholars (in geography, sociology, and planning) have looked at condo conversion only sporadically. A number of studies were conducted in the 1980s, mostly in Europe (van Weesep 1984; Hamnett and Randolph 1984, 1988). Only a few studies have been conducted since, most in the early 2000s (Hamnett 2004; Hamnett and Whitelegg 2007; Huron 2012). Although these works are important, they are too temporally and spatially disparate to have formed a central thesis on the process.

This book aims to fill these gaps by undertaking a broad, citywide assessment of TOPA. To fill gaps on the TOPA process, I examine the degree to which the statute meets its primary goal—mitigating displacement. Specifically, I examine a representative sample of seven properties with a total of 1,179 units that went through the TOPA process between 2003 and 2013. The buildings were chosen to account for variation in location, size, socioeconomic status, and outcome in the TOPA process. For each building, I interviewed the leader(s) of its tenants' association to identify how many people in each building stayed put through the TOPA process and to determine how smoothly the process unfolded in each. I also consulted official documents relating to each conversion and, when necessary, the attorney representing the tenants. I also put these findings into greater relief by examining the ten-year legal battle that began after a local landlord sold eleven of his rental properties without informing tenants of their right to refuse the sale. These tenants' struggle to right their landlord's wrong suggests that the statute's success also depends on factors external to the law.

To fill the gaps related to condo conversion writ large, I also consider my results in the context of three broad literatures. The first is largely theoretical and focuses on the role that condos and condo conversions play in neoliberalism broadly and gentrification more specifically. The second, on local autonomy, is empirical and political. It examines the ways communities can take ownership of gentrification and the reinvestment that comes with it. The third, which concerns how to measure displacement, is methodological *and* political inasmuch as it challenges gentrification scholars to expand how they measure displacement and assess its impacts on vulnerable populations.

The Role of Condos in Gentrification

The condominium is a relatively new form of property in the United States. Although people have been able to purchase apartments in multifamily buildings since the late 1800s, the practice was concentrated in a few large cities like New York and Los Angeles until 1961, when Congress allowed the Federal Housing Administration (FHA) to insure mortgages for property inside multifamily dwellings (Lasner 2009, 2012; Harris 2011). The change encouraged banks to offer credit to people interested in buying condos and, by spurring demand, also attracted housing developers willing to meet it. For readers interested in learning more about the history of condos, as well as how they are structured and internally governed, Appendix 2 provides a short review.

Although condominiums came into existence before neoliberalism did, scholars argue that condominiums comported well with neoliberal logic. When neoliberal regimes took root, so did condominium development (N. Smith 1996; Kern 2010). City governments were particularly interested in encouraging condominium development for two reasons. First, most cities lacked sufficient empty space for development, or they had vacant space that was poorly configured for horizontal development—usually small, disconnected parcels. The vertical density of condos made working with small spaces easier and guaranteed that a profit could be made by developing on them. Second, by the mid-eighties and early nineties, many cities had experienced decades of decline brought about by suburbanization, middle-class flight, rioting, and severe disinvestment. In this context, cities were happy do the leg work for developers, changing zoning codes to allow for greater density, tracking down owners of abandoned properties, clearing title disputes, and using eminent domain to create parcels large enough for development.

Condos were, however, more than an escape hatch for cash-strapped cities. They were also indicative of an emerging trend in capitalist relations favoring accumulation over social reproduction (N. Smith 1996). In the housing sphere governments began scaling back on subsidized housing at the same time they started subsidizing condo and market-rate apartment developments. In this regard, scholars argue that condominiums are not a neutral form of housing but one that comes at the expense of other forms of housing. They are a physical manifestation of what Neil Smith (1996) called the revanchist city. As Leslie Kern and Gerda Wekerle explain, "Condominium development articulates with the revanchist project of anesthetizing and commodifying the city, of diverting resources from public projects, of encouraging privatized lifestyles for city dwellers and of privatizing practices of social reproduction" (2008, 242).

Scholars who embrace Smith's notion of the revanchist city have also turned their attention to condo owners. They argue that condos are developed, priced, and marketed with an "ideal" neoliberal citizen in mind (Miles 2012; Mitchell 2001; MacLeod 2002; Kern 2010; Kern and Wekerle 2008). And to the extent that condos can increase the number of ideal residents, they can also remake cities in a more neoliberal image.

In neoliberal ideology an ideal citizen is characterized by several traits. The most important is the ability and desire to own rather than rent. Neoliberals view ownership as a bastion against dependency because it requires people to take responsibility for their own housing (Blomley 2005, 2008). They also believe condo ownership encourages entrepreneurial behavior because people who buy condos are investing their money rather than "throwing it down the drain"—a common refrain used to disparage renting.

Citizens who can contribute more to the city in taxes than they take in services are also considered ideal urban residents. Kern and Wekerle (2008) observe, for example, that condos are usually marketed to demographic categories—empty nesters, professionals, dual-income families—whose members can purchase services and thus are unlikely to make demands on public services like schools, playgrounds, or health clinics (see also Lee and Webster 2006). Leslie Kern's (2010) study of the growing importance of professional women in the Toronto condo market provides a case in point. In many ways, the growth in female property ownership represents a flip of the standard script in which men are property owners and wives come along for the ride. However, the positioning of condos "as a way of achieving gender equality" has its limits (2010, 71). As Kern argues, condos empower only women who can afford to purchase them. Moreover, the conflation of female autonomy with property means that other issues of importance to women in the housing market (e.g., access to affordable housing, discrimination against female-headed households, etc.) are ignored or left unchallenged.[15]

Although urban scholars have written about condo conversion only sporadically, their views are largely consistent with those articulated vis-à-vis condos more generally. As noted previously, Neil Smith describes condo conversion as central to gentrification:

> Condominium and cooperative conversions in the US, tenure conversions in London and international capital investments in

---

15. Kern also observes that the marketing strategy aimed at women may ultimately contradict the ideology that gives rise to it. Most marketing campaigns, for example, sell condos as starter homes for women. Once women get married or have children, they are expected to move. By positioning condos as a temporary way station to adulthood, it is possible condo owners will end up embodying many of the same tendencies that renters are criticized for and for which cities hope to protect against.

central-city luxury accommodations were increasingly the residential component of a larger set of shifts that brought an office boom to London's canary wharf . . . and New York's Battery Park City . . . and the construction of new recreational and retail landscapes from Sydney's Darling Harbour to Oslo's Ackebrygge. (1996, 36)

Despite the acknowledgment that condo conversions are an integral part of gentrification, there has been only sporadic empirical analysis of the process (van Weesep 1984; Hamnett and Randolph 1988; Hamnett 2004; Hamnett and Whitelegg 2007; Huron 2012). Probably the most well-known scholar to study condo conversion is Chris Hamnett, a British geographer. With different coauthors, Hamnett has analyzed Britain's "flat [apartment] break-up market" as well as the conversion of factories into lofts for sale in London.

Hamnett's earliest work on flat breakups, with coauthor William Randolph, found that between 1914 and 1975 the stock of privately rented housing in Great Britain fell from 7.1 to 2.9 million units (Hamnett and Randolph 1988). They argue that the decline was driven by supply- rather than demand-side dynamics. In particular, they note that increased investment in London in the late eighties, coupled with changes in mortgage financing (which made getting a mortgage easier), encouraged landlords to sell off individual flats rather than maintain ownership of an entire building and rent out its units.

Hamnett and Randolph (1988) also argue that flat breakups were detrimental to the poor and working classes. The transformation narrowed the choices available to many families who could not afford to purchase homes: "Private renting is no longer a real option: the dwellings simply do not exist. They are therefore forced either to buy, or if they cannot afford ownership occupation, to move into the council [public housing] sector" (1988, 10).

Hamnett has also argued that there are significant problems in how flats were transformed into property. In Britain, property can be owned under two terms—freehold and leasehold. Under freehold terms, a buyer owns the structure and the land beneath it. In a leasehold purchase a buyer buys a long-term lease on a flat usually set at 99 years but permissible up to 999 years. When flat breakups began in the 1980s, units were turned into property under leasehold rather than freehold arrangements. And because leasehold property owners do not own a share in the common elements of the freehold property in which their unit is located, a tenant-landlord relationship often emerges between leasehold and freehold owners (Hamnett 2004).

In more recent work Hamnett and Drew Whitelegg (2007) examine the conversion of factories into lofts in the Clerkenwell neighborhood of

London. They argue that the transformation of factories and other industrial spaces into residential use is indicative of a wider process of occupational restructuring in Western cities. London, for example, was historically a city of factory workers, but as Great Britain deindustrialized in the late seventies and eighties, the city's working-class population shrunk and was replaced by professional workers. They also argue, in contrast to Hamnett's earlier work with Randolph (1988), that both supply- and demand-side dynamics drive the conversion of former industrial spaces into lofts. On the supply side the closure of factories and attendant infrastructure, such as canals, warehouses, storage facilities, and railway distribution centers during deindustrialization, opened up land for redevelopment. On the demand side Hamnett and Whitelegg note that the "dramatic changes in land uses" did not happen "of their own volition" (2007, 108). Rather, a demand for those spaces had to exist for developers to transform them. The authors specifically reference London's new workers—the "professional, managerial, and creative middle class"—who have "both the demand and the financial resources to pay for central area living and proximity to work" (107).

Hamnett and Whitelegg's (2007) stance on the connection between condo conversion and displacement is also different from the one Hamnett put forward with Randolph almost twenty years earlier. While Hamnett and Randolph (1988) saw a clear connection between flat breakups and displacement, Hamnett and Whitelegg argue that loft conversions occur "on a clean social slate" (2007, 106). That is, because the loft conversions occurred on property that was previously industrial, they involve no displacement.

Although Hamnett and Whitelegg's (2007) study has come under criticism for how it measures displacement—an assertion with which I agree and discuss in the next section—it does provide an opening for asking whether condo conversion is as singular a process as it is often presented in the literature. This study tests the presumed singularity of condo-conversion processes by assessing how and to what degree tenant-led conversions diverge from the patterns predicted in the literature.

Local Autonomy in the Context of Gentrification

TOPA also speaks to a body of literature about (re)building local autonomy in the context of neoliberalism (DeFilippis 2004; Blomley 2008; Saegert 2006; Huron 2012; Springer 2012). Although this literature is quite large, I draw on a subset devoted to developing mechanisms for community control over housing (DeFilippis 2004; Huron 2012; Martin and Pierce 2013). These efforts are especially relevant in the context of gentrification, where a lack of control often results in displacement.

For local-autonomy scholars, capital mobility (brought on by globalization and neoliberal governance) is the driving force behind the loss of community control (DeFilippis 2004). Although urban investment in cities has steadily accelerated since the mid-1990s, city governments, neighborhood organizations, and individual residents now have little ability to control it. Whereas investment capital used to be owned primarily by local or regional interests, it is now more commonly owned by extralocal investors or held in mutual funds with investors spread across the globe. The result is that capital is now invested (and disinvested) with little regard for the localities affected by these capital flows.

For their part, city governments are poorly positioned to challenge these arrangements. Most cities have been forced to adopt an entrepreneurial stance toward investment (Harvey 1989). After decades of disinvestment, cities now see their main job as attracting investment, and many are loath to turn down offers or to make demands that would benefit cities but potentially scare off investors. Although this posture may seem overly deferential, it is worth recognizing that most contemporary mayors have firsthand experience with disinvestment, having come of age when urban decline was the norm. In DC, recent mayors and native sons Adrian Fenty (2007–2011) and Vincent Gray (2011–2015) both lived through the city's crack epidemic, its budget woes, and ultimately its takeover by the control board.

Residents are just as disempowered (DeFilippis 2004). The federal assistance that would allow low-income residents to stay in place despite market fluctuations has been severely diminished over the last thirty years (Hackworth and Smith 2001). The waiting list for public housing in DC provides a stark example. In 2013 there were more than seventy thousand names on the list (DeBonis 2013). The city's inspector general estimates that the average wait for a one-bedroom apartment is about twenty-eight years (Willoughby 2013). In DC as elsewhere, low-income residents are on their own. Most simply cannot absorb the sharp rent increases that accompany reinvestment. Low-income residents who own their own homes are often no better insulated; many are unable to keep up with the sharp property tax hikes that follow gentrification.

In *Unmaking Goliath* (2004), one of the seminal texts on local autonomy, geographer James DeFilippis argues that (re)building local autonomy must begin by limiting capital's mobility and transferring ownership of it to local people and institutions that have a concern not just for growing returns but also for the wider neighborhood where it is invested. DeFilippis explores three structures for developing local ownership—LECs, mutual housing associations, and community land trusts. To determine their effectiveness, he relies on multiple metrics. At the macro level he argues that successful collective ownership must be "infused with a sense of social justice" (2004, 9). Otherwise, gated communities and other forms of exclusive yet also collective ownership could count as acceptable forms of local autonomy. Second, collective ownership must be structured so that its benefits are not just for a particular group of people in time but can carry over to successive owners. LECs, for example, keep unit prices affordable across sales by capping the equity an owner can draw when selling.

At the micro level DeFilippis (2004) argues that collective decision making must be part of the process of both establishing and managing shared housing. People's lives must also be improved through the process of collective ownership. Improvement can be defined as stabilizing residents' housing situation (e.g., making frequent moves unnecessary), limiting their housing costs (e.g., capping rent at 30 percent of net income), and/or guaranteeing maintenance of their homes.

As I demonstrate in Chapter 4, the notion of local autonomy figured centrally in the city council's decision to enact the TOPA statute. TOPA's sponsors on the city council saw the law as a mechanism for giving city tenants control over their housing during intense periods of gentrification. The driving ethos behind TOPA makes it an ideal law to test in terms of the criteria laid out by DeFilippis.

Huron's (2012) recent dissertation on the TOPA law makes an important first stab in this direction. As noted previously, Huron's findings are generally positive. Of the 134 LECs created through the TOPA process since 1980, almost two-thirds (64 percent) are still in existence. And they have accomplished what they were set out to do—maintain affordable housing.

Studies by low-income-housing advocates in DC also present a positive picture of tenants who use city money to buy their buildings through the TOPA process and keep them affordable. A recent study on the city's First Right Purchase Program by the DC Fiscal Policy Institute (Reed 2013a) provides an example. The program provides loans to low-income tenants' associations who want to buy their building through the TOPA process. In the last decade fourteen hundred units were preserved as low-income housing through the program.

Although these studies are important and timely, they focus on narrow slices of the TOPA universe—tenants who use TOPA to keep their buildings affordable. As I discovered during my research, however, many tenants' associations also use the TOPA process to create market-rate condominiums, co-ops, and apartments and worked with for-profit developers to make it happen. The market-oriented nature of these processes notwithstanding, all of them entailed practices that DeFilippis (2004) insists are crucial to building local autonomy during periods of intense gentrification. They are, in a sense, a hybrid of collective and market processes. In the empirical Chapters

6 through 8, I use DeFilippis's criteria to determine whether these practices can still deliver on local autonomy in a market context.

My research contributes to the literature on local autonomy in two interconnected ways. Empirically, this study adds to the small but important literature on TOPA by expanding the analysis to also include conversions that work fully within a market context. This is an important gap to fill. Although the city does not track condo conversion in a way that permits us to delineate between tenants' associations that receive government assistance and those that do not, tenant lawyers I spoke with for this project suggest most conversions occur in a market context.[16] Providing empirical evidence on the potential for success using a hybrid structure—one that adopts collectivist elements while working within market rules—also has political implications. That is, my findings may impel us to rethink the collectivist "possible."

Displacement

The final literature I address in this book concerns debates about whether gentrification can happen without displacement. The fact that scholars now ask this question is fairly remarkable. In fact, the notion that gentrification leads to displacement used to be sacrosanct (Glass 1964; N. Smith 1986, 1996; Zukin 1987). Beginning in the early 2000s, however, a number of scholars and commentators began to question the connection. Today, several argue that gentrification can and frequently does occur without displacement (Duany 2001; Byrne 2003; Vigdor, Massey, and Rivlin 2002; Sternbergh 2009; Weinberger 2011; Hamnett and Butler 2013).

The explanations for displacement-free gentrification vary. Some argue that gentrification happens primarily in empty or underused space (e.g., vacant lots or abandoned factories), so regeneration happens on a "clean social slate" without displacing existing residents (Hamnett and Whitelegg 2007, 106). Others argue that the changing demographics associated with urban revitalization simply mirror our changing class structure (Butler, Hamnett, and Ramsden 2008). As cities deindustrialized, the workforce moved from factory jobs into better-paying professional ones. Thus, the working class has not been displaced so much as replaced.

However, the idea that gentrification can happen without displacement remains contested. In particular, critics argue that assertions of displacement-free gentrification are based on faulty metrics (Slater 2009, 2010; Davidson and Wyly 2012). Specifically, most proponents of the clean-slate view of

---

16. Eric Rome, one of the tenant lawyers I interviewed, argued that LECs and other nonmarket uses of TOPA are not common because they are difficult to create and sustain. See Chapter 5 and Appendix 3 for more information on my interview sources.

gentrification use only one measure—direct displacement—to make their case. Direct displacement happens when tenants leave a rental unit because they cannot afford an annual rent increase or their unit has become uninhabitable because of landlord disinvestment. Critics of the displacement-free view contend that displacement can happen in other ways as well, so multiple measures are needed to capture its existence and scope.

Criticism of Chris Hamnett and Drew Whitelegg's article on factory-to-loft conversions in Clerkenwell in London is a case in point (Slater 2009, 2010; Davidson and Wyly 2012, 2013). As noted previously, Hamnett and Whitelegg argue that even though Clerkenwell's conversions "may well be accompanied by growing feelings of relative deprivation on the part of existing residents who have seen traditional working men's cafes and pubs replaced by swish restaurants, wine bars, kitchen shops, and florists" (2007, 122), they did not involve displacement because none of the factories had been used for residential purposes before conversion. Critic Tom Slater (2009, 2010) contends, however, that this argument ignores forms of displacement that are not only well documented in the literature (he points to Peter Marcuse's 1985 typology of measures) but occur when direct displacement is not present. Referencing the quotation from Hamnett and Whitelegg cited previously, Slater observes:

> What Hamnett and Whitelegg are describing is Marcuse's [1985] displacement pressure—so they have actually uncovered a clear example of gentrification with displacement. It is also a pity that they did not consult the recent scholarship on "indirect displacement" in surrounding neighborhoods as warehouse, industrial and office building conversions elevate rental and sales prices in "up and coming" areas adjacent to those conversions. (2009, 305)

My work here makes a methodological contribution to this debate by employing one of Marcuse's (1985) measures of displacement—exclusionary displacement—in my analysis of TOPA.[17] Exclusionary displacement occurs when a unit is voluntarily vacated but then made unavailable for a renter who could have afforded the unit at its most recent rate. Exclusion can be caused by a steep increase in rent, a tenure change (from rental apartment to condo), or a building's demolition, among other factors. Exclusionary displacement is important because it captures how the low-income housing stock is reduced. It also explains why low-income tenants find it difficult to

---

17. Although many scholars cite Marcuse's work, few have employed his alternative measures of displacement in empirical work.

make intracity moves (whether to be closer to a new job, accommodate the birth of a baby, or downsize after divorce) and why their children cannot establish new households in the city when they come of age.

The exclusionary displacement measure is especially relevant to my work here because tenants who vacate their units during a TOPA process do so willingly and in a context where staying in place is a viable option. Bought-out units cannot, therefore, be counted as cases of direct displacement. However, since developers take ownership of these units once they are bought out and vacated, the units are subject to changes (e.g., sharp rent hikes or a tenure change) that may result in exclusionary displacement. My assessment of TOPA, then, not only tracks how many people can stay in place during a TOPA process but also how many units vacated via buyouts are subject to exclusionary displacement.

Overview of the Book

To explain TOPA and the arguments it addresses, this book takes a semi-ethnographic approach. I collected most of the data for this book by interviewing tenant leaders and their attorneys about the process of invoking TOPA rights. Although the book is not ethnography in the purest sense of the word, the goal is to uncover the process by letting tenant leaders describe it in their own words. My hope is that, academic arguments aside, this book will be readable and relatable to everyday citizens in the District who are interested in TOPA and the fate of their city.

The remainder of the book is divided into three sections. The first section—Chapters 2 and 3—provides DC's backstory. Chapter 2 details the social and economic changes that have occurred in the city and describes how the city went from rock bottom to booming metropolis in a span of fifteen years. Chapter 3 examines how residents across the city's trenchant race and class divides interpret the gentrification in their midst.

The second section of this book serves as a sort of connective tissue, bridging the citywide story discussed in Chapters 2 and 3 to the TOPA experiences of specific buildings related in Chapters 6–8. In Chapter 4 readers are treated to a crash course on the logistics of RHCSA. In particular, I outline the mechanics of the legislation and the varied ways that tenants use it. Chapter 5 introduces readers to the sample properties my empirical analysis relies on as well as the metrics of analysis I use to assess the statute's success at meeting its key goal of displacement mitigation.

In the third section of the book—Chapters 6, 7, and 8—I assess the TOPA process by measuring the statute's ability to mitigate displacement, evaluating the city's regulatory efforts to ensure tenants can use the statute as its architects intended, and detailing abuses of the statute by landlords and their attorneys. In Chapter 9, I summarize my empirical findings and consider them in light of the three debates discussed previously. I then make a final political assessment of TOPA, asking and answering whether the politics of staying put offered through the TOPA statute is worth supporting.

2

From Bullets to Cocktails

A Capital Transformation

At some point in the late 1980s or early 1990s city residents began referring to DC as "Dodge City." The name was suggestive—DC was like a frontier town with a lot of violence and little law and order. It was also literal—in neighborhoods like U Street and Columbia Heights you could find yourself dodging bullets some nights. Twenty years later, in April 2010, a bar named Dodge City opened on U Street. By then, the name conjured an era few new residents knew about (Crockett 2012a). In fact, now the main things to dodge on U Street at night are tipsy millennials and cars lined up in front of valet stands.

In this chapter I describe DC's transformation from a decaying city to a vibrant, increasingly exclusive city. I begin by providing a brief statistical overview of DC's changes and comparing them to changes in the wider metro area. I then offer a brief explanation for why American cities, and DC in particular, adopted neoliberalism. As I demonstrate here, most cities initially found neoliberalism unattractive. Finally, I devote the remainder of the chapter to tracing the actions DC leaders took after the city hit rock bottom in 1995 and was placed in federal receivership.

In providing this overview I have two goals. The first is to provide readers with important background on DC. Although DC's adoption of neoliberal reforms is broadly consistent with the approach taken by other U.S. cities, its story is unique in two ways. First, unlike most cities in the United States, DC was forced to adopt neoliberal reforms by an external agent, the so-called control board. Second, though DC was not alone in trying to grow its tax base, it was far more constrained in how it could do so. Most cities could court new industries (or subsidize expansion in existing ones) and hope workers followed, bringing in new tax revenue from business profits as well as personal income and real estate purchases. However, DC's largest employer, the federal government, is beyond the city's control. DC cannot tax the federal government or direct its actions. In this context, DC's turnaround plan had to focus on the residential tax base, an emphasis that gave precedence to the role of real estate. The centrality of real estate would in turn be magnified by the early 2000s housing bubble.

My second goal is to highlight why a statute like TOPA is so important in DC. A recent study on gentrification in the magazine *Governing* clearly demonstrates the stakes (Maciag 2015). Although gentrification remains a fairly concentrated phenomenon in the United States as a whole, DC ranks second among cities where gentrification is considered extensive. Nearly 52 percent of the city's low-income tracts have been gentrified since 2000. Only Portland, Oregon, has a larger percentage (58 percent) of gentrified tracts (Maciag 2015). In this context, TOPA is often the only line of defense for low-income residents who want to stay put, whether in their individual units or in the city as a whole.

Statistically Documenting DC's Gentrification

To demonstrate the depth and scope of change in DC, I examine two broad categories of data. I begin with socioeconomic data, charting changes in income and poverty as well as in the black and white share of the city's population.[1] Although race and class do not overlap perfectly in the United States, their intersection remains strong. White people continue to have more wealth and greater spending power than minorities and are thus more likely than minorities to be gentrifiers. None of this is to suggest that minorities cannot be gentrifiers—they can and are. However, a declining minority population concomitant with an increasing white one is common in gentrifying places. As I demonstrate in the next chapter, race is also the key variable around which gentrification is interpreted in the city by both its long-term, mostly black residents and its new, mostly white ones.

The second category of data I use to sketch the spread of gentrification in the city is housing. In particular, I focus on changes in tenure and cost. Although tenure changes are not central to the definition of gentrification, most

---

1. The census collects racial data using the terms "Black/African American" and "White Non-Hispanic." In the interest of space and readability I use "black" and "white" to describe these two categories.

scholars agree that gentrification is associated with a shift away from renting and toward ownership (Hamnett and Randolph 1988). And of course, rising rents and home prices are well-established ways to identify neighborhoods undergoing gentrification.

For each category of data I begin with a citywide description of change.[2] I then look at change in a sample of ten census tracts.[3] These tracts were selected for scrutiny because they are located around the city's condo-conversion center of gravity, a statistical measure that determines the median location from a data set of multiple locations. Figure 2.1 shows this center of gravity and is based on data provided to the author by the city's Department of Consumer and Regulatory Affairs. It includes condo conversions approved in the city between 2000 and 2008. Each small dot on the map represents a property that has converted to condo. The larger dot represents the median location of all these conversions. The circle around it is a standard distance circle, a measure roughly analogous to standard deviation. Figure 2.2 shows the sample census tracts selected for further scrutiny from within this circle. Focusing on tracts within one standard distance of the median condo conversion ensures that we do not look at tracts that are outliers in the distribution of condo conversions. These data demonstrate that the pace of change in selected tracts tends to be greater than change in the city as a whole.

A Whiter, Wealthier City with Persistent Poverty

During the last decade, three trends stand out regarding the socioeconomic changes in the city. First, DC is much wealthier than it was ten years ago. The median household income in 2000 was $40,127. The estimate for 2010 was $61,835—a more than 50 percent increase. The average family income also grew, though to a smaller degree, from $102,342 in 2000 (adjusted to 2010 dollars) to an estimated $117,664 in 2010—an increase of 15 percent.[4] However, increases in the average family income in sample tracts were much

---

2. Unless otherwise noted, all citywide data presented here were dynamically generated from the U.S. Census Bureau's American FactFinder website at http://factfinder2.census.gov. Income and poverty data on the FactFinder website rely on American Community Survey five-year estimates (2007–2011). At the time of writing the 2010 full-count census data on income and poverty were not yet published.
3. Unless otherwise noted, sample tract data were taken from the website of Neighborhood Info DC (http://www.neighborhoodinfodc.org/index.html), an initiative sponsored by the Urban Institute and the Washington DC Local Initiatives Support Corporation (LISC). Neighborhood Info DC compiles data from multiple sources (U.S. Census Bureau, real estate research firms, etc.) and stores them in one location.
4. I use Neighborhood Info DC data on average family income because 2000 numbers were adjusted to 2010 dollars. This calculation is not available on the census website.

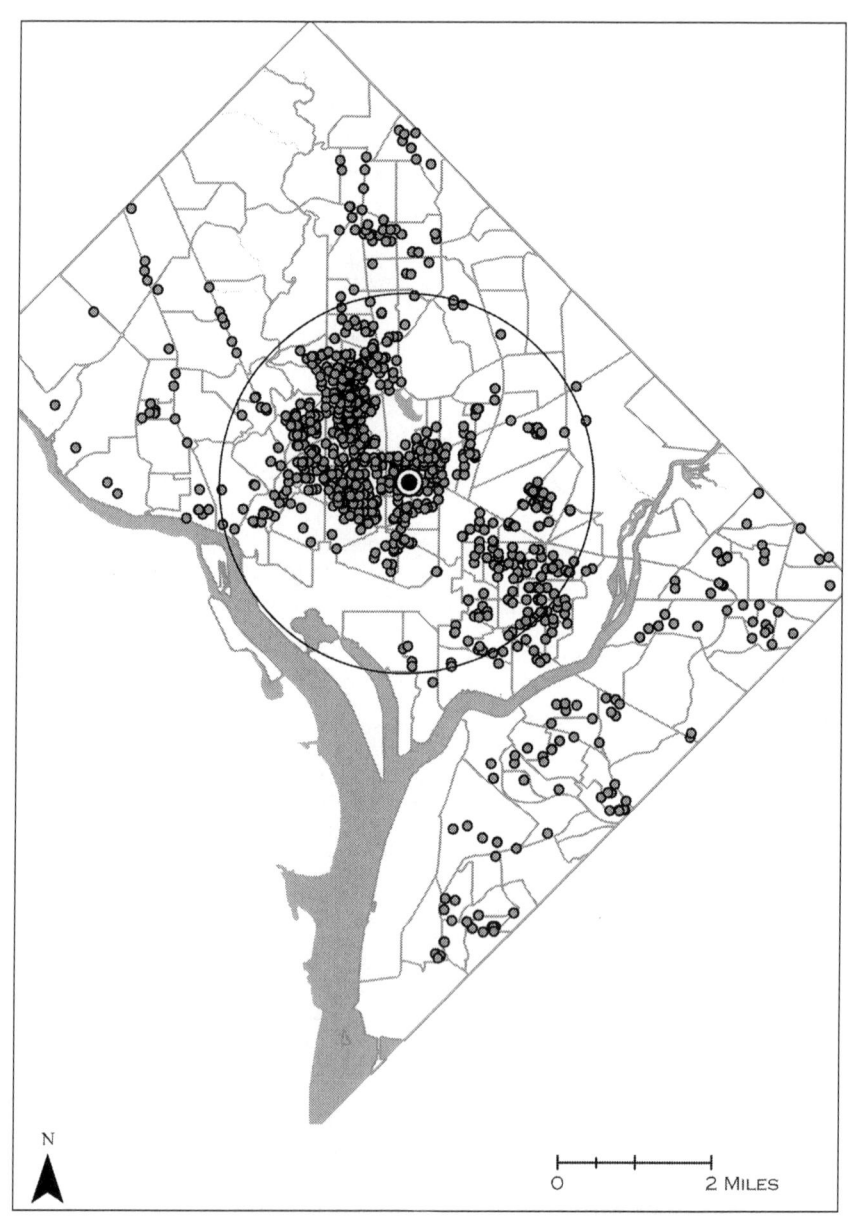

Figure 2.1 Condo-conversion center of gravity and one standard distance in Washington, DC. (Map by Meagan Snow.)

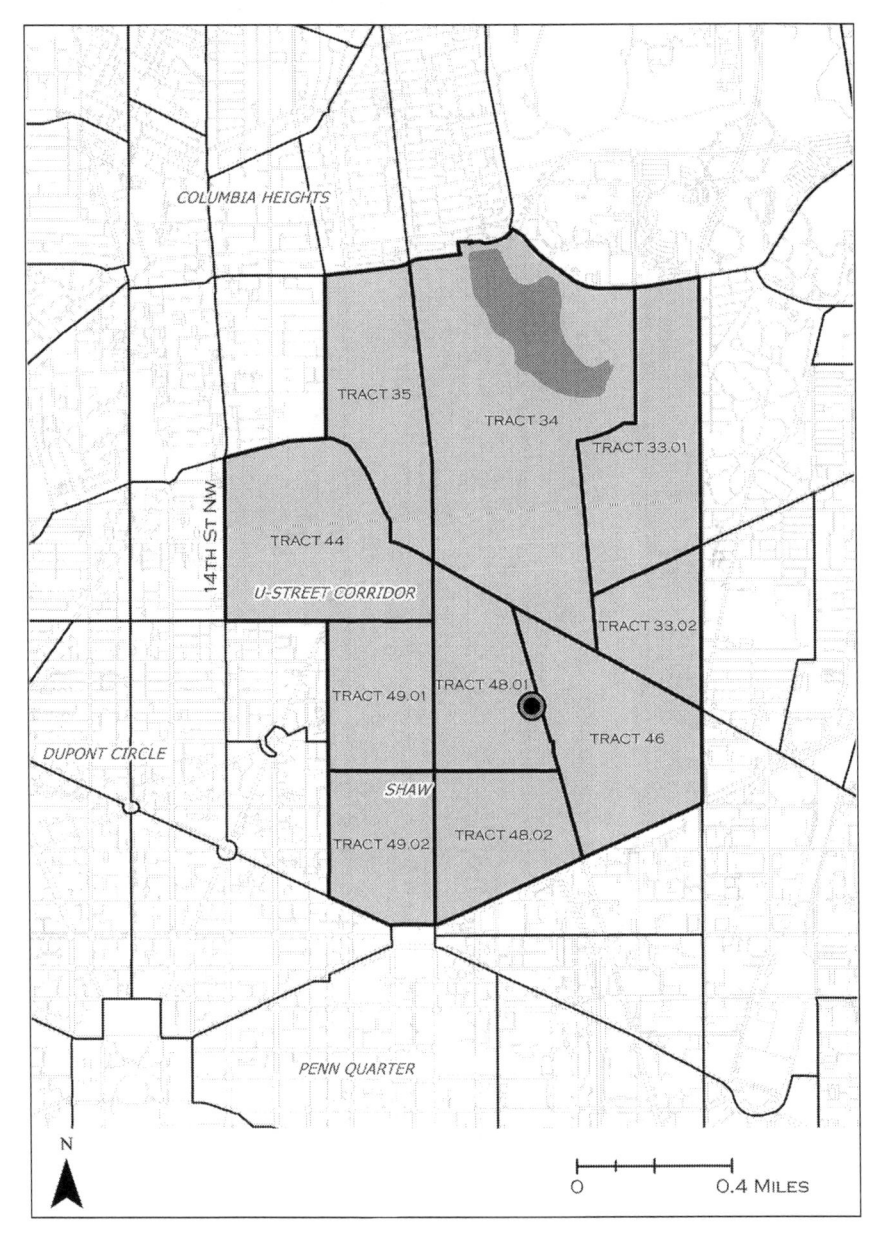

Figure 2.2 Sample tracts in Washington, DC. (Map by Meagan Snow.)

TABLE 2.1 AVERAGE FAMILY INCOME IN SAMPLE TRACTS, 1999 AND 2005–2009

Tract	1999 (2010 $)	2005–2009 (2010 $)	Increase between 1999 and 2005–2009 (%)
DC	102,342	117,645	15
33.01	76,692	173,985	126
33.02	80,286	93,613	17
34	41,577	52,340	26
35	42,119	61,974	47
44	62,904	125,042	99
46	54,478	72,528	33
48.01	59,498	125,005	110
48.02	52,562	73,886	41
49.01	44,791	82,680	85
49.02	77,307	93,796	21

larger than in the city as a whole. The average increase, 60.5 percent, was four times as large (Table 2.1).

The city's income gains mask the fact that the city continues to have stubbornly high poverty. Indeed, this second trend of persistent poverty seems to contradict the first. The percentage of the population below the poverty level decreased only 2 percent between 2000 and 2010, from 20 percent to 18 percent. The persistence of poverty in an increasingly wealthy city is at least partly a result of the 2008 recession. At the height of the recession, the city recorded an unemployment rate of nearly 12 percent (Reed 2010), and the rate remains stubbornly high. The March 2015 unemployment rate for DC was 7.3 percent (Bureau of Labor Statistics 2015). Recovering from the recession's economic hit has been especially difficult for the city's minority populations. Minorities across the country saw greater losses in income and assets than white residents did, leading some scholars to describe the 2008 recession as a depression for minorities (Fletcher 2015; Patterson 2010). The disparate effects of the recession along racial lines may also explain why sample tracts, which became whiter over the last decade, bucked the city trend regarding poverty, recording an average decrease of 5.3 percent (Table 2.2).

The third trend is the shifting balance between the city's two largest racial groups—black and white residents. Although the black share of the population is still larger than the white share, the city is becoming a whiter place. Between 2000 and 2010, for example, the black share of the population declined by nearly 10 percent, from 60.0 percent to 50.7 percent. It was the steepest decennial decline in the black share of the city's population since the census first began recording population by race in 1800. Though the black

TABLE 2.2 PERCENTAGE BELOW POVERTY LEVEL IN SAMPLE TRACTS, 2000 AND 2005–2009

Tract	2000 (%)	2005–2009 (%)	Change in percentage between 2000 and 2005–2009
DC	20.2	18.2	−2
33.01	23.3	20.2	−3.1
33.02	15.1	14.2	−0.9
34	40.2	42.5	2.3
35	35.9	24.9	−11
44	20.3	11.9	−8.4
46	24.2	22.4	−1.8
48.01	29.9	11.6	−18.3
48.02	21.0	27.0	6
49.01	35.3	15.3	−20
49.02	18.6	18.5	−0.1

share of the city's population reached its peak in 1970, at 71.1 percent, its average decennial decline between 1970 and 2000 was 3.7 percent. The drop over the last decade was almost three times as large.

In early 2011, the city's black population dropped below 50 percent (Tavernise 2011). It was the first time in fifty years that black residents made up less than a majority of the city's population. It was also a symbolic loss for a city that had proudly embraced the "Chocolate City" moniker. Perhaps not surprisingly, news organizations had a linguistic field day with the news. NPR described DC as "more vanilla" (Kellogg 2011), while the *Washington Examiner* claimed that Chocolate City "was melting" (Rosiak 2011).

Other minority groups in the city avoided population decline but experienced only minimal growth. The second- and third-largest ethnic groups in the city—Hispanics and Asians, respectively—saw their share of the population increase by 1.2 percent and 0.8 percent, respectively. These increases pale in comparison to the growth of Hispanics and Asians in other U.S. cities (see Dardick and Mack 2011 for information on Chicago). In stark contrast to the shifts found in the city's minority populations, the white share of the population grew substantially, with a 7.7 percent increase. Their share of the city's population in 2010 was 38.5 percent.

When we look at the sample tracts just discussed, the concomitant decline in the black share of the population and the rise in the white share is even starker. In sample tracts the black share of the population declined by an average of 26.3 percent—more than double the decline in the city as a whole. Likewise, the white share of the population increased an average of 23.72 percent—three times the rise for the city as a whole (Table 2.3).

TABLE 2.3 WHITE AND BLACK SHARE OF THE POPULATION IN SAMPLE TRACTS, 2000 AND 2010

Tract	White population, 2000 (%)	White population, 2010 (%)	Change in percentage of white population between 2000 and 2010	Black population, 2000 (%)	Black population, 2010 (%)	Change in percentage of black population between 2000 and 2010
DC	30.8	38.5	7.7	60.0	50.7	−9.3
33.01	4.1	28.0	23.9	90.0	64.0	−26.0
33.02	6.2	32.0	25.8	91.0	59.0	−32.0
34	0.8	12.0	11.2	94.0	79.0	−15.0
35	1.0	14.0	13.0	87.0	72.0	−15.0
44	22.0	61.0	39.0	58.0	22.0	−36.0
46	3.4	23.0	19.6	92.0	65.0	−27.0
48.01	4.5	36.0	31.5	78.0	47.0	−31.0
48.02	7.8	27.0	19.2	76.0	51.0	−25.0
49.01	13.0	33.0	20.0	81.0	52.0	−29.0
49.02	11.0	45.0	34.0	58.0	31.0	−27.0

More and Costlier Housing

After World War II, Americans began their great suburban trek (Jackson 1985). In DC this march translated into fewer residents and, over time, less housing as buildings were vacated and eventually demolished. When DC began to rebound in the late 1990s, developers returned. Between 2000 and 2010 the city added 27,124 new housing units (District of Columbia Office of Planning 2012).

Tenancy (whether one owns or rents) also tilted toward owning rather than renting. In the city as a whole, the shift (from 40.8 percent to 42.0 percent) was quite small—a 1.2 percent increase in the number of owner-occupied housing units. However, in sample tracts, the shift was much larger.[5] While two tracts saw slight decreases in owner occupation, eight tracts witnessed an average increase of 7.3 percent (Table 2.4).

Between 2000 and 2010 home prices also skyrocketed in the District. Although gentrification involves adding value to property, the sharp increase in home value during the decade is most likely the result of the housing bubble that began in the early 2000s. In ten years, the median sale price for a single-family home in DC increased by 170 percent, from $203,000 to $549,000.[6] Price increases were even sharper in sample tracts, most of which had a median sales price below the city's average in 2000 (Table 2.5). On

---

5. Data on owner occupancy for sample tracts are from the American FactFinder website because Neighborhood Info DC does not include the relevant data for 2010.
6. Data on median house prices are from Neighborhood Info DC because they are not yet available from the census.

TABLE 2.4   PERCENTAGE OF OWNER-OCCUPIED HOUSING UNITS IN SAMPLE TRACTS, 2000 AND 2010

Tract	2000 (%)	2010 (%)	Change in percentage between 2000 and 2010
DC	40.8	42.0	1.2
33.01	62.8	60.0	-2.8
33.02	59.3	59.9	0.6
34	33.2	42.5	9.3
35	27.9	35.3	7.4
44	45.0	53.5	8.5
46	45.7	43.9	1.8
48.01	39.2	41.9	2.7
48.02	14.9	21.5	6.6
49.01	29.2	28.8	-0.4
49.02	10.1	31.8	21.7

TABLE 2.5   MEDIAN SALES PRICES FOR SINGLE-FAMILY HOMES IN SAMPLE TRACTS, 2000 AND 2010

Tract	2000 ($)	2010 ($)	Increase between 2000 and 2010 (%)
DC	203,000	549,000	170
33.01	219,000	416,000	89
33.02	196,000	448,000	129
34	179,000	458,000	155
44	202,000	681,000	237
46	124,000	406,000	227
48.01	135,000	557,000	313
49.01	252,000	632,000	151

Note: Data were not available for tracts 35, 48.02, and 49.02.

average, the median sales price increased by 185 percent in sample tracts for which there are available data.

Renting an apartment also became more expensive during the decade. The DC Fiscal Policy Institute notes that the proportion of low-, medium-, and high-rent places in the city's rental stock has tilted toward the luxury market (Reed 2012). Between 2000 and 2010 the number of low-cost units in the city declined by 51 percent, while the number of high-cost units "more than tripled" (Reed 2012).

DC in Relation to the Wider Metropolitan Area

While the descriptive statistics just presented are suggestive of gentrification, we must ask if these changes are confined to DC or hold true for the wider metropolitan area.[7] If these changes occurred across the metro area, something besides gentrification could explain the city's growing wealth. A number of indicators, however, demonstrate that the changes in DC either ran counter to trends in the metro region as a whole or followed the trend lines but to a greater degree.

Change to the racial mix is an example of the first case. While the city's white population grew by 7.70 percent, the metro area's white population actually declined by 4.57 percent. As DC was becoming whiter, the metro area was becoming less so. Moreover, while DC's black population declined by nearly 10 percent, the region's black population saw only a slight decline of less than 1 percent (−0.069%).

Shifts in owner occupancy provide another example of changes in DC running counter to those of the region as a whole. While owner occupancy increased slightly in the District (1.2 percent), it decreased in the region as a whole. The metro area's average owner occupancy between 2005 and 2007, for example, was 67.4 percent. Between 2011 and 2013 it declined to 63.1 percent.[8] The difference between the city and the metro area as a whole is likely related to the fact that incidents of foreclosures were greater in the metro area's eastern suburbs and exurban areas than in its center (Hendey et al. 2011).

Income figures provide an example of the second case, where DC's changes moved in the same direction as those in the region as a whole, but more starkly. Between 2000 and 2007, for example, personal income per capita in the District grew (in current dollars) from $33,369 to $53,606—an increase of 60.65 percent.[9] In the metro area as a whole, personal income per capita also rose, but more modestly, from $40,673 to $54,971—an increase of 35.15 percent.

Neoliberal Remedies

The extensive changes in DC could not have happened without the active participation of city officials. Though we often think about gentrification

---

7. The wider metropolitan area is called the Washington-Arlington-Alexandria, DC-VA-MD-WV metro area by the U.S. Census Bureau. Unless otherwise noted, metro-level data reported in this section can be found in the U.S. Census Bureau's (2010) *State and Metropolitan Area Data Book: 2010*.
8. These data are from the American FactFinder website.
9. The *State and Metropolitan Area Data Book: 2010* does not compare other forms of income, so I use personal income here, which the census defines as "the sum of wage and salary disbursements, supplements to wages and salaries, proprietors' income with inventory valuation and capital consumption adjustments, rental income of persons with capital consumption adjustment, personal dividend income, personal interest income, and personal current transfer receipts, less contributions for government social insurance" (U.S. Census Bureau 2010, A-74).

as a process driven by individuals—the new guy fixing up the old Miller place, the young couple who moved into the vacant row house and have not stopped hammering since—wider forces are often necessary to entice individuals to make these sorts of moves.

The United States has experienced three stages of gentrification since the end of World War II (Hackworth and Smith 2001), and in each of them the state has had a role to play. Although there is considerable variation in each stage, the most notable differences lie in the shifting balance between federal, state, and municipal involvement. In the first two stages (1968–1978 and 1979–1993) the federal government was an active participant, often driving local efforts by providing tax incentives or federal subsidies for cities hoping to rejuvenate downtown areas, particular neighborhoods, or retail corridors. By the time the third and ongoing phase began (roughly 1994), federal involvement was limited. Municipal governments were leading the charge (Harvey 1989).

The shift from the federal to municipal level of government is primarily the result of the decline of so-called Keynesianism.[10] Keynesianism was crafted in response to the Great Depression and the devastation it wrought (Stiglitz 2003). Its proponents argued that the Depression proved that unregulated markets can (and often do) work poorly (see Harvey 2005 for a cogent review). As a result the state could and *should* intervene in the market to stimulate demand (Stiglitz 2003). Over time, state intervention centered on three goals—stimulating economic growth, guaranteeing full (or near-full) employment, and ensuring a base level of social welfare (Harvey 2005).

What developed in the post–World War II era was a "virtuous circle" between capital, labor, and the state (Lipietz 1992, 17). Capitalists agreed to stop abusing their employees and instead view them as potential consumers—often of the very products they were making—and pay them accordingly. Likewise, workers agreed to increase productivity if their bosses shared the gains from it (e.g., with raises, vacation time, or other benefits). Although many of these changes began well before World War II, they were consolidated in state policies after it.

For its part, the federal government agreed to guarantee the agreement between capital and labor (Lipietz 1992). In particular, it would pass legislation to ensure workers *could* be consumers. Minimum-wage laws, for example, guaranteed a base level of earnings, and periodic increases in the minimum wage ensured that the laws would continue to do so. Likewise, the government permitted and managed collective bargaining through

---

10. Keynesianism is an economic model named after its key proponent, John Maynard Keynes. It also goes by other names, including "embedded liberalism" (Harvey 2005, 11) and "Fordism" (Lipietz 1992, 1).

institutions like the National Labor Relations Board to avoid costly strikes. Finally, and perhaps most relevant to cities like DC (which had no manufacturing base to speak of), the state ensured that workers "remained consumers even when they were prevented from 'earning their living' through illness, retirement, unemployment or the like" (Lipietz 1992, 7). Unemployment insurance, for example, helped workers make ends meet during layoffs. The food stamp program ensured people could still buy groceries during tough times. And programs like Medicaid (launched in 1965) helped states cover health-care costs of low-income residents.

The federal government also made forays into the housing sphere, ensuring that low-income residents would have decent shelter. The federal government subsidized the construction of public housing complexes in cities across the United States and later provided subsidies to families trying to rent in market-rate housing (Section 8 assistance[11]). As noted previously, the federal government also got involved in trying to eradicate neighborhood-level blight by offering block grants to cities interested in attracting new businesses and residents.

By the early 1970s, however, the Keynesian model was beginning to collapse. In political economic terms, it was the victim of a crisis of accumulation (Arrighi 1978; Lipietz 1992; Harvey 2005). Although scholars argue that the capitalist system is inherently crisis prone, the specific crisis in the Keynesian model involved a declining rate of profit.[12] In response to falling profits, corporations closed factories or began to move them to places with cheaper labor. Unemployment began to rise in response. Inflation also emerged, reaching double-digit territory by the late 1970s.

Although the specific causes of the crisis, which also included international shocks like the 1973 Organization of the Petroleum Exporting Companies (OPEC) oil embargo, are beyond our scope here, the effect on cities *is* relevant. The seventies and eighties are often regarded as lost decades in urban America, when once-thriving neighborhoods morphed into settings for open-air drug markets, gang violence, disinvestment, and dereliction. Although the crisis did not cause urban decline—a process that began much earlier—it certainly exacerbated it and contributed to other trends already harming cities, most notably suburbanization (Jackson 1985; Thabit 2003).

---

11. Although Section 8 is now officially called the Housing Choice Voucher Program, it is still widely referred to as "Section 8."
12. Giovanni Arrighi argues that capitalism can also experience "realization crises," which happen when "the rate of exploitation (the relation between the portion of social product which is appropriated by capital and the portion retained by the workers) is 'too high' to allow the realization of surplus-value" (1978, 4).

The urban response writ large was the adoption of neoliberalism. It was a major departure from Keynesianism. At a philosophical level, neoliberalism is an ideology given form by distrust of government and a parallel faith in the free market (Harvey 2000, 2005). Neoliberals believe that the private sector is more efficient than the public sector at allocating and managing resources, including basic elements of survival (food, water) as well as modern conveniences (transportation, electricity, etc.). Neoliberals take an equally dim view of government efforts to ensure social reproduction—those ancillary services that make working possible, including shelter, education, good health, and child care (Abramovitz 2010). Indeed, for neoliberals, state guarantees create a dependent class of people content to "mooch" off the government rather than contribute to society.[13]

Neoliberal ideology also comes with its own ideas about social order (Harvey 2005). For neoliberals, the individual's freedom is a paramount social virtue. However, individuals are also responsible for the consequences of their freedom. That is, while people are free to make their own decisions (e.g., quit college, take out a mortgage, or invest in a particular company), they are also responsible for handling the fallout from bad ones. This means that neoliberal ideology takes a dim view of government efforts to ensure particular social outcomes, such as (and using the previous examples) college completion, home ownership, or guaranteed returns on investments. Such efforts are deemed suspect because they are viewed as creating dependency. In neoliberal ideology dependent people are less likely to take risks, which grow the economy, or to take personal responsibility, which fosters improved decision making.

The only truly acceptable role of the state in neoliberal ideology is to ensure capital accumulation. And the best way for the state to do that is by getting out of the way. Of course, on the ground, distant from abstract theory, neoliberalism requires and even demands state involvement (Peck, Theodore, and Brenner 2009). However, the state in question is now often municipal. In the wake of federal retreat, cities were all but forced to respond to the problems caused by the crisis of Keynesianism (Harvey 1989). That is, cities could live with the dereliction, or they could try to stop and ultimately reverse it.

---

13. Criticizing recipients of government aid can be politically risky. Attacking social security beneficiaries as undeserving, for example, often translates into "an attack on Grandma." Thus, advocates of neoliberalism often focus their *public* ire on the government for creating dependency. However, negative views of recipients continue to frame their *private* critiques. When he was running for president in 2012, for example, Republican candidate Mitt Romney told a closed-door meeting of donors that he did not expect to get the vote of the 47 percent of the population who felt "entitled to health care, to food, to housing, to you-name-it. . . . I'll never convince them they should take personal responsibility and care for their lives" (Corn 2012).

Why Neoliberalism Prevails

Although neoliberalism congealed in urban areas quite quickly, during the 1990s it was not a foregone conclusion that it would supplant Keynesianism. In fact, most American cities have large constituencies who have neither liked nor benefited from neoliberal policies, including factory workers, municipal employees, and the poor (Harvey 2000, 2005). However, cities often found themselves in a weak position to thwart the growing dominance of neoliberalism.

A key reason cities adopted neoliberalism was political. By the late seventies Keynesian defenders were facing competition on the political battlefield. Most notable in this regard was Ronald Reagan, who spent much of the sixties and seventies using his political bully pulpit as governor and then presidential candidate to discursively frame Keynesian programs as morally suspect. During his 1976 campaign for the Republican presidential nomination, Reagan routinely described government programs as lavish and their recipients as undeserving. At a campaign stop in New Hampshire, for example, Reagan described Taino Towers, a public housing complex in New York, this way: "If you are a slum dweller, you can get an apartment with 11-foot ceilings, with a 20-foot balcony, a swimming pool and gymnasium, laundry room and play room, and the rent begins at $113.20 and that includes utilities" ("'Welfare Queen' Becomes Issue" 1976, 51). He also recounted the story of a woman caught gaming the welfare system:

> There's a woman in Chicago. She has 80 names, 30 addresses, 12 Social Security cards and is collecting veterans' benefits on four nonexisting deceased husbands. And she's collecting Social Security on her cards. She's got Medicaid, getting food stamps and she is collecting welfare under each of her names. Her tax-free cash income alone is over $150,000. ("'Welfare Queen' Becomes Issue" 1976, 51)

Both stories were factually inaccurate. Taino Towers was neither luxurious nor as cheap as Reagan had claimed. And the woman caught bilking the system in Chicago actually managed to get a little over $8,000 before she was caught ("'Welfare Queen' Becomes Issue" 1976). But when amplified and contrasted with stories of "hardworking" Americans, these stories made once-popular government assistance programs look like handouts to the undeserving. When Reagan finally became president in 1980, he made good on his word to put the brakes on what he viewed as Keynesian excess. Reagan used his first year in office (1981), for example, to cut in half the funds allocated to public housing and Section 8 (Dreier 2011).

By the time Bill Clinton came to the White House, hopes that the Democrats would reverse course, at least in urban American, were muted. After the 1994 midterm elections President Clinton found himself boxed in by an activist Republican Congress. The 1994 Republican "Contract with America," for example, made no mention of urban America, but many of the policies it outlined, such as welfare reform, sent a clear signal to mayors grappling with persistent poverty and unemployment—"you are on your own." And the growing fear that Clinton was a "closet" neoliberal was cemented in 1996 when he used his State of the Union address to declare that "the era of big government is over" (Clinton 1997, 79). Indeed, within a year Clinton approved a welfare reform package that cut benefits and limited the time recipients could receive them. The effect on cities was costly. People kicked off the rolls often ended up placing greater demands on locally financed public services such as homeless shelters and foster-care programs.

Cities also found themselves economically unable to hold neoliberalism at bay by replacing it with local variants of Keynesianism. Some cities, like DC, were near bankruptcy and had no money left to spend (Barras 1998; Gillette 2006). By the late 1980s the District's government was relying on accounting gimmicks to balance its budgets (Abramowitz and Greene 1989). Even solvent cities faced bleak long-term prospects. Continued suburbanization meant declining population, and as a result, a shrinking tax base. The fact that people who stayed behind tended to be poorer, sicker, and less educated than those who left also meant that increased local spending would at best stabilize problems but not solve them.

Cities also could not borrow their way back to Keynesianism (Phillips-Fein 2013; Sinclair 1994). Before the 1990s, cities often issued bonds to finance "public goods," a catchall category that included utilities, roads, and public housing, among other things. However, after several urban bankruptcies and near defaults in the seventies and eighties, banks grew pickier about buying bonds issued by cities (see Phillips-Fein 2013 for information on New York). In particular, banks began relying more heavily on credit-rating agencies to determine whether city bonds were financially sound investments. And bond-rating agencies started holding evidence of urban decline against cities as they assessed municipal bond offerings. Instead of focusing on a city's financials—its budget, its ability to raise taxes for repayment if necessary—the agencies started including factors beyond cities' immediate control, including high poverty rates, the balance between professional and unskilled labor, and long-term population projections. Moody's, for example, downgraded Detroit's bond rating in 1992, using factors such as population loss, high unemployment, and high taxes to justify its decision (Sinclair

1994). Since then, credit-rating agencies have continued to use external factors to downgrade urban bonds (Walsh 2009).

Given these constraints, most cities had little option but to adopt a business-like posture. However, the way cities adopted this new approach was subject to variation. There was no neoliberal how-to manual for cities to consult.[14] Instead, cities had a menu of options before them—bureaucracy reduction, privatization, business-friendly tax and zoning reform, and public-private partnerships—but little instruction on how to implement them. It was an open question, for example, how cities should pair menu items (privatize bureaucratic functions and reduce services or privatize bureaucratic functions and keep services stable?) or apportion them (privatize a little or a lot?).[15]

In many ways DC is no different from other cities that had to grapple (or are still grappling) with the pressures just outlined. However, DC also faced an added layer of constraints. As DC's license plate tagline "taxation without representation" suggests, the city has unique political constraints.

Why Neoliberalism Prevails in DC

When the U.S. Constitution was written in 1776, the fledgling country did not have a permanent capital. The founders wanted one, though, and gave the new government the authority to establish one. Specifically, Article 1, Section 8, granted Congress the following powers:

> To exercise exclusive Legislation in all Cases whatsoever, over such District (not exceeding ten Miles square) as may, by Cession of particular States, and the Acceptance of Congress, become the Seat of the Government of the United States, and to exercise like Authority over all Places purchased by the Consent of the Legislature of the State in which the Same shall be, for the Erection of Forts, Magazines, Arsenals, dock-Yards, and other needful Buildings.

---

14. Neil Brenner, Jamie Peck, and Nik Theodore argue that neoliberalism is a "rascal concept" because it is "promiscuously pervasive, yet inconsistently defined, empirically imprecise and frequently contested" (2010, 182). Although this comment refers to scholarly definitions of neoliberalism, their point is applicable here inasmuch as there has never been one understanding or definition for the implementation of neoliberal policies in urban settings.
15. Privatization after the 1982 debt crisis provides a useful, if international, reminder of the imprecision that attends the application of neoliberalism on the ground. After the 1982 crisis, for example, African countries privatized more slowly than their Latin American counterparts (Simmons, Dobbins, and Garrett 2007). Likewise, minority populations in Africa were more heavily involved in asset purchase than those in Latin America were (Starr 1988).

As this excerpt makes clear, Congress did not see the District as equivalent to a state. In many ways this view is not surprising. When the Constitution was written, there was no such district in place. And when the first president, George Washington, selected territory for the District, it was largely uninhabited. The proposed ten-square-mile site, carved out of land from Maryland and Virginia and bisected by the Potomac River, contained only two small settlements—Alexandria and Georgetown.

Once the proposed city was built, however, new residents began to arrive. By 1800 the District had a respectable population (just over 11,000) by the standards of the day (Gibson 1998). The city's population also grew rapidly after the Civil War. In 1860, when the war began, just over 61,000 residents lived in the city. Twenty years later, the city's population had more than doubled to 147,000 (Gibson 1998). Many of the city's new arrivals were freed slaves. Indeed, a third of city residents were black according to the 1880 census (Williams 2009).

It was not until 1973 that the District was given a measure of autonomy over its internal affairs. That year Congress passed the District of Columbia Home Rule Act. It allowed the city to elect a mayor and a city council with eight geographic seats and five at large. However, the act also explicitly laid out several restrictions on the new city government, including but not limited to taxing the federal government or its workers who live in other jurisdictions, running deficits, or issuing bonds over 17 percent of annual revenue.

Although the Home Rule Act partially solved the problem of local disenfranchisement, the problem of federal disenfranchisement persists. Citizens in the District of Columbia still do not have voting members in either the Senate or House of Representatives. And Congress continues to have the power to veto legislation passed by the city council.

This context is important for understanding DC's embrace of neoliberalism. When DC found itself in dire straits in the early 1990s, it did not have the same wiggle room that other similarly struggling cities had. None of this is to suggest, of course, that any cities struggling with suburbanization, deindustrialization, and/or disinvestment had good options before them. However, unlike other cities, DC was prohibited by law from running deficits or declaring bankruptcy. It was also severely restricted in using taxation to improve its circumstances (i.e., it cannot tax its largest business). Most important, the structure of home rule meant that Congress could intervene in the city's financial affairs if its budget was in or near arrears, which is exactly what it did in 1995 when it imposed the unpopular District of Columbia Financial Responsibility and Management Assistance Act on the city. In short, DC had no say over whether or when it adopted neoliberal reforms.

In the next section I look at the concrete steps that DC has taken in its adoption and implementation of neoliberalism. Specifically, I focus on two steps the city took to turn itself around. The first was strategic: developing an approach to growing its tax base. The second was tactical and imposed initially by the control board: reorienting the city's budget away from social safety net provision.

It is worth noting that these steps did not constitute a formal a priori plan for development. The control board's approach, at least initially, was single-minded—to balance the city's budget. Efforts to rebuild the city were developed later. There is also no one person responsible for instituting neoliberalism in the city. The control board instituted the city's austerity plan, but the plan was implemented and buttressed by four mayors, including Marion Barry (1995–1999), Anthony Williams (1999–2007), Adrian Fenty (2007–2011), and Vincent Gray (2011–2015), as well as a series of city councils.

Finally, this history is brief and thus incomplete. Space constraints prevent a detailed account of important issues like changes to the zoning code or the creation of business improvement districts (BIDs). Suffice it to say that the goal of this history is not to present a technical, nuts-and-bolts review of how redevelopment occurred. Rather, through vignettes of particular programs, policies, and decisions, I highlight the new priorities that attended the city's shift toward neoliberalism.

Urban Neoliberal Governance: The Case of DC

Growing the Population

Perhaps the first and most important element of the District's recovery plan was the effort to grow its population. The city's population began a steady decline after hitting a peak of just over eight hundred thousand in 1950. Outmigration had many negative effects, but the most important for the city was the contraction of its tax base. And unfortunately, DC was constrained in how it could fill the gap, since home rule prevented DC from making up the shortfall by taxing either its largest employer or the commuters who worked for it.

A declining tax base was also bad news for a city required to provide both city- and state-level services. Indeed, the year the control board was established, DC was responsible for running a Medicaid program (usually a state function), two prisons (the city jail and a facility in Lorton, Virginia[16]), two court systems (local and appellate), and a university (DC Appleseed Center 1997).

---

16. In 1997 Congress allowed DC to transfer convicted felons into the federal Bureau of Prisons and close its Lorton facility (Shin 2001).

Given the restrictions on what and who DC could tax, as well as its hefty service obligations, the city decided to focus on growing its residential tax base. In particular, it hoped to entice people to the city from adjacent suburbs in Maryland and Virginia. The big question, of course, was how to get people to come (or return) to the city.

In 1995 DC was not considered an especially attractive place to live. The year before the control board took over, the city recorded 399 homicides—lower than the "murder city" years but still disturbingly high. The city's bureaucracy was also in shambles. City services were routinely described as "failing" in the *Washington Post* (Garreau 1995, C1; Loeb 1995a, B3; 1995b, A1; Locy 1995, A1). During the first five months of 1995 two city agencies were put into federal receivership. In January the city lost control over its public housing (Loeb 1995a), and in May a federal court seized control of the city's child welfare system—"the first time any court in the nation has seized control of an entire child welfare system" (Locy 1995, A1). City schools were not under federal receivership, but conditions were just as bleak. A 1995 report on the city's education system described it as "needing millions of dollars in repairs," having "inadequate supplies and outdated textbooks," and struggling under "an oppressive bureaucracy" (Horwitz 1995, B1). In short, headlines from the city's paper of record were often eye-popping, if unintentional, advertisements for why people should stay away. Given the negative buzz surrounding the city in 1995, its leaders would obviously have to do more than hang a welcome shingle on Key Bridge. They would have to develop a strategy for whom to attract to the city and how to entice them. They would also need to figure out how to finance those efforts.

In a 2001 Brookings Institution report about DC's options for increasing its tax base, Carol O'Cleireacain and Alice Rivlin (a former control board member), outlined two potential strategies the city could adopt—the "adult strategy" and the "family strategy" (5).[17] The adult strategy was designed to attract people in two overlapping categories—people with high incomes and people with no (or adult) children. The report suggested the city could attract these groups by selling its "cultural amenities, restaurants, nightlife, and racial, ethnic, and income diversity" (5). This strategy was based on the idea that high-income, childless adults would increase the city's income tax base and eventually its real estate tax base. As wealthier residents moved in, they would presumably improve their homes, increasing their tax value and in the process boosting city tax coffers. Rising home

---

17. These strategies are best seen as ideal types, or generalized approaches to redevelopment, rather than concrete plans. Moreover, the authors caution that "the point [of this exercise] is not to choose one or the other, but to understand more clearly where policy choices might lead" (5).

values would in turn encourage developers to build new housing, which the city could also tax.

The family strategy was designed to attract middle-class families back to the city. The term "middle class" is, of course, notoriously vague. O'Cleireacain and Rivlin described the group occupationally, as "teachers, law-enforcement officers, nurses and other medical service providers, university faculty and staff, and professional, technical, and clerical workers in both government and the private sector" (2001, 6). The family strategy would presumably require less new housing than the adult strategy, since each household would have more members (e.g., two adults and two children instead of one adult). And the infusion of new school-age children in the district could stop (and potentially reverse) erosion in the public school system's enrollment. More middle-class families in the school system could also help stabilize the system.

Although both strategies came with benefits, O'Cleireacain and Rivlin (2001) argued that the family strategy would be the harder of the two plans to implement. It would also cost significantly more money. A quick look at the process and cost of each strategy explains why.

According to O'Cleireacain and Rivlin (2001), the adult strategy could largely be implemented through the city's extant planning process. A key ingredient for the strategy—more housing—could be accomplished with three easy policy fixes. The first was to ease the permitting and zoning procedures for developers interested in building housing in the city. The second was to help developers "assemble packages of land for development" (5). Specifically, O'Cleireacain and Rivlin suggested that the city could use its condemnation powers to seize long-vacant properties. Many neighborhoods had entire blocks of vacant properties, so condemned parcels could be easily consolidated for large-scale development. Third, the city could open up waterfront areas along the Potomac and Anacostia Rivers for high-density residential development.

The adult strategy would also entail limited costs, most of which could be borne by developers. O'Cleireacain and Rivlin (2001) noted that developers were already interested in the city but needed help getting started. Moreover, even though new residents would strain some city services—notably trash collection and vehicle registrations—they would have little to no impact on more costly services, such as education and welfare, because they have high incomes and no school-age children.

In contrast to the adult strategy, the family strategy would be more complicated and expensive to enact. In fact, because of the complications, O'Cleireacain and Rivlin (2001) suggested the strategy be implemented neighborhood by neighborhood rather than citywide all at once. They listed four policies that would have to be applied to make the family strategy work.

The first would be to target a selection of neighborhoods for implementation. Ideally, these areas would have an anchor institution, such as a university or hospital that the city could partner with to build middle-class housing, first for anchor institution employees and later for similar workers at other institutions. Second, public schools in targeted neighborhoods would need to be improved. Ideally, these schools would also be integrated with other community services, such as senior or day-care centers, effectively becoming a second-tier anchor. Third, the city would need to encourage affordable-housing construction and protect low-income families from displacement. These goals could be accomplished through a mix of subsidies (to developers willing to build affordable housing) and regulations (to limit rent and property tax increases). The final policy entailed bringing back city employees currently living outside the city. O'Cleireacain and Rivlin observed, for example, that most of the city's firefighters, teachers, and police live in suburban Maryland or Virginia.

The projected costs of implementing the family strategy were also much higher than those for the adult strategy. The primary reason is that middle-class families typically use more services and bring in fewer tax dollars than wealthier, childless households. The majority of costs would be incurred by the school system, already troubled by years of neglect and mismanagement. O'Cleireacain and Rivlin (2001) estimated, for example, that singles and childless couples would provide a yearly net economic benefit to the city (between $4,343 and $12,950), while families would create a net loss (between $6,253 and $16,583).

While O'Cleireacain and Rivlin (2001) acknowledged the higher price tag of the family strategy, they also noted that the adult strategy would come at an important social cost. As they explained, it "poses a serious risk of exacerbating racial and class tensions and widening the gulf between rich and poor in the city" (6), since new residents are more likely than existing residents to be white, wealthy, and young.

Given that both strategies pose serious risks, albeit very different ones, O'Cleireacain and Rivlin (2001) suggested that the city adopt a middle path to attract singles, childless couples, and families with children. In many ways, DC has followed this advice, adopting key components of both plans.

In terms of the adult strategy, for example, DC made good on calls to increase the city's housing stock. Between 2000 and 2010, some 27,124 new housing units were built in the city. And the building boom is ongoing. In April 2012, there were 8,704 units under construction and another 33,444 in the "planning and conceptual" stage (District of Columbia Office of Planning 2012). These changes are easily seen on the landscape, as entire blocks, vacant or in disrepair ten years ago, have been transformed into mixed-used developments—usually mid-rise apartment buildings with street-level retail. Cranes regularly punctuate the skyline in neighborhoods like NOMA (North of Massachusetts) and the New York Avenue corridor.

However, the city has also made efforts to attract families back to the district. The earliest effort came in 1997, when Anthony Williams lobbied Congress for tax incentives that would encourage people to buy homes in the District. He argued that home ownership in central-city areas would help "the alleviation of urban decay and the stabilization of central city neighborhoods" in DC (Tong 2005, 2). The program was passed as part of the 1997 Taxpayer Relief Act. While the tax credit was open to any first-time home buyer, it was targeted to low- and middle-income home buyers because the credit declined incrementally for incomes above $70,000 for singles and $110,000 for couples. A study by Fannie Mae Foundation in 2005 found that the program was successful (Tong 2005). It not only encouraged home ownership among targeted groups but also contributed to appreciation of home values in the city, which in turn helped low-income residents build equity.

The city also opted to take on the central task necessary to make the family strategy work—school reform. And rather than tackle the problem one school at a time, as O'Cleireacain and Rivlin (2001) had suggested, the city went big, initiating a systemwide reform effort. In the spring of 2007 the city council approved a reform package proposed by then mayor Adrian Fenty. Fenty and his supporters had argued that the city's schools were in poor condition in large part because the Board of Education, which ran the system, was more responsive to the teachers' union than to students. Under the new legislation, the mayor was put in charge of the school system's budget and given the power to hire (and fire) the school superintendent (Nakamura 2007).

After the reform passed, Fenty hired Michelle Rhee, a then little-known school reformer, to run the system. Rhee would use her bully pulpit in DC to catapult herself and urban education reform into the national spotlight. Under her leadership, DC became a test site for several controversial reforms, including tying teachers' pay to students' test performance. Rhee was a divisive figure in DC, and it is too soon to tell whether her efforts will improve the system, but Fenty's decision to take over the schools—long considered one of the city's most intractable problems—and to hire a dynamic superintendent with a take-no-prisoners attitude suggests the city was at least willing to do something to keep families in the city who could not afford its tony private schools.

Despite the blend of adult and family strategies employed by the city, outcomes have not been evenly balanced between the two. Patterns in the city's growth indicate the city's approach has tended to tilt (whether purposively or not) toward the adult strategy. This tilt is evident even when we look at policies seemingly consistent with the family strategy outlined by O'Cleireacain and Rivlin (2001). Some of these policies were too small or too poorly funded to make a big impact. Others ended up helping families, but primarily wealthy ones not in need of a boost.

Perhaps the most important sign that the adult strategy is prevailing is the decline in the number of families living in the district. In 2000, for example, 46 percent of households in the District were classified as "family households." Ten years later the percentage was 42.3. Census data on the number of households with individuals under eighteen years of age are also telling. Between 2000 and 2010 the total number of households with individuals under eighteen declined by nearly 4 percent, from 24.6 percent to 20.7 percent.[18]

A recent story in the real estate section of the *Washington Post* puts a face on the change by highlighting one of the city's newest residents, Amy (Dietsch 2013). If the adult strategy were a movie, Amy would be straight out of central casting. In her early sixties, she moved to the district after a divorce. Her former home, a four-bedroom split-level in nearby Bethesda, felt too big, so she bought a seventeen hundred–square-foot bungalow in the city's Tenleytown neighborhood. Amy is, the article notes, "part of a growing wave of one-person households" in the city—up to 45 percent, according to census data from the 2011 American Community Survey (Dietsch 2013, E1). And if we use purchasing power as evidence, Amy is also wealthy. Her new house costs $740,000, and she spent another $124,000 renovating it (Dietsch 2013).

Another piece of evidence that city efforts to grow its population have tilted toward the adult strategy can be found in how the city has tried to mitigate displacement. Recall that the family strategy calls for subsidies to ensure that the supply of affordable housing keeps pace with demand from low- and middle-income residents. While the city does have programs in place to address affordable housing needs, they are not sufficient to the task.

During the time period considered here, the city's primary vehicle for subsidizing affordable housing was the Housing Production Trust Fund. The fund has been in existence since 1988 but was basically a do-nothing entity for the first twelve years of its life because it lacked a stable source of financing. In 2002, Mayor Anthony Williams approved legislation to finally provide the fund with a permanent source of financing—15 percent of the city's proceeds from deed recording and transfer taxes were earmarked for the fund.

The fund is generally used in two ways: to fund developers willing to build or renovate affordable housing and to subsidize tenants interested in buying their buildings through the TOPA process. When Williams signed the legislation, the city was just entering a real estate boom, so the fund was flush for several years. Estimates suggest that it has been used to build or

---

18. These data are from the American FactFinder website.

preserve between seventy-five hundred (Reed 2013b) and eighty-nine hundred (DePillis 2010c) affordable units since 2002.

While the fund has been used to build or preserve some affordable housing, it has not been enough to seriously mitigate displacement or provide a counterweight to the new market-rate construction. The executive director of a local nonprofit, the Coalition for Nonprofit Housing and Economic Development, put it succinctly when he told a *Washington Post* reporter that "it is a fraction of what's needed" (Pierre 2007, B2). Indeed, the estimated number of preserved units is about one-third the number of new market-rate units produced in a similar time frame.

When the recession hit in 2008, the city's housing market came to a virtual standstill, and city revenues from real estate transactions dried up. As a result, so did the fund (Biegler 2012). When the housing market began improving in 2010, affordable-housing advocates hoped the city would replenish the fund. Instead, Mayor Vincent Gray opted to borrow money from the fund for another city-sponsored affordable-housing initiative—essentially "robbing Peter to pay Paul," as one local blogger put it (Baer 2012). The move was surprising, not just because the funds were transferred between affordable housing programs but also because Gray had been a vocal critic of the way gentrification was unfolding in the city. His 2010 mayoral campaign slogan—"One City"—was widely viewed as a rejoinder to Mayor Adrian Fenty, whose policies were often seen as favoring the city's white, wealthy wards over its poorer, minority wards. Although the city council restored a portion of the money taken from the fund in its 2013 budget (Weiner 2013) and provided a one-time infusion of $63 million for fiscal year 2014, the fact that the fund's financing depends on a healthy real estate market and is often short of what is needed suggests that the fund was never intended to serve as an engine for preserving, let alone expanding, middle-class housing in the city. Rather, it was "built small," designed to make an impact on the margins but not the center.

A final piece of evidence that the city's approach to growing its population has tilted toward the adult strategy can be seen in the way school reform has affected enrollment in the District of Columbia Public School System (DCPS). Reforming the school system was supposed to keep existing schoolchildren in the system (especially in middle school when attrition is highest) and entice young professionals transitioning to parenthood into it. Despite its goals, the city's approach to school reform has had a counterintuitive effect on DCPS enrollment. Rather than growth, the system experienced an initial contraction in enrollment.

Registration in DCPS reached its zenith in 1967 when 146,000 students attended schools in the system. For the next forty years, enrollment declined steadily. When I arrived in the city in the fall of 1998, for example, just over

70,000 students were enrolled in DCPS (Filardo et al. 2008). By the fall of 2006, just before Rhee took over the system, DCPS's enrollment was 52,107, almost twenty thousand fewer students. In the two years after Rhee took over the system, enrollment continued to drop.[19] In the fall of 2008, for example, enrollment was at 45,120. In the fall of 2009 it fell to 44,620.[20]

Enrollment drops after Rhee took over the system (in part, with a mission to increase them) are due in large part to her decision to make cost cutting an integral part of the reform effort. Of particular interest here is Rhee's decision to trim costs by closing underpopulated schools. Rhee reasoned that it was more costly to run a low-enrolled school than to combine it with another and use the savings for core spending priorities. However, many families with children at schools set to close responded by taking their children out of DCPS. An analysis of the effect of the closings by a consortium of think thanks found that many parents opted not to place their children in designated receiving schools because they were "poorer performing" than the closing school, geographically distant, and/or difficult to get to (21st Century School Fund, Urban Institute, and Brookings Institution 2009, 11). Parents interviewed in a *Washington Post* story about the closings expressed similar concerns. One parent complained that her son's new receiving school was in a "dangerous neighborhood" and "too far away" for him to walk there (Labbé and Nakamura 2008, B1). Many parents moved their children to public charter schools after the closings. The consortium's analysis found that "students from closed schools attended charters at more than double the rate of students from non-closed schools" (21st Century School Fund, Urban Institute, and Brookings Institution 2009, 7).

None of this review is meant to suggest that Rhee is behind the city's charter school growth or that the shift to charters is bad (or good). The move to charters began well before Rhee's decision to close schools and has continued since. The debate over the merits of charter schools is also well beyond the scope of this book. However, the school-closing decision can be evaluated in relation to the city's attempts to grow its population. And those efforts are inconsistent with the family strategy. In particular, the closure of public schools is contrary to O'Cleireacain and Rivlin's (2001) idea that improving neighborhood schools can anchor low- and middle-income families in the city while also attracting new residents of similar income levels. Closed schools cannot serve as anchors, and it remains an open question whether charter schools can. Indeed, most charter schools rent their instructional space and, thus, frequently move in search of cheaper rents, improved space, and so on. Charter advocates argue that the city should allow charters to rent

---

19. Post-2000 DCPS enrollment data were taken from Neighborhood Info DC.
20. Enrollments began to stabilize in 2012 and have grown incrementally since (Turque 2012).

the city's shuttered schools, but DCPS's current chancellor wants to keep the schools available should enrollment increase (Brown 2013). Unless charters can find a way to ground themselves in neighborhoods, their ability to fulfill the neighborhood anchor role is questionable.

It is also worth noting the negative symbolism attached to the DCPS closures. All but one of the twenty-three schools on Rhee's closure list were east of Rock Creek Park, and six were east of the Anacostia River (recall that wealth declines as one moves from west to east in the city). Parents with children in closed schools did not, therefore, see the neighborhood benefits attached to improved schools. Instead, they saw the improvements as weighted to the west in areas where the white share of the population was greatest and incomes were higher than the city average.

Cutting the Fat: Human Services

A second plank in the city's recovery plan involved taking a scalpel to its bloated budget. Three principles governed the process. First, although cuts were made across the board, they were concentrated in human services. Second, decisions about what to cut were driven, at least initially, by the control board. Third, though individuals set to lose their jobs complained bitterly about the cuts, city residents were more sanguine about them. Journalists, for example, had long observed that the city's bureaucratic expansion contributed to inefficiency because new positions were designed to create jobs, not improve services (Fisher 2011; Loeb 1995b; Montgomery 1999). Most city residents hated dealing with the city's unruly bureaucracy. Officials were widely seen as lazy, inept, and often hostile. A *Washington Post* story on the state of the city's bureaucracy four years after the control board was created is telling. Although things had begun to improve, many problems lingered. One resident told a reporter she was "totally dreading" her trip to the Department of Motor Vehicles (DMV). Another described city employees as "nasty, just for the sake of being nasty." The mayor had equally harsh words, telling the reporter that "we need to free ourselves from the tyranny of those DMV lines" (Montgomery 1999, A1).

It is impossible to cover all of the cuts the city has made since 1995. Here, I highlight two particularly contentious examples of the process. The first is the city's 2001 decision to shut down its public hospital, DC General. The second is the city's 2007 decision to close the Franklin School, a downtown homeless shelter. The results were mixed.

DC General

In 1995, when the control board was created, the District financed and ran its own public hospital, DC General. The hospital was open to all city residents and, unlike other hospitals in the city, provided comprehensive care to the uninsured. The hospital was, however, plagued with long-standing managerial problems and poor patient outcomes.

In 1997 the city converted DC General into a public benefit corporation (PBC). The goal of the conversion was to give the hospital more control over the money it received from the city and allow it to keep insurance payments from paying patients. While the PBC structure did allow the hospital more control over its finances, many of the hospital's long-standing managerial problems persisted. The hospital's billing office remained a mess—informal audits found evidence of under- and overbilling—and administrators were unable or unwilling to stay within allotted budgets (Meyer et al. 2010).

At another time, things might have continued on as they were. DC General had been poorly run for decades without much intervention. However, city finances were now being scrutinized from above. According to a Brookings Institution report about DC General's closure (Meyer et al. 2010), the hospital's problems were discussed at a summer 2000 meeting between the control board and the congressional subcommittee overseeing it. The subcommittee told the control board that it would no longer permit deficit spending at DC General and that the city would need to find a better way to meet the health needs of its uninsured population. During the budget process later that fall Congress formalized its message in a directive to the city's chief financial officer (CFO), Natwar Ghandi (Meyer et al. 2010).[21] After receiving the directive, Ghandi alerted city officials that DC General would run out of funds by March of the following year.

Initially, Mayor Anthony Williams proposed expanding the city's Medicaid program to include all residents making up to 200 percent of the federal poverty limit. Williams's plan received a cool reception on the city council, however. In addition to concerns about costs, the city council doubted city officials could successfully implement an expansion in the short time span within which it was working.

As a result, the city adopted a private-sector solution that contained two major changes. First, the city would no longer provide health care directly to its residents. Instead, the city would contract with private health-care providers to deliver services to the city's uninsured population. Two companies received contracts—DC Chartered Health Plan and UnitedHealthcare. The city manages enrollment in the system, which is modeled after a

---

21. The CFO position was created as part of the 1995 District of Columbia Financial Responsibility and Management Assistance Act. The new position was placed at the same level as the mayor on the executive office organizational chart, and the person filling it reported directly to the control board. The position, which took over key financial powers from the mayor's office, was essentially a shadow mayor for budgetary issues.

health maintenance organization (HMO), and pays its two providers a lump sum per year to deliver care. Second, the city decided to close DC General. Patients are now seen wherever participating doctors work.

The hospital's closing was met with anxiety and anger by its primarily African American clientele (Mencimer 2001). Although many of DC General's patients knew firsthand how poor the services were, they doubted the city's other, often-elite hospitals would take them in. The other hospitals were seen as geographically and culturally distant. DC General, located next to the Anacostia River, was in a majority black neighborhood. The Georgetown University Medical Center—one of the hospitals slated to receive DC General's patients—was located on the far western edge of town in a wealthy white neighborhood.

For their part, the city's other hospitals worried their emergency rooms would be inundated with uninsured patients. Hospitals would have to staff more doctors and nurses, and they worried that costs of care would not be reimbursed. Indeed, the reason that DC General was closed—budget cuts—left many hospital administrators doubtful.

Although many residents' worst fears were never realized, the city's experience privatizing its health-care system has been mixed. On the positive side, the city has significantly increased the percentage of residents with health insurance. Between October 2003 and March 2009, enrollment in the city's two plans nearly tripled, from 17,573 to 52,384 participants (Meyer et al. 2010).

However, many problems remain. One of the new system's biggest problems is that it has had difficulty attracting sufficient numbers of physicians to the network (Meyer et al. 2010). Its patients also continue to have poor health outcomes, likely because the new system is not set up to address "the social determinants of health, such as personal behavior, income, education and environmental factors" (4).

The corporate behavior of one of the program's contractors, DC Chartered Health Plan, also created problems for the city. In 2008 the city's Department of Insurance Securities and Banking issued an audit of DC Chartered's financial condition. Although the audit found no substantial problems with the company or its dealing with the city, it did shed unflattering light on the company's organizational structure. Specifically, the audit reported that DC Chartered was owned by a holding company, D.C. Healthcare Systems, whose sole proprietor was a local businessman named Jeffrey Thompson (DeBonis 2012c). Moreover, the report indicated that DC Chartered Health Plan's charter required it to pay annual dividends to its holding company (effectively Thompson as its sole owner). Between 2006 and 2008, Thompson received nearly $7.5 million in dividend payments (DeBonis 2012b, 2012c).

In March 2008, shortly after the report was filed, the city sued DC Chartered for overbilling on Medicaid claims (Suderman 2011). The city eventually dropped the case after DC Chartered agreed to return $12 million to the city. However, the settlement put a crimp in Thompson's personal bottom line. In 2009, DC Chartered ran a deficit, and the next year's profit was too small for Thompson to receive a dividend (DeBonis 2012c).

In 2012 Jeffrey Thompson also found himself at the center of a political scandal. The problems began in March when federal agents raided his home and office. Prosecutors alleged that Thompson had masterminded a shadow campaign for Vincent Gray's 2010 mayoral run, funneling thousands of dollars in off-the-book donations to Gray's campaign staff. Thompson was allegedly angry at the Fenty administration's lawsuit over Medicaid overbilling and wanted to install a friendlier mayor in the Wilson Building (Steward 2013).[22]

Things only got worse for Thompson as the year went on. In October the city petitioned the Superior Court of the District of Columbia to put Thompson's company into receivership. A city audit had uncovered "significant irregularities" in the company's financial records (District of Columbia Department of Insurance, Securities and Banking 2012). And after the company submitted amended financial statements, the city successfully argued in court that the company could not fulfill its contractual obligations.

Although few people want to return to DC General's emergency-room-as-primary-care model, the decision to privatize its low-income health care has been no panacea for the city. Expanding insurance coverage was a positive move for the city. However, critics rightly note that the city's taxpayers were poorly served by its arrangement with DC Chartered. The millions of dollars in dividends paid to Thompson could have and should have been invested in patient care.

Franklin School Homeless Shelter

The second example of DC's exercise in budget cutting—the closure of a homeless shelter in the city's historic Franklin School—provides a recent, post–control board look at the process and offers a glimpse of what a more severe application of neoliberalism looks like. As its name suggests, the shelter was initially a school. Built in 1869, the Benjamin Franklin School was designed to be the flagship of the city's then new public education system (Dutra 2002).

The school was closed in 1925. In the decades that followed, city officials used the building only intermittently, and it fell into disrepair. In 2002 the city decided to convert the former school into a men's homeless shelter

---

22. Thompson signed a plea agreement with prosecutors in 2014 acknowledging his role in the shadow campaign (Brown and Fisher 2014).

Figure 2.3 The Franklin shelter in Washington, DC, February 2013. (Photo by the author.)

(Figure 2.3). At the time, the building's location downtown was ideal for a shelter, since most of the city's homeless population and numerous charities serving them were already clustered downtown.

Five years later, in 2007, Mayor Adrian Fenty decided to close the shelter. He argued that conditions at the shelter were abysmal. The building needed major repair work and was dangerously overcrowded. It also had a bedbug infestation and lacked proper fire escapes (Greenwood 2011). Speaking to a local journalist, a city administrator described the closing as a "humane act": "It's finally time to close a terrible place." He also argued that the city wanted to move away from "warehousing" the city's homeless population in shelters and focus instead on moving them into transitional housing. As the official explained, "What we've been doing for 30 years isn't working. You can in fact cure this problem for some people." As an example, he cited efforts to clear a homeless encampment near Interstate 395. "We took 10 people off the median strip of I-395. . . . A year later, all 10 are in apartments, and no one has asked to go back to the median strip" (Fisher 2008, B1).

Opponents of the closure saw the city's motives for closing the shelter differently. They argued that it was part of the city's effort to consolidate redevelopment in downtown, paving the way for even more high-end housing and retail developments. The shelter's location, two blocks east of the White House, had been in a relatively dead part of town—busy with federal workers during the day but empty at night. By 2007, however, the area's nightlife was picking up. The shelter was within walking distance of the revamped Penn Quarter neighborhood and the Verizon Center, where the city's Major League Hockey and National Basketball Association teams (the Capitals and the Wizards) play.

However one interprets the Fenty administration's motivations, the shelter's closing created numerous problems for the homeless men who used it. The city's remaining shelter space was not large enough to absorb all the men who lost beds at the center, and though the city promised to find accommodation for them before the shelter closed, it did not have alternatives in place on the shelter's final day (Nakamura 2008).

The Fenty administration was also forced to revert to the so-called warehousing model after the 2008 recession, when the city experienced a sharp spike in homelessness, especially among working families with no history of prior homelessness (Cherkis 2013; Gowen 2011). In the winter of 2008, for example, the city decided to repurpose the old DC General building to serve as a hypothermia center for homeless families.[23] Three years later, more than two hundred families were calling DC General home (Cherkis 2013). The shelter is still in use at the time of writing (winter 2015), having morphed into a permanent shelter with year-round residents, but the city council recently voted to close it in the near future.

Although the city's homeless population has increased rapidly since the 2008 recession, the city has no plans to repair and reopen the Franklin shelter. Indeed, a few weeks after the shelter was closed, the Fenty administration issued a solicitation for developers interested in working with the city to redevelop the site (O'Connell 2009). As of the winter of 2015, the city had yet to find a partner. The building's interior is in bad shape—crumbling ceilings, old pipes, and faulty electrical wiring. The property is also listed as a

---

23. DC has a right-to-shelter law that requires the District to provide homeless residents access to shelter when the temperature drops below 32°F. Before 2007 the city used DC General sporadically as an overflow space for homeless residents during the hypothermia season. In the winter of 2007–2008, however, the city substantially increased the bed capacity at the hospital.

National Historic Landmark, meaning renovations must follow guidelines for historic properties, which tend to be costly and limit how interior space can be repurposed.

What Does DC's Neoliberal Turn Mean for Tenants?

If we think about urban neoliberalism on a spectrum ranging from less to more extreme, DC's experience would fall on the less extreme side of the spectrum. Although the city made significant cuts to social services after the control board was created, it has maintained a commitment to ensuring key aspects of the social safety net. The most obvious example is the city's approach to low-income health-care provision. While the city closed DC General—a move that created fear and anxiety among the city's low-income population and had negative symbolic fallout as well—it did not abandon its effort to subsidize low-income health care. It moved away from the de facto emergency-room-as-primary-care model that DC General entailed and toward a subsidized HMO approach. Today, the city's rate of uninsured citizens is lower than it was when DC General was closed. Moreover, its rate is among the lowest in the metropolitan region (U.S. Census Bureau 2013). The greatest criticism of the new approach is that city contracts for provision of care were subject to corporate malfeasance and greed—significant problems but ones that have not yet, at least, involved cuts to patient care. The lesson here is that the dictates of neoliberalism notwithstanding, cities can continue to maintain so-called Keynesian goals under neoliberal structures. Scholars of neoliberalism will not find this surprising (Brenner and Theodore 2002; Brenner, Peck, and Theodore 2010), but the point is worth highlighting because it demonstrates that cities, and individuals within them, can respond to the broad mandates of neoliberalism in ways that deviate from its ideological imperatives.

However, it is also true that the city has done very little to keep its most vulnerable citizens in place as the city gentrifies. Though we cannot fault the city's initial efforts to grow its population, we can fault its response to the negative side effects that resulted. When confronted with obvious and direct evidence of displacement, the city's response has been insufficient and in some cases hostile.

The Housing Production Trust Fund demonstrates the insufficient nature of the city's response. The program does not have a stable source of funding; nor is its budget, even in the best of years, capable of meeting more than a fraction of the need it is meant to address. These problems have been well documented for years. The city's response has been to ignore them. Even large, one-time infusions of cash will not solve its long-term problems.

The city's decision to close the Franklin shelter demonstrates the hostility that has sometimes attended the city's neoliberal reforms. While no one can fault the city for wanting to move its homeless population into cleaner, healthier spaces, the city closed the shelter without having replacement spots ready for those negatively impacted by it. Moreover, the city's continued use of the warehousing model for dealing with homelessness suggests the Franklin shelter's closing was at least as much about clearing the space for redevelopment as it was about protecting the homeless from the hazards of shelter life.

The growth in the city's homeless population was also, at least partially, caused by the city's failure to respond to the negative consequences of its revitalization efforts. Some of the increase, of course, is due to the 2008 recession, which upended the budgets of many families who had no prior history of homelessness. However, the city's population of homeless families has continued to grow even as the recession wanes. Between 2008 and 2012, for example, the city's homeless family population increased 46 percent (Harding 2012). By the winter of 2014 the old DC General was sheltering even more families than it did in 2011—288 families in total, including 600 children (Gowen 2013; Cherkis 2013).

Amber Harding (2012), an attorney with the Washington Legal Clinic for the Homeless, argues that the steep increase in the city's homeless families despite the waning recession is due to the city's decision to change how it allocates money reserved for affordable housing. Specifically, the city has shifted resources from programs like the Local Rent Supplement Program, which provides long-term rent subsidies to eligible residents, to programs like the city's new Rapid Rehousing Program, which provides short-term rent subsidies (usually for a year) to families willing to move out of its shelters. The idea behind Rapid Rehousing—that a family could go from being homeless to paying market rate rents in one year—is overly optimistic at best and naïve at worst. Even some city officials involved in the program acknowledge as much. In a *Washington Post* story on the program, one official stated, "Frankly, with the cost of rent in the city, I don't know if [staying in the apartment in which they were housed] is the best outcome for a lot of people" (Samuels 2014, B1). Given the rapid loss of affordable housing in the city over the last decade (Reed 2012), it is not a stretch to think the Rapid Rehousing Program was designed to move low-income residents not only out of shelters but also out of the city.

TOPA takes on heightened importance in this context. Indeed, it is one of a diminishing set of options low-income tenants have to hold on to their spots in the city and to negotiate for terms that make staying put in them possible. This context also highlights why we need to examine not only whether

TOPA prevents direct displacement but also whether it prevents exclusionary displacement. The loss of affordable housing in the city means there is virtually no give in the housing market for low-income people. People down on their luck who might have been able in previous years to keep a roof over their head by downsizing or finding a cheaper apartment simply cannot do so anymore. In the next chapter I discuss how city residents themselves view these changes and others like them. As I demonstrate, there is a huge chasm between how the city's longtime, mostly black residents view these changes and how its newly arrived, mostly white residents see them.

3

Gentrification and Its Discontents

In DC gentrification often feels like the front line of a war zone. The war is fought with words, but it is no less intense. And the flash points can erupt around everyday activities that by themselves have nothing to do with gentrification. Take snow and efforts to dig out from underneath it. The District does not receive a lot of snow. Many winters bring little more than flurries. When it does snow, however, it often packs a wallop, and city residents who park on the street have to dig out their cars. Shoveling out from a snowstorm became a front line in the city's gentrification wars after a 2012 snowstorm. Carl Foster, a longtime resident of Columbia Heights, wrote to the *Washington Post* to complain about the response he received from a new neighbor whose car he had helped extract from the snow:

> One of the newbies got stuck in the snow. I helped push him out. As soon as he was free, he jumped out and offered me $5. Did it cross his mind that the black man giving him a hand was his neighbor and was just being neighborly? I told him I was sorry I helped him and walked away. (Foster 2012, C6)

Gentrification is, at root, a class-based phenomenon. It occurs when middle- and upper-income residents move into working-class, or low-income, neighborhoods. As the quotation by Foster demonstrates, however, gentrification also has a racial and ethnic dimension. Although race is not the driving impetus behind gentrification—gentrifiers do not move into neighborhoods with the goal of turning them white any more than cities intentionally set out to attract only white residents—it is often experienced that way.

In many ways, the racial element of gentrification is not surprising. In DC, race has long been an important part of the city's demographic and political fabric. During the Civil War, the city was a sanctuary for fleeing slaves (Masur 2010). It continued to attract African Americans during the Reconstruction period and later during the Great Migration. Perhaps not surprisingly, DC was regarded as a physical and symbolic safe haven for African Americans.

However, if the space itself nurtured the black community, its political structures limited and confounded them. Until 1973 the city was run by a federally appointed board of commissioners, who were always white. The 1973 Home Rule Act finally provided the city with a local government, but it did not give the city voting representation in Congress itself.

This local context, and the ongoing civil rights struggle, meant the city's first black leaders often saw politics through a racial lens. The late Marion Barry, who served four terms as mayor and several stints as a council member, is especially indicative of this trend. As Jonetta Rose Barras (1998) notes in her political biography of Barry, his childhood in Mississippi and, later, Memphis, Tennessee, provided a formative lesson that was hard to shake—no matter how smart or deserving you were, white people would hold being black against you. His experience and those of other contemporary black leaders eventually morphed into what political scientists came to call "black politics." The philosophy behind it created a hierarchy for black political leaders' focus. As Barras explains:

> There could be no doubt about priority: If it was for and about blacks, then it had to be number one. If a black person was in charge, then it was okay. If it advanced blacks at the expense of whites, so much the better. Race was the prism through which everything was first viewed. Class came next. (1998, 112)

Not surprisingly, many African Americans developed views of gentrification against this larger political backdrop. And for white people moving into a city where their presence was and sometimes still is greeted with resentment, if not anger, it is not surprising that they would offer counter-interpretations also framed via race. In short, gentrification in DC is largely talked about, and ultimately interpreted, through racial frames.

To be fair, seeing gentrification through a racial lens is not confined to DC. The specter of race haunts discussions of gentrification in cities across the country (Freeman 2011). However, racial tropes do appear to be peculiarly American. In European cities, for example, discontent tends to be expressed in more explicitly class-based rhetoric. A recent scholarly article on gentrification in London (Slater 2009) provides a case in point. A photo at the beginning of the article shows a graffiti tag from the Hackney neighborhood—"Middle Class Scum Fuck Off! Class War!"

In the remainder of this chapter I discuss the racial frames used to understand gentrification in DC. I begin with a brief aside about earlier discursive efforts to frame gentrifiers as urban pioneers. This interpretation, which sees gentrifiers as "civilizing" unruly places, provides an early example of the tendency in the United States to see gentrification in cultural rather than class-based terms. I then present the racial frames used to understand gentrification in the District, drawing on newspaper and blog accounts for illustration. The city has an active array of blogs and news sites devoted in part or whole to gentrification.[1] Several columnists with the *Washington Post* and the alternative weekly the *Washington City Paper* have also covered gentrification extensively, with intimate portraits of the change affecting specific neighborhoods and even individual buildings. I also include excerpts from interviews I conducted with some of the prominent writers in these outlets.

My goal here is not, however, to referee these disputes. Rather, I have three objectives in mind. First, I want readers to get a sense of how gentrification plays out in DC. Too often, our understanding of gentrification in the United States is based on the experiences of large cities like New York. Although the basic processes of gentrification are the same in most Western cities, DC's unique political and racial history gives its interpretive repertoires an idiosyncratic, "only in DC" feel. I also lay out these debates because they infuse how condos are viewed in the city—often, if sometimes obliquely as housing for white newcomers. These views in turn highlight TOPA's potential to counter not just displacement but the wider cultural pain that attends it in DC.

---

1. See, for example, *Greater Greater Washington* (http://greatergreaterwashington.org), *PoPville* (http://www.popville.com), the *Root* (http://www.theroot.com), *In Shaw* (http://blog.inshaw.com), *Housing Complex* (http://www.washingtoncitypaper.com/blogs/housingcomplex), *D.C. Wire* (http://www.washingtonpost.com/blogs/dc-wire), *Black Snob* (http://blacksnob.com), *DCist* (http://dcist.com), the *District Curmudgeon* (http://www.distcurm.blogspot.com), and the now-shuttered *DCentric* (http://dcentric.wamu.org).

Taming the Frontier

In the 1980s urban boosters embraced triumphalist discourses to forgive gentrification's excesses (N. Smith 1996, 1986). Gentrification was often described as a process of "settling" or "taming" the city and those doing the taming as its "urban pioneers" (N. Smith 1996, 11–12). Neil Smith (1996) argues that the gentrification-as-settlement discourse borrows heavily from American frontier myths. As he explains, "The new urban pioneers were expected to do for the flagging national spirit what the old ones did: to lead the nation into a new world where the problems of the old world are left behind" (xvi). Urban pioneers would clean up American cities and restore national pride. While pioneers were depicted as brave souls doing difficult work, inner-city residents were described as native people were before them, as unruly, savage, and incapable of using the land to its fullest potential.

These settlement and pioneering discourses came under withering critique from a host of groups—inner-city residents, academics, and housing activists (Zukin 1987; N. Smith 1996; Pérez 2002; Boyd 2005). Critics observed that urban pioneering could be understood, much like westward expansion was by Native American groups, as a form of invasion (N. Smith 1996; Zukin 1987). And like their metaphoric siblings on the American frontier, urban pioneers were deemed culpable for the sorrow their presence caused (N. Smith 1996). Others observed that the pioneer rhetoric is problematic because it "implicitly labels those long-time residents (who are often poor blacks and Latinos) as socially disorganized, unmanageable populations likely to benefit from the presence of middle-class, white urban pioneers" (Boyd 2005, 268).

Although settlement and pioneer discourses came to be seen as loaded, even by gentrification boosters, they have periodically reemerged on gentrification's discursive terrain. A recent advertisement for a new apartment complex in the District's H Street corridor (dubbed the "Atlas District" by developers) provides a case in point. The web page announcing the complex, the Flats at Atlas, beckons potential residents:

> Urban pioneers, rejoice—here's your chance to move into DC's most intriguing new neighborhood. At the Flats, you're part of H Street's ongoing evolution as a hot spot for dining, exploring, partying, and relaxing. Dynamic and eclectic, the area blends historical charm with a forward-thinking attitude. H Street has come alive, earning praise even at the national level.[2]

---

2. See the page at http://flatsatatlas.com/neighborhood.

The ad sparked an exasperated response on a local blog, the *District Curmudgeon*:

> The "Urban Pioneers" branding that the Flats at Atlas has chosen essentially says "Hey, nothing was here before you. This place has no history, there was nothing of importance before YOU moved in." That's myopic, shallow, and simplistic. (IMGoph 2012)

I turn now to a description of how extant and new residents view such developments and the wider gentrification of which they are a part. As I demonstrate, the process is understood primarily in racial terms.

Uncommon Currency: Interpreting Gentrification across DC's Racial Divides

Because DC is a city of long-standing racial division, there are few tropes shared by black and white residents. Rather, distinct frames circulate among the city's longtime (largely black) residents and its new (primarily white) arrivals. I begin with a discussion of tropes commonly used by longtime residents and then turn to those used by newcomers.

The Plan

"The Plan" is a common frame through which longtime, black residents interpret gentrification in the city (Prince 2014). The phrase is shorthand for an alleged plot to kick black people out of the District. Courtland Milloy, a metro columnist for the *Washington Post*, notes that "back in the 1970s, many low-income black D.C. residents began expressing fears that a nefarious scheme was afoot to push them out of the city. They called it 'The Plan'" (2012, B1). Clinton Yates, another *Washington Post* journalist, described The Plan in a similar way in my interview with him. He told me that people who believe in The Plan think that "the goal was to let the city bottom out. White folks would move out first; black folks would move out second. You rebuild the city, and then the whites repopulate the city as it once was before home rule. That's The Plan."[3]

As the descriptions by Milloy and Yates suggest, The Plan predates the current period of gentrification by decades. Harry Jaffe (2010), a journalist with the *Washington Examiner*, notes that The Plan was first mentioned by Lillian Wiggins in the *Washington Afro-American* newspaper. According to

---

3. For a list of interviewees and the dates the interviews were conducted, see Appendix 3.

Jaffe, Wiggins saw The Plan as an attempt to undermine the city's elected black leaders and eventually reclaim power for the white minority:

> We can thank Lillian Wiggins for first articulating this particular conspiracy theory. A columnist for the *Washington Afro-American* in 1979, she wrote: "Many residents believe that the Marion Barry era may be the last time Washington will have a black mayor. If negative programming and characterization of black leadership are allowed to continue in the city of Washington and especially the black community, there is a strong possibility of the 'master plan' which I have so often spoken about maturing in the 1980s." Drop the master and you have "the plan." (2010)

When I asked Clinton Yates, who grew up in DC, what people would point to as evidence that The Plan existed, he responded, "The FBI busting in on Marion Barry." In 1990 an FBI sting caught the mayor smoking crack with a former paramour, who was working undercover for federal authorities (LaFraniere 1990). The initial investigation, which involved the U.S. attorney for the District of Columbia, the FBI, and local police, was centered on public corruption, but Barry's arrest, and later conviction, was for the narcotics violation. Indeed, Barry was eventually acquitted of the corruption charges brought against him (Barras 1998). Most African Americans knew the mayor had a drug problem, but they saw his arrest as a dirty trick. In the absence of compelling evidence of corruption, the "Feds" resorted to exploiting personal weaknesses (drugs and women) to get their man. As Yates put it, "I mean, when everybody knew that he had been doing drugs all around the city for, oh, the better part of fifteen years? You know what I mean?"

Although Marion Barry and reaction to him helped animate The Plan for many city residents, the trope persisted even as Barry's power and influence waned. Instead, it has been updated to fit the current context. In its new iteration the goal of The Plan remains the same—to kick low-income black residents out of the city. However, and perhaps fittingly for neoliberal times, the reasons behind the goal are no longer seen as political but economic. In the story's contemporary telling, The Plan's instigators are greedy developers who want to kick poor black people out of their homes so they can turn their buildings into high-priced housing for white residents. And their enablers are as likely to be black as white.

Washington Post metro columnist Courtland Milloy (2012) fleshed out The Plan's new contours in a recent column about a city proposal to build a bus depot in Ivy City, a poor, black neighborhood in the city's northeast quadrant. Tour bus operators working out of nearby Union Station wanted better parking options, and merchants at the station hoped more predictable tour times would increase traffic in the station and thus their shops. The tiny neighborhood nestled between a major commuter route, a cemetery, and Gallaudet University is historic but run down. And, for Milloy, that made it an ideal spot for city officials working to implement The Plan:

> As the saying goes, just because you're paranoid doesn't mean they aren't out to get you. Take the case of Ivy City residents, whose legal battles with the D.C. government offer evidence that The Plan is not some figment of poor folks' imagination. And, in many ways, it's even more dastardly than they thought. In temporarily halting a District plan to put a bus depot in Ivy City, D.C. Superior Court Judge Judith N. Macaluso ruled Monday that Mayor Vincent C. Gray's administration had "deliberately disregarded" laws requiring that residents be informed about how they would be affected by the move. Even worse, the judge found that developers had "evaded environmental screening by mischaracterizing the project" on city documents. The only difference between this plan and The Plan as low-income people envisioned it is that instead of being pushed out by whites returning to take over the city, they were being pushed out by black elected officials operating as if in the employ of developers. (2012, B1)

Matthew Yglesias, a writer for *Slate*, has also talked about The Plan in a contemporary setting. Yglesias, however, set his sights not on the Ivy City bus depot but the city's efforts to grow its population. As he explains, "Gray's denials aside, there very clearly is such a plan and the evidence for it is all over his administration's planning documents which clearly foresee that the past fifteen years or so of population growth in the District will continue" (2012). For Yglesias, it is a numbers game:

> You see, if you take a city where most people are black and locate it in a country where most people are white then a plan for a growing population is a plan for whitening your city. After all, only about 12.6% of the American population is black. So if there's a random influx of people into the District that influx is going to be much less black than the city as a whole. Even if the people moving to DC aren't a random sample, even if they're three times as likely to be black as the average American then their movement into the city will have a blanching effect on the District's demographics. By the same token, even in the context of net population growth there's always churn and always going to be some people leaving the district. And since most people living in the district are African-American, it's natural

that most of the people churning out of DC (like Courtland Milloy![4]) will be black. (2012)

Despite the temporal durability of The Plan, it is often dismissed and sometimes derided by white and new residents. Harry Jaffe, a white columnist for the *Washington Examiner*, for example, calls The Plan a "conspiracy theory" (2010). In the comments section of the online version of Milloy's (2012) article about The Plan in Ivy City, a reader with the handle "doggedreader" accuses him of fighting a "race war." Another reader, Spence Thompson, had this snarky offering: "If any DC Native does not like how the city is changing with its new residents: I left a spot open in Pennsylvania Amish Country for you."

White residents are not, however, the only people to keep their distance from The Plan.[5] Clinton Yates, who is African American, told me that he used to hear about The Plan when he was growing up in the city during the late 1980s and early 1990s. As he explained, among "black professionals at dinner parties, this was the conversation of the day!" In our interview Clinton described how he reacts today when he hears people talking about The Plan:

> It's just kinda like, "Alright, this crazy dude is talking about The Plan." You know what I mean? And you're just kinda like, "Is this really productive?" The Plan is emblematic of, again, a mind-set and a conspiratorial sort of belief that a lot of people just don't buy into, never mind whether or not they care about it.

So, is there a Plan? I do not know. However, for my purposes it matters less whether it exists than whether people think it does, and clearly some do. The continued salience of The Plan suggests that gentrification is understood by many African Americans in the first instance as a racial process. For them gentrification is but the most recent in a long list of obstacles crafted by white residents unwilling to accept black power in the city.

Swagger Jacking

Like all good turns of phrase, "swagger jacking" works because it captures a process or phenomenon right under our noses but not yet named. The

---

[4]. Milloy does not live in the District, a fact cited by detractors (Welch 2010) and supporters (Yglesias 2012) alike.
[5]. See Sabiyha Prince's discussion (2014) of the complicated ways that the city's African American population views The Plan.

term was first used in rap and hip-hop circles to describe musicians copying or trying to steal the swagger of fellow artists. In an April 2008 episode of the *Parker Report*, a periodic segment on the *MTV Jams* program, host Eric Parker sat down with three members of the Diplomats—Jim Jones, Freaky Zeeky, and Juelz Santana—to talk about swagger jacking. Specifically, he wanted to know what it was. Freaky Zeeky offered the most succinct definition: "Swagger jacking is if you stole somebody's style and then coming out like it's yours."[6]

In DC swagger jacking has become part of the city's gentrification script. However, it is no longer about musicians nicking each other's style points. Rather, it captures the appropriation of black culture by white businessmen in a city where black people are increasingly not around to partake of it. The ground zero for swagger jacking is U Street, once dubbed "the black Broadway" for its concentration of black music and theater. The U Street corridor is, like the city as a whole, no longer majority black. Indeed, the black share of the population in the census tract at the heart of the area, tract 44, was only 22 percent in 2010, down from 77 percent in 1990 (Neighborhood Info DC 2015). In a post on the *Root DC* blog, Stephen A. Crockett Jr. laments:

> Look. I get it. The Chocolate City has changed. It isn't what it used to be, and I don't know what's worse: the fact that D.C. was once so marred by murder that it was nicknamed Dodge City or that there is now a hipster bar on U St. that holds the same name. Point is, there is a certain cultural vulturalism, an African American historical "swagger-jacking," going on on U Street. It's an inappropriate tradition of sorts that has rent increasing, black folks moving further out—sometimes by choice, sometimes not—while a faux black ethos remains. In a six-block stretch, we have Brixton, Busboys and Poets, Eatonville, Patty Boom Boom, Blackbyrd and Marvin. All are based on some facet of black history, some memory of blackness that feels artificially done and palatable. (2012a)

Although U Street is ground zero for swagger jacking, examples of it are not confined there. A few months after Crockett wrote his essay, the proprietor of an about-to-open doughnut shop, Cool Disco Donut, abruptly changed the store's name after an outcry of protest in social media. Cool Disco Dan is the tag name of an African American graffiti artist, Dan Hogg, who was active in DC during the 1980s (Yates 2013). The shop's owner, Aaron Gordon, who is white, grew up in DC and saw the name as a way to honor

---

6. The interview clip is available at http://www.mtv.com/videos/misc/225874/swagger-jackin.jhtml.

an artist whose work he saw growing up, but other fans of Cool Disco Dan saw it differently (Judkis 2013). One of the graffiti artist's young fans set up a Facebook page (Society for the Preservation of Cool "Disco" Dan) in protest. The group threatened to cause a ruckus outside the store when it opened if it bore Cool Disco Dan's name (Judkis 2013).

The fan who started the web page explained his motives in an interview with the *Washington Post*: "To a guy on the street, his name is everything, particularly for a graffiti artist, and to have it diminished and changed into the name of a doughnut shop is not really very respectful to me" (quoted in Judkis 2013). After the grand opening, the group complained on Facebook that the shop—now Zeke's D.C. Donutz—was selling T-shirts with the shop's original name printed on them, prompting replies from commentators, such as "On the back of the black" and "They need to cut their losses and quit that shit."[7] Journalists covering the story described it as the city's most recent example of swagger jacking (Austermuhle 2013; Judkis 2013).

In a short time, swagger jacking has become part of the city's cultural lexicon about gentrification. So how best to understand and ultimately place it? At one level those charging businesses with swagger jacking are engaging in a long-standing ritual of cultural protection—one common to all cultures but more prevalent among minority communities, who worry their culture will be swallowed whole or nicked without so much as a nod by mainstream culture. However, such efforts are also about mourning culture's geography. Although culture is transmitted by humans across time and place, culture is often lived and experienced in place. It is the feeling you get that culture is a place, and vice versa. Crockett admits as much in an essay penned in response to the overwhelming feedback he received from his essay (the online version received well over seven hundred comments).

> D.C. has traditionally been unique in its big-city charm but small-town feel. It was a place where the people who stayed—after so many thousands left—felt pride when a high school basketball star named Lawrence Moten rocked his high socks at Syracuse, because it meant something bigger than just fashion. It was a nod to where he was from and how we did it. It made us little people here proud. And, I can't just relocate my connection to this city—yes, the way it was—anymore than I can unattach my skin. (2012b)

Finally, swagger jacking is a comment on profit. In particular, it gives voice to the frustrating sense that outsiders, and white ones at that, are turning

---

7. These comments were posted by Facebook users Chaka Freeman on February 11, 2013, and Robb Burch on February 12, 2013, respectively.

profit from experiences that were not only less than ideal but also not theirs. For Crockett and others, there is just something distasteful about new arrivals making money from difficult experiences, and the community building that resulted, when they were not even there, and the people who were are now figuratively and literally out of the picture.

Myopic Little Twits (a.k.a. Adrian Fenty's White Supporters)

If gentrification in the District could be personified by any one person, it would be former mayor Adrian Fenty. Fenty was a one-term mayor and in many ways had far less impact on the city than Anthony Williams, who had more than a decade, first as CFO and then as a two-term mayor, to shape the district's gentrification. But Williams is a baby boomer and far too understated to fit the bill. Fenty, however, seemed to embody all that was changing in the city. He was young—only thirty-five—when he ran for mayor. He was also a "wonk" who interned on the Hill and worked for a city council member before running for office. Fenty was hard charging, just like the ambitious professionals who voted for him. Richard Florida would be hard pressed to craft a better icon to represent his creative class.

To be fair, Fenty is in many ways more Chocolate City than his reputation would suggest. Unlike Williams, for example, Fenty was born and raised in DC. He attended DCPS schools and a private Catholic academy in the city and received a JD degree from Howard University. Fenty is also black; even though his mother is white, he is considered black by city residents. In American culture blackness tends to be defined, even if only implicitly, by the "one-drop rule." Fenty's wife is also black, a fact that has symbolic import, especially among African American women in the District (see Belton 2010). Unlike his predecessor, Anthony Williams, who frequently dealt with public commentary questioning whether he was "black enough" (Jenkins 1999), Fenty's race has never been in question.

When Fenty ran for mayor in 2006, he won all 142 of the city's voting precincts. He was seen as energetic and unfailingly polite. By the time he ran in the Democratic primary election four years later, however, he was frequently described as "a jerk" and an "arrogant prick" (Suderman 2010). In the summer leading up to the election, an anonymous group started passing out fliers with the caption "slap this brat" underneath a picture of a toddler (with Fenty's superimposed face) riding a hobby horse (Craig 2010). After one candidate forum, Mark Plotkin, a fixture in the local commentariat, even queried whether Fenty had had a "personality transplant" (Orvetti 2010).

Fenty lost the 2010 Democratic primary in large part because his support among black voters declined sharply over the course of his term (Stewart and Mays 2010). He went from being regarded as a native son to an outsider.

Fairly or not, Fenty was seen as insensitive to the city's African American residents, and his policies were viewed as detrimental for them. Fenty was criticized, for example, for further downsizing the city's bureaucracy, long a source of middle-class employment for the city's African American population. He was also blamed for his school superintendent Michelle Rhee's decision to close schools in the city's eastern, largely black wards while sparing those on the western, mostly white side of the city. Fenty drew fire as well for snubbing DC activist Dorothy Height and the poet Maya Angelou in early 2010. The pair had requested a meeting with the mayor to speak on behalf of a nonprofit run by the estranged wife of Marion Barry that was set to be evicted from city property. Fenty's staff put the failure to meet down to scheduling difficulties, but others argued it was intentional and especially disrespectful given the age and prominence of both women (Hopkins 2010).

Fenty also got little credit among the city's black population for his accomplishments. One of Fenty's signature achievements was to improve and add to the city's recreational offerings (Craig 2009). Fenty, an avid triathlete, made it his mission to speed up the city's process for repairing recreation facilities and building new ones. In 2009, for example, he ensured that the city's Tenleytown pool was finally rebuilt. The pool was shut down in 2003 after a wall collapsed in the building housing it. Although plans for a new pool were drawn up shortly after the wall fell, the city's Department of Parks and Recreation never completed the bidding process for a builder. Fenty saw that the bidding process went forward and that the new pool was an Olympic-sized facility. He also spearheaded the construction of a new recreational facility with a pool, playing fields, and community center in the Deanwood neighborhood, a working-class, black neighborhood in the northeastern section of the city.

While the city's pools are used by residents of all races—facility usage mirrors the demographics of the neighborhoods where they are based—improvements to them were seen as reflecting white priorities. After the Deanwood pool was built, for example, a resident of the area told the *Washington Examiner* that the pool was not for the area's black residents: "Fenty is getting ready for white people moving into the community" (Klopott 2010).

Other livability initiatives spearheaded by the Fenty administration were also viewed as for white residents. Colbert I. King, who writes a weekly editorial for the *Washington Post*, observed the sentiment firsthand at a candidates' forum he moderated in mostly African American Ward 4 before the 2010 mayoral election:

> In questions submitted by the audience, and in barbs hurled at the mayor by lesser-known mayoral candidates, three expressions of

derision directed toward Fenty were used almost interchangeably: "The Washington Post" (which endorsed him), "dog parks" and "bike lanes" (both of which he champions). These are three thinly disguised code words for white influence. They also reflect a mindset that holds that the city's dwindling black majority is being kicked to the curb. (2010, A13)

The equation of white people with livability initiatives was crystallized, however, after the primary election when longtime *Washington Post* metro columnist Courtland Milloy penned an acerbic essay celebrating Fenty's loss. Although Milloy (2010) described the loss as the result of a "populist revolt," it was clear he saw the revolt in racial terms. The people at the barricades and those on the other side were of different races.

Fenty boasted of being a hard-charging, can-do mayor. But he couldn't find time to meet with 98-year-old Dorothy Height and 82-year-old Maya Angelou. Respect for elders—that's too old school for Fenty. Dis the sistas—his supporters will understand. Watch them at the chic new eateries, Fenty's hip newly arrived "creative class" firing up their "social media" networks whenever he's under attack: Why should the mayor have to stop his work just to meet with some old biddies, they tweet. Who cares if the mayor is arrogant as long as he gets the job done? Myopic little twits. And lordy don't complain about [school chancellor Michelle] Rhee. She's creating a "world-class school system," they text. As for you blacks: Don't you, like, even know what's good for you? So what if Fenty reneged on his promise to strengthen the city from the inside by helping the working poor move into the middle class. Nobody cares that he has opted to import a middle class, mostly young whites who can afford to pay high rent for condos that replaced affordable apartments. (Milloy 2010, B1)

Milloy's sobriquet for the city's new residents won the *Washington City Paper*'s "best new political label" of 2011 (Schaffer 2011). Not surprisingly, the "myopic little twits" were not amused by Milloy's less-than-affectionate nickname. They called Milloy "racist" and referred to his article as a "screed" (Morrissey 2011). One Twitter user responded with language unsuitable for a family newspaper: "I'm white; own a house in #BloomingdaleDC for 4 years now; added value to it; raising a family. Fuck you Courtland Milloy" (quoted in R. Smith 2010). Despite the negative feedback, a year later Milloy was unrepentant. In an interview with the *Washington City Paper*, journalist Rend Smith asked Milloy if he regretted his choice of words. Millroy responded:

Yeah, another year and the Myopic Twits are older, blinder and wise-asser. I did notice that a few volunteered to help spruce up some DCPS buildings before classes began. So miracles do happen. The rest of them seem more interested in bringing a 19th century flava to the city, with their gas lamps and trolley cars. Then again, when you're on their side of the wealth gap, inheritance gap, employment gap, education gap, you can act like landed gentry. (Quoted in R. Smith 2011)

Although Fenty's successor, Mayor Vincent Gray, was not scorned by the black community in the same way that his predecessor came to be, the equation of livability initiatives with whiteness lingers on. After Gray announced a sustainability initiative for the city in 2012 (see Gray 2012), a councilman in the city's Ward 4 district, Vincent Orange, told the mayor in a debriefing session that he had fielded numerous calls from worried residents: "People in the African American community were scared to death of this thing. They thought this was another attempt to move them out of the city" (quoted in DePillis 2012b). The equation of white and sustainability was also not lost on a journalist covering the initiative's unveiling:

While the kickoff event drew 440 people, only 25—count 'em—were African American. Sure, all meetings have their racial imbalances, but that one's pretty severe (it's not like all Gray's shindigs are lily white; 44 percent of the 1,700 attendees at the One City Summit were black). (DePillis 2012b)

Gentrifiers as Ethnically Diverse

The city's new residents, many though not all of whom are white, have also developed race-centric tropes to understand gentrification. In many ways the race-centric nature of their tropes is to be expected. Outside gentrifying neighborhoods, moving house does not require an interpretive discourse. People move for all sorts of reasons—they get a new job in another city; they get married and have kids; their nest empties out; their current house has bad karma or possibly even ghosts. In a gentrifying neighborhood, however, moving, whether in or out, can be fraught with meaning—often overdetermined meaning. Many new residents arrive in the city with the label "gentrifier" and the baggage that comes with it already affixed. Of course, some new residents remain blissfully unaware or purposefully ignorant of how their arrival affects others. Interns and students are constantly cycling through the city. Many know they will return home at the end of an internship or degree program and spend little time getting to know the city. But others move to the city with no planned exit date. They come to stay, at least for the foreseeable future, and as they get to know the city, they discover that their presence is much discussed and sometimes much maligned. It is into this charged space that the city's newcomers, often though not always white, come to interpret their presence in the city.

One of the most common tropes newcomers (and their advocates) use to situate their presence is to assert that they are, as a whole, a diverse and multiethnic group. In an essay in *City Journal*, for example, Jerry Weinberger (2011) celebrates the city's "new" diversity. Though he acknowledges that the city has experienced a sizable black exodus—he estimates one hundred thousand since 1990—he argues that their departure is akin to working- and middle-class white people leaving for the suburbs in the 1950s and 1960s. Moreover, because the newcomers are not a racially uniform lot, Weinberger argues that the city's demographic shift is not a mere replacement of white with black. To demonstrate, he describes a recent visit he took to Yards Park, near the new Nationals' stadium:

> What a human hodgepodge: one little girl was watched over by tattooed parents sporting green and bright-red hair. For all I know, they could have been stockbrokers or physicists: it's getting harder and harder in America to tell a book by its cover. Two black kids were supervised by their dad. One little Jewish girl was overseen and photographed by her Orthodox parents (he with kipah and tzitzit, she with long dress and a wig). Some Iranians were minding their kids. Young people abounded, but plenty of middle-aged and older people were there, too. (Weinberger 2011)

For Weinberger, these demographics suggest a once-segregated city is becoming desegregated. Indeed, though Weinberger acknowledges that desegregation has to date been concentrated in the city's formerly black neighborhoods, it will, he contends, move west to the city's white enclaves. Thus, worries about gentrification's racial divides are misplaced. As he concludes, "Gentrification won't mean whiteification" (Weinberger 2011).

Garance Franke-Ruta (2012), a correspondent for the *Atlantic*, has also offered up a spirited defense of gentrification as a multiethnic process. Her article, a critique of Stephen Crockett's essay on swagger jacking, makes many points, but the one of relevance here is her position that the adoption of black cultural icons by city businessmen is a recognition of the city's long-ignored black history and something from which people of other races can learn:

D.C. has enough statues of white men and venues and buildings named in their honor. Lord knows it has a boatload of statues of white men on horses. It does not, in the grand scheme of things, have many statues of major figures in African-American history. The U Street area is not Chinatown, where banks and random non-Chinese stores are fronted by a script that outsiders cannot read, while since the late 1990s the heart of the local Chinese-immigrant community has been in suburban Maryland. And it is not Clarendon, Va., or even Cleveland Park. It is a real living, breathing, multi-ethnic, multi-racial neighborhood and cultural melting pot whose establishments have realized the mid-90s dream of reconnecting D.C.'s future to memories of its past. (2012)

Although it is frequently self-defined white gentrifiers who defend gentrification as a multiethnic process, black gentrifiers have also added their voice to the gentrification-is-multiethnic chorus. In her article "Confessions of a Black Gentrifier" for the *Washington City Paper*, Shani Hilton (2011) explores what it means to be both a gentrifier and black, in part by interviewing other black gentrifiers. One woman, Aisha Moore, moved to Congress Heights in 2009 from California. She told Hilton she was frustrated by the equation of gentrification with whiteness:

> I get it, in terms of numbers, but it's annoying. The story over here, east of the river, is all about black gentrification. Black people are moving back to Anacostia and the Congress Heights area. . . . There are different types of people here, but that doesn't water down the chocolate. (Hilton 2011)

Hilton was less sanguine than Moore about her role as a gentrifier. Hilton recounts that when she first moved to the district in 2002 to attend Howard University, white people were just beginning to move into the area:

> White professionals and hipsters trickled in, slowly, visible even through the bubble of being a black college student, surrounded by 10,000 other black college students, in a largely black neighborhood, in a mostly black city. By 2004, they were regularly spotted making their way to and from the Shaw-Howard University Metrorail station. And, by the time I graduated, white people were jogging up 4th Street NW through the campus, and walking their large dogs on the green lawn of Howard's Louis Stokes Health Sciences Library—something longtime black residents never did. (2011)

After graduation Hilton left the city for work in New Jersey. She returned a few years later and found an apartment near her old campus. Things were very different. As she explained, "To put it bluntly: There were white people, everywhere" (Hilton 2011).

Hilton acknowledges she initially felt unsettled by the change, writing that it was "disconcerting." She was also alarmed to realize that she was part of it:

> More disconcerting, though, is that five years later, I walk my own large dog on the library's green lawn. The story of the black gentrifier, at least from this black gentrifier's perspective, is often a story about being simultaneously invisible and self-conscious. The conversation about the phenomenon remains a strict narrative of young whites displacing blacks who have lived here for generations. But a young black gentrifier gets lumped in with both groups, often depending on what she's wearing and where she's drinking. She is always aware of that fact. (Hilton 2011)

Is This Seat Taken? Filling Vacant Space

The city's new residents are often sensitive to being labeled "displacers." The word "displacement" has a racial connotation in DC (as elsewhere in the country). As Hilton's comments illustrate, displacers are depicted as white, while displacees are described as black. The term is also burdened with negative connotation. Displacement is viewed as an aggressive process. Though displacers rarely meet those they displace, their very act of moving into a neighborhood is often described as forcing or impelling others to leave. Thus, when a new resident, especially a white one, is accused of being a displacer, his or her transgression is seen in both economic and racial terms. In this context, the city's new residents often take great pains to demonstrate that they are not displacing anyone. Rather, they are filling vacant space.

In her critique of Stephen Crockett's essay on swagger jacking, for example, Franke-Ruta (2012) rejects Crockett's depiction of white people pushing black residents out of the U Street corridor. Citing census tract 44, which is in the center of the area, she argues that black residents left the neighborhood long before white people started moving in:

> More than 1,100 people left the neighborhood between 1980 and 2000—a third of the population. That is a profound population loss, and coincided with a time when just about the only new major development in the area was Marion Barry's Frank D. Reeves Center project, a government building that's had something of a troubled history. (2012)

Franke-Ruta argues that white people did not push black people out but moved into spaces that black people left vacant:

> I've lived upstairs from Busboys and Poets since it was a lonely beacon in the night on a corner that was dark on the three other sides, and all the way down 14th toward U Street, too. I was so grateful it stayed open late or else my block would have been nothing but vacant lots, shuttered stores and abandoned properties at night that first year. Most of my building was built on a vacant lot. There was probably a building there before the riots, but by the time I got to D.C. in 1997, whatever had been there was long since razed and the spot was paved and being used for weekday parking and a weekend flea market cum junk sale. (2012)

Franke-Ruta extends the vacancy argument to the area's storefronts. Citing the Brixton, one of the establishments Crockett calls out for swagger jacking, she argues:

> Again: the bulk of the black U Street population loss happened by 2000, more than a decade before the Brixton came onto the scene. That's doubtless why the property that now houses the Brixton was standing empty (excuse me, was an "eyesore") and why it was available to become something new. (2012)

When I asked the Prince of Petworth, the pen name of Dan Silverman, a white newcomer who chronicles the city's gentrification on his blog *PoPville*, to respond to Crockett's argument about swagger jacking, he also raised the specter of vacancy. In fact, he asked me if I had read Franke-Ruta's (2012) article. "I agree with her 100 percent," he told me. And like Franke-Ruta, Silverman emphasized the fact that much of the city's growth, in U Street and beyond, has occurred on vacant property: "There's another element to DC that needs to be addressed, which is, I guess it would stem originally from the riots. What I came to when I moved here, and [what] most people [who] moved here [came to], is the vacant properties." Silverman also feels that the process of moving into vacant properties or into new buildings built on vacant land is not the same as the displacement Crockett (2012a) decries. As Silverman explained:

> So, there's a big difference between having an apartment building and tearing it down and charging three thousand dollars for rent when it was seven hundred [dollars] for the rent versus having a vacant lot where there was nothing and an apartment building is built.

Like Franke-Ruta (2012), Silverman also extended the argument to the Brixton: "There's a big difference in my mind when there's a vacant storefront, like the Brixton was, that he [Stephen Crockett] uses as an example of swagger jacking. It was a boarded-up liquor store."

While the Prince of Petworth and Franke-Ruta reject the displacement argument, preferring instead to see gentrification as largely a process of filling empty space, they have not done so by harkening back to eighties-era urban pioneer rhetoric. Although some developers still sell their projects this way (e.g., the Atlas Flats), those who write on behalf of the city's gentrifiers prefer to see themselves as part of a hip mélange of races, incomes, and backgrounds. Franke-Ruta captures the sentiment succinctly when she says her neighborhood is much like a *Washington Post* journalist described it in 1996: "a Benetton boardwalk scene—black, white, Latin, gay and straight" (2012).

Are Condos for White People?

Condos are emblematic of gentrification, so it bears asking if city residents think condos are for white people. In DC, condos are owned by people from various racial and ethnic backgrounds. Normally, the racial background of home owners in a given neighborhood, community, or census tract roughly matches the racial makeup of the area as a whole. However, like much else about gentrification in DC, condos are often understood in racial terms. The connection, though, is more oblique than the one drawn between white people and dog parks/bike lanes and illustrated in earlier quotations (King 2010). Rather, it happens through a series of associations and relies on some taken-for-granted assumptions. The first is the association of condos with professionals. The second is the association of professionals with whiteness. With these notions in place, people simply imagine condos as places where white people live. The taken-for-granted nature of these assumptions means, however, that the equation of condos with white people is unspoken. It just is.

To understand how condos came to be associated with white people, we need to begin with the recent history of housing starts in the city.[8] During the 1990s DC saw very little new residential construction. Between 1990 and 1998, for example, the number of housing starts in the District hovered well below five hundred per year. In one of those years—1996—the city did not record a single new housing start (Phillips, Beasley, and Rodgers 2005). This slump is not surprising. By 1990, the city was beginning its fourth decade of population decline, and its ability to govern itself was being called into question (Abramowitz and Greene 1989; *Financial Status* 1994). Moreover,

---

8. In urban areas housing starts are usually in multifamily buildings.

the control board's initial focus on austerity meant developers were taking a wait-and-see approach to investment in the city.

New residential construction finally started to tick up in the late 1990s. In 1999, new housing starts surpassed the five hundred mark for the first time in nearly a decade, and by 2002 they had exceeded fifteen hundred (Phillips, Beasley, and Rodgers 2005). In purely functional terms, these data mean that the city's new housing is closely associated with the city's gentrification. There was, of course, nothing that required developers to reserve their housing for the professionals suddenly flocking to the city. However, the impression that condos are for these newcomers is often encouraged by developers themselves.

The target market for most condo developers in DC is a status-conscious, well-heeled, young (or older and childless) professional. Developers are not shy about admitting it either. Indeed, they do so routinely in the city's real estate magazines and blogs, usually when they are promoting an upcoming property. David Gorman, one of the principals at Lock 7 Development, told *UrbanTurf* that "the majority of buyers we see for our units are young professionals without children who want to be near shopping, restaurants and downtown" (Turner 2014). Howard Riker, the managing director of Hines, the firm behind the CityCenterDC development, described it as "a slightly higher end product." The project's condos, which range in price from $500,000 to $3.2 million, are described as part of "an urban oasis, with landscaped roof parks, sunbathing lounges with water foundations, and dining alfresco" (Meyer 2013, 92).

In fact, efforts to stand out from the pack notwithstanding, there is a tedious conformity to the catchwords and phrases these and other developers use in their marketing campaigns. The word "luxury" is now nearly ubiquitous in advertisements for new condos. Words like "boutique," "sleek," and "modern" are almost as common.[9] Developers also state their preference for the professional crowd in more subtle ways, through the types of amenities they offer. Instead of day-care services, for example, new condos emphasize hotel-like services. The K at City Vista provides its owners with a dry-cleaning concierge service as well as a notary public. Owners at the City Market at O have a dog run and a rooftop infinity pool as well as an exclusive gym and spa.

Although well-heeled professionals can hail from anywhere in the county and belong to any racial or ethnic group, the racial shifts that have accompanied their influx into DC mean that most residents assume they are white.

---

9. A new condominium complex along the C&O canal in Georgetown, 1055 High, is described as a "boutique" property on its website (see http://1055high.com). A property highlighted in the September 2014 edition of the *Washingtonian* magazine is described as "sleek" and "modern" (Thomas 2014).

A recent blog post in the online version of the *Washington City Paper* provides a case in point. In "Four Ways of the Condo," writer Perry Stein (2014) divides the names of the city's new luxury condos into four categories. The first three poke fun at the naming conventions of developers. The Barcelona and Calistoga, for example, belong in the "Faraway Lands" category. "Prepositions" covers the aforementioned K at City Vista and City Market at O. Meanwhile, the Lyric, Calistoga, and Matrix are emblematic of the "nonsensically pretentious." The final category, "Swagger Jacking," speaks to the presumed whiteness of the city's new condo stock. The three names in the category—the Ellington, Langston Lofts, and the Fitzgerald—all reference black artists.[10] Although Stein does not provide the racial composition of any of the three buildings, the assumption is clear—white people live in these buildings. Indeed, their residents have to be white for the swagger-jacking label to apply, and Stein does not need to prove it. The whiteness of these buildings is a given.[11]

Race, Class, and TOPA

Although condos are frequently seen as being for newcomers, and thus for white people, there is no similar equation operating in the context of TOPA. Two reasons explain why. First, as I detail in Chapter 4, TOPA defies easy categorization. Even thirty years after the bill's introduction, there is no consensus on what it is, who it helps, or how it helps them.

Second, as I discovered during the process of my research, most city tenants have never heard of the TOPA statute. Blake Biles, one of the lawyers interviewed for this project told me, for example, that low-income tenants' default assumption is that a building sale means they will have to move. Others have only a vague sense that DC is tenant friendly. Most tenants find out about TOPA and the rights that it affords them only after their buildings have been contracted for sale.

None of this is to suggest, of course, that TOPA unfolds in race-blind ways. By helping people stay put in low-income neighborhoods that are or were recently majority black, TOPA plays a part in preserving a place in the city for low-income black residents. Indeed, low-income housing advocates who help minority populations use their TOPA rights certainly see

---

10. The Ellington references DC native and jazz musician Duke Ellington. The Langston Lofts and the Fitzgerald refer to the poet Langston Hughes and the jazz vocalist Ella Fitzgerald, respectively.
11. The census does not provide data at the building level, so I cannot ascertain the racial makeup of any of these buildings. However, my wider point is not that Stein's observation is (or is not) correct but that the assumption is so firmly in place that it can go unquestioned.

their efforts in this wider context (see Kathryn Leigh Howell's 2013 work on Columbia Heights). And not surprisingly, minority tenants who go through a successful TOPA process also frequently come to see TOPA in these terms, as a way to prevent outsiders/white people/developers from kicking "us"/black people/workers out of the city.

In my later analysis, however, I largely focus on TOPA's effect on the city's class dynamics. None of this means, of course, that I ignore tenants who see TOPA's benefits through a racial lens. I do not. However, I also do not confine my interpretation of TOPA to its impact on race in the city for several reasons. The first is practical. Charting racial change at the building level is difficult. Because of privacy concerns the census does not publish data at the building level. Moreover, even when I asked tenant leaders to estimate the racial composition of their buildings pre-TOPA, most responded with generalizations (e.g., "about half," "a lot," or "some"). Without a baseline, I was unable to chart changes in buildings' racial composition post-TOPA.

Second, emphasizing race over or at the exclusion of class would miss important categories of people harmed by the city's gentrification. Through my research I found that a building sale prompted anxiety for people of all races. Two of the buildings in my sample, for example, were located in upper northwest DC, where the population is predominantly white and wealthy. However, both buildings contained near-elderly residents (people roughly between the ages of fifty-five and sixty-five) who had lived in their individual units for decades and were paying below-market rates. They felt vulnerable to gentrification despite their race.

Across the city public schoolteachers and people working in nonprofits can also be found in rent-controlled apartments. People of all races fill these positions, and though they can usually afford rent-controlled rates, the luxury market is well out of their reach. Likewise, it is not uncommon for immigrant families to cram into one-bedroom apartments in the city's wealthier neighborhoods in order to send their kids to the city's best public schools. A building sale can trigger anxiety and disruption as these families search for comparably priced rents, which can be hard to do for those whose arrival predates the city's boom.

Finally, emphasizing the racial dynamics of gentrification tends to direct the political focus for "fixes" onto individual gentrifiers (i.e., the mostly white newcomers). In the spring of 2012, for example, the *Washington City Paper* published "A Guide for the Responsible Gentrifier" (Schaffer 2012). The author, Michael Schaffer, prefaced the guide with a surrender of sorts:

> Absent significant interventions that carry their own consequences, most of the things elected officialdom could do to slow gentrification is stuff no one wants: Crime could soar again, or schools could get

even worse. Those changes, of course, would hurt existing residents way more than up-market house-hunters. (2012)

As a result, the author proposes an individualized solution to the problems that surround gentrification—a guide for how gentrifiers can better blend into their neighborhoods. And though Schaffer uses terms such as "newcomer" and "old-timer" instead of race-specific categories, the piece is clearly designed to help young, white professionals navigate their interactions with middle-aged and elderly black people:

> One question that comes up repeatedly in Washington is what ethical onus lies with you, the newcomer? Must you defer regularly to prevailing neighborhood norms? Given that you're now just as much of a resident as the old-timer next door, can you push back without guilt? It's complicated! (Schaffer 2012)

The guide recommends that new arrivals treat neighbors with respect (no loud parties), show common courtesy (say hello to people on the sidewalk), and get involved in civic groups (go to Advisory Neighborhood Commission [ANC] meetings).[12] The list is essentially a how to guide for being a good neighbor, and would apply to new arrivals anywhere in the city, even in nongentrified areas.

The problem is that none of these fixes does anything to mitigate displacement. And to be fair, there is little newcomers of any race can do to stop displacement. Therefore, the onus for mitigating displacement, and thus keeping a place for low-income black residents in the city, should focus on those who can actually do something about it—notably, city officials. Indeed, Schaffer's (2012) contention that city efforts to slow gentrification will mark a return to the bad old days is debatable. As I have already explained, the city's lack of intervention has actually contributed to a presumably old-school problem—homelessness and the social dysfunction that comes with it. It is a false choice to suggest, as Schaffer does, that the city can either stand out of the way or go back to the bad old days. The city can clearly make meaningful interventions, of which TOPA is but one example.

I now turn to the second section of this book. In it I lay out the history of the TOPA process and describe the methods I use to analyze it. Readers should see it as a connective tissue of sorts, bridging this first, largely historical part of the book and the third, deeply empirical portion of it.

---

12. The city currently has forty-one ANCs, which are subdivisions of the city's eight wards. Each ANC has an elected commissioner whose primary job is to serve as an interface between residents and the ward's city council member.

4

The Rental Housing Conversion and Sale Act of 1980

In this chapter I introduce the Rental Housing Conversion and Sale Act (RHCSA). I outline its basic provisions and describe how the right of first refusal works in practice. I also contextualize the act, explaining why the city enacted it and how Congress, which can prevent city legislation from taking effect, responded to it. In so doing, I have three goals. First, I want to highlight the social-justice ethos motivating the bill's sponsors. They saw condo conversions in a negative light, as driving displacement and gutting the city's affordable-housing stock. The right of first refusal was an antidote, a way to level the playing field by giving tenants some control when their buildings were put up for sale and conversion. In this regard, RHCSA fits squarely within the local autonomy paradigm discussed in Chapter 1.

Second, I want to demonstrate the limits DC officials faced as they developed the bill. As I describe later in the chapter, an earlier effort, a moratorium to stop condo conversion, tried to protect the city's low-income residents by temporarily removing their housing from the sway of market forces. A lawsuit against the ban, however, forced the city to consider an alternative method of help. That method, RHCSA, was a compromise of sorts, a tool that helped tenants but within rather than against market logic. The pairing of social justice and market logic means that RHCSA is something of a hybrid.

RHCSA's hybrid nature gives rise to my third goal. Despite its hybrid nature, RHCSA has long been defined as antimarket. In the congressional hearing detailed here, for example, RHCSA was often conflated with rent control, even though the two statutes govern different practices (building sales versus annual rent increases) and intervene in the market in different ways (preferencing particular buyers versus limiting rents). This misreading continues to inform how RHCSA's critics view the act today. RHCSA's hybridity is, however, central not only to the legislation but also to my decision to study it in the context of local autonomy. Indeed, DC's history demonstrates that even in the early 1980s, before neoliberalism had taken root, stepping completely outside the market was difficult. And in DC's case, these difficulties were compounded by congressional interference in city affairs. The only way DC could address the conversion problem was through a hybrid model. Given the impetus behind RHCSA and the support for it among the city's low-income housing advocates, it bears asking whether, how, and to what extent it contributes to local autonomy.

I conclude by assessing the degree to which the bill's history comports with the critiques of condos and condo conversion laid out in the first chapter. Although condo conversion is often depicted as a singular process, RHCSA's hybridity means that tenants can use a condo-conversion mechanism in multiple ways. This multiplicity further suggests the need to nuance our theories about the role of condo conversion in the gentrification process.

A Brief Summary of the Bill

The DC city council enacted RHCSA in 1980. The act contained two parts: Conversion of Rental Housing to Condominium or Cooperative (CRHCC) and the Tenants Opportunity to Purchase Act (TOPA).

The first part of the act, CRHCC, governs the conditions under which owners of multiresident apartment buildings may convert to condominium. The law stipulates that landlords who want to convert an apartment building to condo must hold an election in which 50 percent (plus 1) of current residents support conversion. And to prevent strong-arming by landlords, elections may occur only once every twelve months.

The second part of the act, TOPA, governs the rights that tenants in residential buildings have when a landlord decides to sell the property. In particular, the law stipulates that tenants must be given the right to purchase the property if or when a landlord decides to sell it. Landlords may inform tenants before listing the property for sale or after the landlord and a third party have signed a contract of sale for the property. This process is referred to as issuing a TOPA notice. In the latter case, TOPA allows tenants to invoke the "right of first refusal." This right lets tenants refuse a contracted sale and purchase the building instead for the same price. Tenants are also allowed to allot their right of first refusal to a third party—usually a developer or nonprofit—who will help them purchase the building.

The rights that stem from TOPA are also collective for buildings with five or more units. To refuse a sale, tenants must first form a tenants' association (if one does not already exist), register it with the city, and hold an election in which a majority of tenants vote to refuse a sale. Properties with established tenants' associations have 30 days to refuse a sale. Buildings without associations are given 45 days to form an association and refuse the sale. After a sale has been refused, residents have 120 days to arrange financing to purchase the building themselves or in conjunction with a developer or nonprofit group. Once a purchase is completed, tenants may opt to keep a building rental or convert to condo or co-op. Buildings opting to convert must hold a vote (per CRHCC guidelines) to approve conversion. Although the outcome—remaining rental or converting—is usually worked out in advance of a vote during negotiations with third-party developers, the city will allow former rental properties to register as condominiums or cooperatives only after a formal election is held.[1]

How the Process Works

When a landlord decides to sell his or her building, the process can unfold in a variety of ways. As noted previously, landlords may invite tenants to purchase their building before a sale has been made or notify them of their right of first refusal after a sale has already been contracted. The former is uncommon except in cases in which the residential building in question is small (around four units). Indeed, until recently, most of the city's multifamily housing stock was owned by family businesses with little development experience.

Once a landlord notifies tenants that a sale has been contracted, there are generally two responses tenants can make (see Figure 4.1 for a flowchart of how the process can unfold). The first is to do nothing. Inaction usually happens because tenants are apathetic, disorganized, in disagreement, or financially unable to purchase their building. The second involves tenants getting organized—forming a tenants' association, invoking their right of first refusal, searching for a developer, and ultimately choosing their property's tenure status. Although tenants may buy their building without outside help, most cannot afford to do so. It is nearly impossible for tenants' associations to secure loans on the open market since most have no business

---

1. CRHCC can also protect tenants who are unable to invoke their TOPA rights (e.g., because of disorganization or disagreements) by ensuring that they still have a say on their building's fate under a new owner.

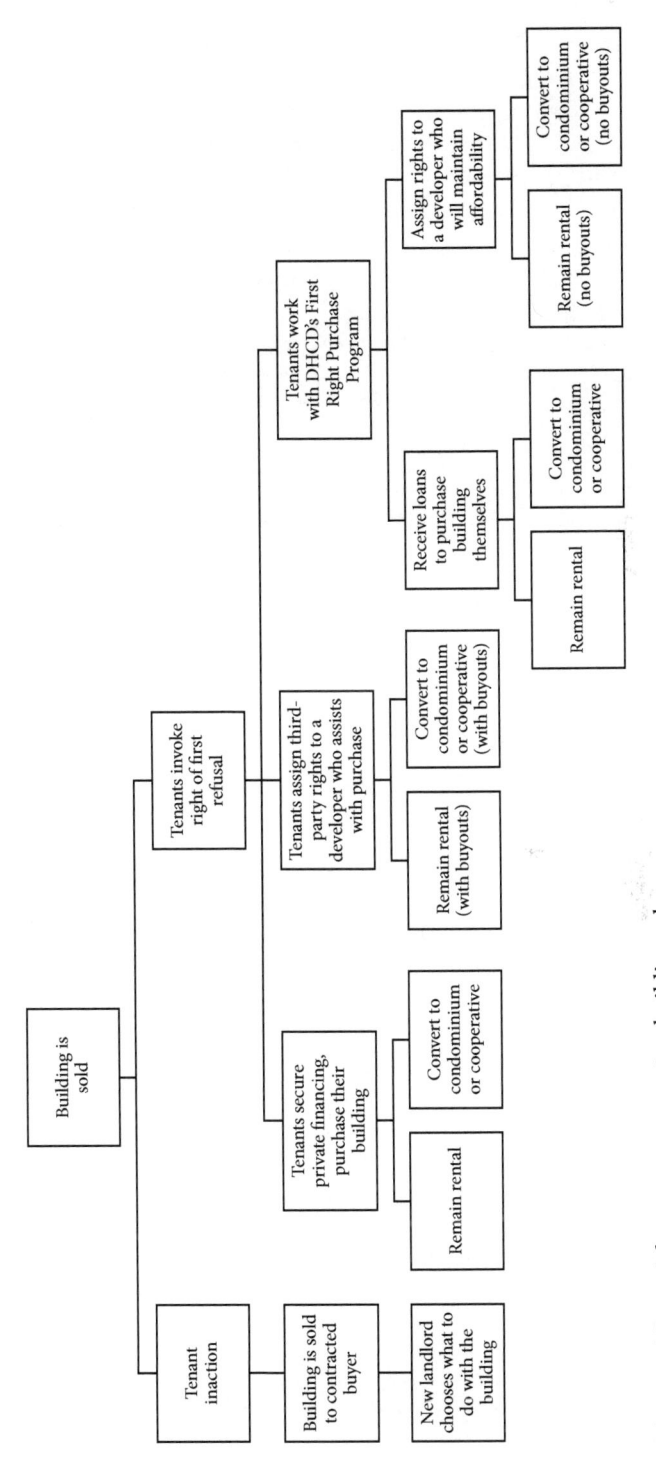

Figure 4.1 Potential tenant responses to a building sale

experience or credit history. Thus, the great majority of tenants' associations assign their right of refusal to a third-party developer to receive assistance with financing. The city's Department of Housing and Community Development (DHCD) does, however, provide tenants that meet the city's low-income criteria with access to low-interest loans through its First Right Purchase Program. Tenants can use these loans to purchase their property outright and to make repairs on it. Tenants using First Right Purchase can also assign their rights to a nonprofit developer. In these cases, the loan goes to the developer on the condition that he or she agrees to keep units affordable, whether as condos or rentals (Reed 2013a).

As Figure 4.1 demonstrates, there are two typical outcomes for residential buildings that are sold. The first is for the building to convert to a condominium or cooperative. The second option is for the building to stay rental. The outcome—to convert or remain rental—usually depends on four factors. The first is the condition of the housing market at the time of sale. During the boom years (2000–2007) when real estate prices were increasing rapidly, conversions were common. In the aftermath of the 2008 recession, however, a flat or declining condo market made converting to condo too risky for developers and their tenant partners.[2]

The second factor is the degree to which tenants' desires converge. In some buildings tenants tend to want the same thing. In middle-income buildings where tenants are well established in their neighborhoods, for example, the ownership option is often popular. In other buildings where residents are transient or have low incomes, renting tends to be more attractive. Of course, many buildings in the city have diverse demographics, so exceptions abound.

A third factor is an association's financial resources. Because most tenants' associations lack sufficient funds to purchase their own buildings, they have to find a third party willing to provide financial assistance. TOPA regulations give tenants 120 days to complete a building purchase, and when things go smoothly, four months is a sufficient amount of time to find a third-party developer and arrange a deal. But negotiations can and do get delayed for all sorts of reasons, and at crunch time tenants may have less leeway to select their preferred option.

A fourth and related factor is how the negotiation process between tenants and potential third-party partners unfolds. Tenant negotiations with potential third-party partners usually involve a good deal of horse trading. Tenants ask for common element improvements and insider (i.e.,

---

2. Eric Rome, a prominent tenants' association attorney, cited a saturated condo market as the main reason behind the switch in our summer 2013 interview. See Appendix 3 for a list of interviewees and interview dates.

below-market) prices for those staying put, while developers demand the right to offer buyouts to current tenants so they can sell or rent some units at market rates. The degree to which the final outcome favors tenants' initial wishes depends on a host of variables, including but not limited to tenant unity, the savvy of their attorneys, and the alignment of market forces with tenants' desires.

Context

Local Context

RHCSA was enacted in 1980 as a response to a wave of condo conversions then ongoing in the city. DC was not the only big city to see an uptick in condo conversions. Kay Stray-Gundersen (1981) argues that several factors converged in the mid-1970s to facilitate the conversion trend. The first was a backlash against rent control. Landlords in cities with rent-control statutes complained that caps on annual rent increases meant they could not raise sufficient capital to make repairs on aging buildings.[3] Many decided to convert their buildings or sell them to developers who could afford the upfront costs of conversion (Day and Fogel 1981). In DC, a backlash against rent control was in full swing by the late 1970s. The *Washington Post*'s editorial board, for example, described rent control in a 1980 editorial as having a "death grip on the city's rental housing market" ("Rent Control" 1980, A22).

Another factor behind the rising number of conversions was the lack of space for new condo construction. At the time, most municipal zoning ordinances had few areas zoned for multifamily housing, and finding empty land inside these zones was difficult. Investment in rental housing had also become less profitable after a series of tax reforms during the previous decade (Stray-Gunderson 1981).

In DC city officials viewed the conversion trend with apprehension. In the list of legislative findings justifying the act, for example, the bill's sponsors argued that the city was experiencing a "housing crisis" because of condo conversions:

> Since 1977, more than eight thousand (8,000) rental units in the District of Columbia have been converted to condominiums and cooperatives, more than (9,000) additional units have not yet been

---

3. Although most U.S. cities do not have rent control, those that do tend to have large populations, high rates of renting, and a sizable inventory of multifamily apartment buildings. In the late 1970s, rent-control statutes were primarily found in cities on the East Coast and in California (Day and Fogel 1981).

converted but have been declared eligible to do so and applications for six thousand (6,000) more units are pending. The eight thousand (8,000) units which have been converted represent 4.5% of the D.C. 1977 rental stock, and the fifteen thousand (15,000) units subject to conversion represent an additional 8.3%. (*Rental Housing* 1980, 4)

The council also noted that the negative impacts of conversions were not randomly distributed. Rather, they were concentrated among "lower income tenants, particularly elderly tenants," who were forced to move when their buildings converted and who often found limited options for other, low-income housing nearby (*Rental Housing* 1980, 4).

Given the human costs of condo conversion, RHCSA's sponsors positioned their bill first and foremost as an effort to mitigate displacement. Of the seven goals listed in the act's preamble, displacement ranked at the top of the list.

> It is the purpose of the Act to discourage the displacement of tenants through conversion or sale of rental property, and to strengthen the bargaining position of tenants towards that and without unduly interfering with the rights of property owners to the due process of law. (*Rental Housing* 1980, 3)

The second goal was to "preserve rental housing which can be afforded by lower income tenants in the District" (*Rental Housing* 1980, 3). While offering tenants a right-to-buy could reduce the total number of rental units and inflate housing costs—insider prices are often a bargain only in relative terms when compared to prices in a "hot" real estate market—the act's sponsors believed two mechanisms would allow RHCSA to preserve affordable housing. The first was the limit placed on conversions in the first part of the act (CRHCC). By requiring that 50 percent (plus 1) of tenants support conversion and limiting elections to once a year, the bill's sponsors hoped to impede conversions in buildings with active tenants' associations and slow them down in places without them. The second was a built-in assumption that nonprofit groups would help tenants purchase their buildings and operate them as affordable rentals rather than converting them.[4] The act's remaining goals were designed to assist the implementation of these two goals.[5]

---

4. The assumption that nonprofits would help tenants purchase their buildings and keep them low-income rentals never materialized. As I note in Chapter 2, the city's main vehicle for helping tenants use their TOPA rights—the Housing Production Trust Fund—was given a dedicated source of funding only in 2002.
5. The third goal, for example, is to limit displacement of the elderly. This goal was listed separately because prior iterations of the bill, which did not include provisions protecting

In the act's legislative findings, its authors also observed that RHCSA was necessary because previous legislative efforts had proven ineffective at slowing down conversions and thus displacement. In particular, the city had made three prior legislative stabs at addressing the problem.

The first, the Condominium Act of 1976, was designed to provide some order to the condo-conversion process by stabilizing the rules governing when and under what circumstances a conversion could proceed. It also laid out provisions to help people adversely affected by conversions, including a requirement that converters pay the relocation costs of displaced tenants.[6] Like most first-run attempts at legislating a complex process, however, the act was incomplete.

A year later, the city enacted another bill, the Rental Housing Act of 1977. It was the first law to give DC tenants the right of first refusal. Unfortunately, as Proscio (2012) notes, the legislation did not lay out how tenants could invoke the right or the conditions under which they could do so. As a result, fifteen lawsuits were filed between 1977 and 1980 challenging various aspects of the law or its application.

A third piece of legislation, the Condominium and Cooperative Conversion Stabilization Act of 1979, was more straightforward than the Rental Housing Act of 1977 and had more teeth than the city's previous condominium acts. It established a three-month moratorium on condo conversions in the city, starting in May 1979. The primary goal of the moratorium was to provide immediate relief to tenants and some breathing room for the council to devise a more permanent solution (Richburg 1980). In July the city council extended the moratorium for a second ninety-day period.

Not surprisingly, the moratorium was highly unpopular with landlords and real estate developers. After the second moratorium was issued, the Washington Home Ownership Council, a lobby for local developers, challenged its legality in DC Superior Court (Whitaker and Camp 1979). In both moratoriums the city had used "emergency powers" to move the legislation forward quickly. As I note in Chapter 2, the city's Home Rule Act gives Congress the right to review and reject any legislation passed by the city council.[7]

---

the elderly, created opposition from council members who argued that the elderly were often too poor or aged to secure mortgages. Likewise, the fourth goal—to incentivize new landlords to allow low-income residents to stay in place with similar rents—was aimed at both displacement mitigation and affordability.

6. The city's first law on condos was the 1963 District of Columbia Horizontal Property Act. The act is described as "enabling legislation" because it allowed the provisions of the 1961 National Housing Act to apply in the city (van Weesep 2005). The act does not address condominium conversions.

7. The review period is usually a month. If Congress fails to review an approved bill within the allotted time, the bill automatically becomes law at the end of the period.

However, the act also includes an emergency powers provision that allows the city to fast-track bills that address immediate problems without congressional approval. The Home Ownership Council's suit claimed that the city had used its emergency powers improperly. They argued that condo conversions did not constitute an emergency and that the emergency powers provision had been invoked to bypass the congressional approval process, where the ban would have likely met stiff opposition (Whitaker and Camp 1979).

In October the Home Ownership Council won an initial round in its battle against the city's moratorium when a judge on the DC Superior Court ruled the city had exceeded its home-rule authority by using emergency powers to issue the moratorium. He also ruled that the city could not enforce the legislation during an appeals process (Whitaker and Camp 1979). The city chose to appeal the legislation and, in an aggressive move, voted to extend the moratorium for another ninety days while the appeal was pending ("Barry Signs" 1979).

On June 17, 1980, the city council finally passed a comprehensive law to address condo conversions and tenants' rights in the process leading up to them—RHCSA. It was signed ten days later by Mayor Marion Barry and transmitted to Congress for review. There, it would face one final obstacle—a congressman from Texas.

Congressional Context

On August 25, Representative Charles Wilson (D-Texas) introduced House Concurrent Resolution 420 to disapprove RHCSA and prohibit it from becoming law. On September 4, the Committee on the District of Columbia met to discuss Wilson's resolution.

Although the resolution was voted down by a committee vote, allowing RHCSA to become law, the hearing highlights two important facets of RHCSA's history. The first is the inordinate role that Congress has played in the city's domestic affairs. Indeed, even members who supported the city's Home Rule Act found it difficult to withhold judgment on either RHCSA or the city more generally. This tension, between wanting to protect the city's autonomy and to save it from itself, was perhaps best illustrated by Representative Wilson himself.

Wilson began the hearing by noting that his resolution was not likely to pass. In his prepared statement he noted, "I have no illusions about the prospects of this resolution being favorably acted on by this committee" (*Rental Housing* 1980, 127). Wilson argued, however, that the "substance" of the bill merited a formal hearing. Wilson's first concern with RHCSA was that it would thwart economic development in the city.

We are not only depriving ourselves of taxes but what Washington needs more than anything else: that is meaningful, economically viable jobs. So every consideration from the city's standpoint in my judgment is being ill-served by these ill-advised laws, particularly in destroying the employment opportunites [sic] that would come through refurbishment of old housing stock, employment in hotels, et cetera. (128)

Wilson also argued that the city's decision to spur economic development was putting its federal assistance in jeopardy.

If the tax base of the District of Columbia does not grow the District of Columbia cannot continue to provide the services it hopes to provide without a massive amount of Federal payment. It is my judgment that the amount of Federal payment will not be forthcoming from the Congress as long as the majority of the congress feels that the public policies of the District of Columbia do not stimulate the growth of the District's tax base, thereby requiring less effort on the part of the District and more effort on the part of the Federal Treasury. (127)

Finally, Wilson took issue with a provision in RHCSA that stipulated that "an owner shall not evict or send notices to vacate to an elderly tenant with an annual household income of less than $30,000 per year" (5). As he explained:

In this particular legislation, people are protected that make anywhere below $30,000 a year. Now 96 percent of the people who live in my district make below $30,000 a year and they do not expect any sort of Government protection or subsidy as a result of that income. What this bill does is, again, it subsidizes the middle and upper middle class at the expense of the poor and at the expense of services that the District wants to deliver to its people and at the expense of the financial viability of the District of Columbia and this is going to present in the future a great problem. (129)

Despite Wilson's vigorous attacks against RHCSA, he was also clearly ambivalent about meddling in District affairs. In fact, he was careful to supplement his critical comments with remarks meant to burnish his pro-DC bona fides.

> I would like to further qualify myself as a friend of the District. First of all, I have been one, along with the chairman of this committee, and I believe the ranking minority member, who has publicly and vigorously supported the idea of the district having the authority to levy a commuter tax. Second, I have supported the chairman and the chairman of my subcommittee on Appropriations for the District of Columbia in vigorously opposing the abortion ban that we successfully thwarted yesterday by 10 votes. Third, I voted with the Delegate from the District to establish the Home Rule Charter that we did in 1973. . . . I was 1 of 10 sponsors. (*Rental Housing* 1980, 128)

Wilson's inconsistent tone was mirrored by other committee members. Even members who strongly opposed Wilson's resolution of disapproval were willing to play the role of Greek chorus and disparage RHCSA. Representative Stuart McKinney (R-Connecticut), for example, pledged to fight Wilson's resolution of disapproval "tooth and nail" if it passed a committee vote and progressed to the floor of the House, but he also described RHCSA as a "rotten bill" (*Rental Housing* 1980, 135).

Wilson's hearing also illustrates the difficulty Congress had categorizing the statute. Although the bill was attacked on the grounds that it would stymie economic development, critics made no specific reference to how either RHCSA's rights or its regulations would harm development. It was, for example, deemed antimarket even though the right of first refusal does not prevent building sales (it simply says tenants are first in line to buy them) and requires tenants to match a contracted sales price before proceeding.

In the absence of such details, guilt by association defined RHCSA as antimarket. Specifically, it was equated to rent control, a statute whose reputation for thwarting the market was already firmly established, at least in the congressional mind. In fact, the hearing spent more time discussing rent control than the actual statute under consideration, and when RHCSA was mentioned, it was usually in conjunction with rent control. At the start of his prepared statement, for example, Representative Wilson noted that he had "long felt that rent control and condominium control per se were very damaging to the economic health of a city" (*Rental Housing* 1980, 127). Economist Robert Nathan, an expert witness at the hearing, made a similar conflation: "I believe the condo situation has the same issue that the rent control has, namely it becomes a limiting factor in terms of investment and expansion" (131). Representative McKinney, who opposed Wilson's motion, echoed Nathan's sentiments later in the hearing, complaining about RHCSA by observing that rent control has been an "absolute unmitigated economic disaster" (135).

To some degree this conflation is understandable. Both Wilson and McKinney argued that city's new conversions had put so much pressure on low-income tenants precisely because rent control had stalled new housing construction. McKinney even speculated that "there has not been an apartment unit built in the city of Washington since rent control except with Federal funds" (*Rental Housing* 1980, 135). It is also important to remember that the "the condo situation" Nathan referred to in his testimony was clearly broader than the bill before the committee. It referred to the city's previous attempts to use a conversion moratorium to temporarily halt displacement.

Ultimately, however, rent control was a red herring in the hearing. Both statutes are designed to help tenants, but they do so in fundamentally different ways. RHCSA brings tenants into the market; rent control shields them from it. These differences notwithstanding, the conflation of RHCSA with rent control helped solidify the impression that RHCSA was wholly antimarket. The empirical chapters that follow clearly demonstrate how inaccurate this early view was.

Placing RHCSA's History

Although Chapters 6–8 provide ample material for assessing the degree to which TOPA's contemporary practices comport with criticisms of the role that condos play in processes of gentrification, we can make a first assessment here by looking at the degree to which the bill's history aligns with the arguments laid out in Chapter 1. Let us begin by looking at the arguments posited by scholars who see condos as part and parcel of a revanchist project.

As noted previously, many scholars view condominiums as an "economic strategy for increasing the spaces available for capital investment and accumulation" (Kern 2010, 7). They also argue that investment brings social exclusion and displacement, as the wealthy remake the city in their likeness (N. Smith 1996). There is, however, nothing in RHCSA's initial goals to suggest its authors saw the right of first refusal as a mechanism for spurring development that would lead to social exclusion. In fact, the opposite is true. The bill's authors hoped that RHCSA would give tenants a chance to stay put in their fast-gentrifying city. There is also no evidence that the bill's congressional opponents saw it this way. Again, the opposite is true. The congressional testimony quoted earlier suggests that RHCSA was seen as an extension of rent control, which opponents viewed as a drag on investment.

Although the legislation is now more than thirty years old, many critics continue to view RHCSA as an impediment to development. In a 2004 real estate advice column in the *Washington Post*, columnist Benny Kass observed that landlords view TOPA as a form of "tenant blackmail." The conflation of TOPA with rent control also continues today (see Baschuck 2010).

However, it is also true that some developers have found ways to profit from TOPA. For demonstration, we can refer to numbers from the contemporary period. As I note in Chapter 1, between 2000 and 2007—rough bookends of the 2000s housing bubble—1,147 buildings with 26,645 apartments were converted to condominium in the District of Columbia.[8] These units compose nearly 10 percent of the District's occupied housing units and 18 percent of its rental units.[9] The legislative findings attached to RHCSA found that 4.5 percent of the city's rental stock in 1977 had been converted to condominiums, and another 8.3 percent of units would be affected if pending applications were approved. In short, during the recent housing bubble even more units were subjected to conversion than during the crisis period that begat RHCSA. Most important, this increase happened while RHCSA was in place and would have presumably hindered such investments.

Although the early to mid-2000s property bubble explains much of the increased conversion activity, RHCSA also played a role. Despite the widely held view that the legislation was antimarket, the right of first refusal was structured in a way that allowed, even facilitated, private investment. Specifically, the act's provision that tenants can assign their right of refusal to a third party created a legal pathway for the involvement of private investors. Though RHCSA's advocates hoped most third parties would be nonprofits, the act did not stipulate their involvement in the process or provide enough funding to ensure their dominance in it.

The city does not record how many conversions are conducted by for- and nonprofit developers, so there are no counts to consult. However, the condo-conversion boom numbers provided earlier suggest what experts consulted for this project all told me. Condo conversion became a for-profit development niche during the recent housing bubble. That is, some developers tailored their business around the needs of tenant associations invoking their TOPA rights.

One example is Urban Investment Partners (UIP). A *Washington City Paper* profile of the company in 2012 described the company's investors (in New York and the Netherlands) as having an "insatiable" appetite for apartment buildings in the city. However, instead of buying empty buildings,[10]

---

8. These data were provided to me upon request by the Department of Consumer and Regulatory Affairs, summer 2007.
9. The data to make these calculations were dynamically generated from the U.S. Census Bureau's American FactFinder website (http://factfinder2.census.gov). Specifically, I divided the number of converted units by the number of occupied housing units (in 2000) and number of renter-occupied housing units (in 2000), respectively.
10. If a building has no tenants at the time of a sale, a landlord is not required to extend TOPA rights. Some landlords have responded by trying to empty their buildings of tenants before putting them on the market.

or otherwise trying to circumvent TOPA's mandates, UIP actually markets its services to tenants invoking their TOPA rights. As the profile's author, Lydia DePillis, notes, "UIP's succeeded by making tenant protections work for them" (2012c).

Tenacity Group is another company that has centered its business model on tenants invoking their TOPA rights. In fact, its web page markets its services specifically to these tenants:

> If someone you know is at risk of losing their rental home because the owner is selling, we can help. . . . We are the answer for busy apartment dwellers who must organize a tenant association, elect officers, agree on the price, negotiate with their landlord's sales agent, find purchase funding, and determine a total budget for the property's acquisition, conversion, and rehab. (Tenacity Group 2008)

Although I discuss how groups like UIP and Tenacity make tenant conversion profitable (for developers and tenants) in the next three chapters, suffice it to say here that TOPA's history suggests it does not fit squarely in the revanchist category. Although TOPA has certainly opened up space for capitalist accumulation, investment has not always involved social exclusion and displacement. It is for this reason, perhaps, that even though the business community often decries TOPA, some of its members are also willing to make money through it.

When we view condo conversions in light of the scholarship on neoliberal citizenship, our assessment is equally mixed. As the reader will recall, critics of condos argue that condo ownership often buttresses revanchist views of the city. Not only do they produce owners, neoliberalism's ideal citizens, but they also encourage these same citizens to become inward looking, worrying about property values and perceived threats to property value appreciation, such as the homeless, vagrants, and other so-called undesirables. As residents and neighbors, then, condo owners tear at the community fabric of the city rather than tighten its weave.

The outcomes that RHCSA structures permit, however, are not always in line with neoliberalism's ideal citizen. For example, as I note in Chapter 1, one of the critiques of condo owners is that they are not attached to, and fail to make commitments to, their neighborhoods. They are individuated and atomized rather than part of the community's connective tissue. However, the TOPA process tends to engender community and collectivity. As previously noted, TOPA's architects made the right of first refusal a collective rather than individual right. Thus, any attempt to refuse a sale requires tenants coming together to invoke a group right and ultimately decide what they want to do with the building—convert or remain rental. This process entails a lot of meetings, discussion, and collective decision making, the result of which is that tenants in DC's notoriously anonymous apartment buildings get to know one another.

This truism was certainly the case in my property. I already knew some of my neighbors because we exercised our dogs in a vacant lot behind our complex. After attending the first several meetings of our fledgling tenants' association, I knew many more. By the end of the process, I used to joke that our property was like a dorm—everyone knew everyone else and their business to boot. More than ten years later, I count many of my fellow tenant purchasers as good friends. The experience we went through felt transformative and collective. The tenants' association leaders that I interviewed for this book recount similar experiences.

To be sure, community does not always mean tranquility. Anyone who has ever lived in a small town can testify that knowing all of your neighbors can be a curse as much as a blessing. And the city's deep-seated race- and class-based divides can often be exacerbated in the confines of the forced communities TOPA engenders. One tenant leader I interviewed for this book, Afifa Klouj, told me, for example, that racial tensions were a problem in her association:

> We had tensions in the association. Because I was, you know—even though I don't consider myself white, but I'm also not African American. I am African—North African. I'm from Tunisia. So at one point they started saying, you know—people from the association, the building itself, you know—"You are being led by a white woman."

However, the larger critique of scholars writing about neoliberal citizenship is not that condos lead to fractious relations but rather that few relations are formed in the first place. In this regard, then, the tenant-conversion process does not automatically mesh with the critiques offered of condo owners as revanchist urban citizens. When tenants' associations succeed in organizing their members and enacting their TOPA rights, they do create communities among those staying put.

The second example concerns what tenants can do with their buildings after purchase. One of the primary critiques offered by this literature is that condo conversion undermines renting by reducing the inventory of units available to rent, a drop that disproportionately hurts low-income residents without the financial capacity to buy their own homes. However, as noted previously, tenants' associations can and do use TOPA to keep their buildings rental. A bill with a neoliberal solution—the right-to-buy—ends up, ironically, securing the practice of renting.

Finally, the TOPA process—whether it results in a building remaining rental or converting to condominium—is designed to keep at least some low-income citizens in place. Thus, the condo-conversion process cannot be said to produce a unitary type of urban citizen, even in the abstract sense in which urban revanchism is understood. Rather, it creates a mixture of citizens—preserving the old while also entertaining the new. And in the mix that ensues, it is also possible that new relationships are forged and new, hybrid models of experiencing the city emerge.

So, what does this brief attempt to place TOPA's history in wider debates in the literature tell us? The answer is that condos, and condo conversions, are more variable than typically thought. Indeed, RHCSA's history fits uneasily within the paradigms scholars have developed to interpret the rise of condominiums in the context of gentrification. TOPA contains contradictory elements and produces contradictory results. In Chapters 6–8 I flesh out these contradictions in greater detail. I now turn to the case-study conversions that form the empirical basis of those chapters.

5

Sample Conversions and Metrics of Analysis

This chapter introduces the representative sample of condo conversions I assembled to analyze the TOPA process. I describe the process I used to build my sample and describe the properties in it. I then explain how I measure displacement and TOPA's capacity to foster local autonomy.

Building a Sample

Background

The sample I created for my research is a representative sample of seven buildings in which tenants used the TOPA process to stop a contracted sale of their building. Figure 5.1 is a map of the census tracts where sample properties are located (I use tracts rather than address points to protect an informant requesting anonymity). Table 5.1 provides statistical information for the census tract in which each property is located.

The sample is deliberately small. As I discovered during the course of my research, the city does not collect adequate data on the TOPA process. While the city records how many buildings convert to condo per year,[1] for example, it does not record any data on the process itself. Thus, we do not know what

---

1. The city has data on annual conversions because it charges a conversion fee to any entity converting an apartment building to a condominium or cooperative. The fee is paid for

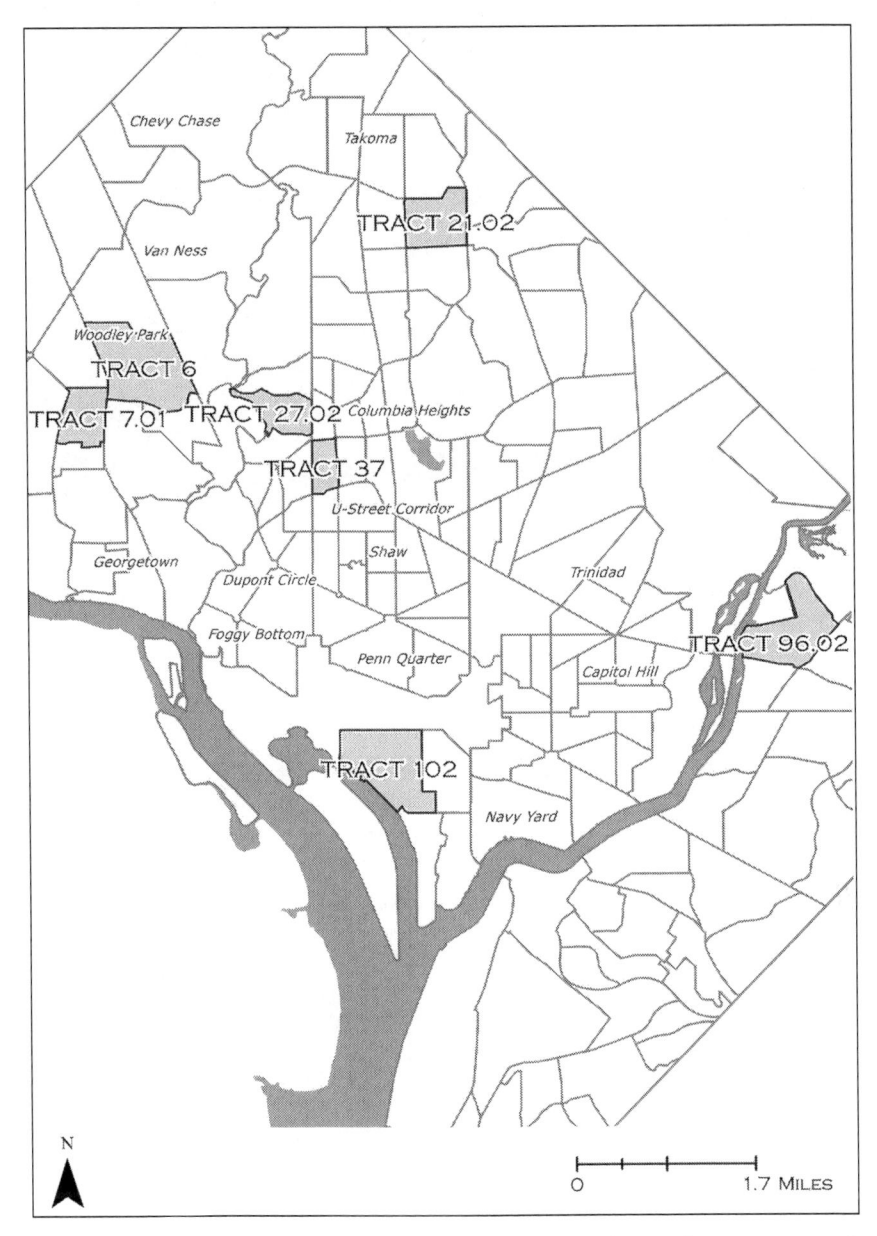

Figure 5.1 Census tracts where sample properties are located. (Map by Meagan Snow.)

TABLE 5.1   STATISTICAL SNAPSHOT OF SAMPLE PROPERTIES
(BY CENSUS TRACT)

Property	Tract number, 2000 census	White non-Hispanic, 2000 (%)	Average family income, 1999 (2010 $)	Percentage below poverty, 2000
DC		28.0	102,342	20.0
Garden Towers	37	8.7	46,503	34.0
Cathedral Court	7.01	80.0	180,070	5.8
Mayfair Mansions	96.02	0.0	36,095	33.0
Kennedy Street	21.02	1.0	71,034	9.1
Town Center	102	31.0	108,978	13.0
The Squire	6	75.0	294,290	4.8
Harvard/Summit	27.02	54.0	92,370	8.4

Note: Data are from Neighborhood Info DC, at http://www.neighborhoodinfodc.org/index.html. Although the map in Figure 5.1 uses 2010 boundaries, the data for Town Center in this table are from its 2000 tract. The 2010 tract is a combination of two separate tracts used in the 2000 census.

percentage of total conversions occur with tenant involvement (i.e., through TOPA) or what percentage of tenants stay put during TOPA conversions. Once I discovered that it would be impossible to track the TOPA process quantitatively, with a large-n study, I decided to opt for greater detail. Instead of making a definitive statement about the total number of DC tenants who have used TOPA to stay put, I would track a small sample of tenants' associations going through the process in order to assess how smoothly the process unfolded; what obstacles, if any, tenants faced; and ultimately how long the process took.

The sample includes only properties sold after 2000 because this period roughly coincides with the most recent wave of gentrification, which Jason Hackworth and Neil Smith (2001) term "third-wave gentrification."[2] The current wave of gentrification is marked by greater municipal involvement in facilitating gentrification and a concomitant increase in corporate investment in urban environments. In DC third-wave gentrification has translated into greater investor interest in the city's multiunit residential housing stock (DePillis 2012c; Gose 2004). Investor interest has also contributed to weak oversight by city officials anxious for the tax dollars redevelopment brings

---

by the entity applying for conversion, which may be a landlord, a developer, or a tenants' association.

2. Hackworth and Smith (2001) theorize that third-wave gentrification begins after the recession of the early 1990s and continues today. DC entered this phase later than many cities because of the financial difficulties discussed in Chapter 2. Although the control board encouraged the city to increase its tax base, its primary focus during the first five years (1995–2000) was on budget cutting.

(Grim 2006a, 2006b). Given the uniqueness of the contemporary period, it makes sense to confine the analysis within it rather than include conversions happening under different political-economic conditions. I do, however, include conversions before and after the 2008 recession so that I can assess how a market shake-up affects various aspects of the process, including tenant bargaining power, developer and tenant access to credit, and the final outcome (rental or condo).

As I put together my sample, I also consulted four experts—a nonprofit developer who works on TOPA conversions (George Rothman at Manna Inc.) and three attorneys (Rick Eisen, Blake Biles, and Eric Rome) who represent tenants during the TOPA process. George Rothman helped me understand the dynamics of tenants working with nonprofit developers. Rick Eisen gave me contact information for tenant leaders at several recent TOPA conversions. I consulted Blake Biles on attempts by landlords and developers to circumvent RHCSA guidelines. Finally, Eric Rome helped fill in my historical gaps on the TOPA process as well as explain the logic behind buyouts and voluntary agreements and how these practices have changed over time.

Sample Properties

The sample contains seven distinct properties, five of which contained multiple buildings. When two or more buildings are sold together, one tenants' association usually represents tenants in all of the buildings slated for sale. Exceptions occur when buildings are spatially distant from one another. In keeping with DC's low height profile, all seven properties contain low-rise (one to five stories) and/or mid-rise (six to twenty stories) buildings.

The first building in my sample is Garden Towers, a mid-rise apartment with 73 units built before World War II (Figure 5.2). Its location, on the eastern edge of Meridian Hill Park between the U Street and Columbia Heights neighborhoods, places it in the heart of the condo-conversion center of gravity (see Figure 2.1).

The second property is Cathedral Court (Figure 5.3). The property contains six buildings located directly across the street from the National Cathedral in one of the wealthiest zip codes in the city. Built in the 1920s, all six buildings are between three and five stories high. There are 177 units on the property. As noted in Chapter 1, I went through a TOPA conversion in this building in 2003. I include it in my sample so that I can draw on my personal experiences with TOPA. My insider experience helped me develop detailed questions about the sequence of steps tenants take to complete the process as well as questions that only an insider would think to ask.

Mayfair Mansions, the third property (Figure 5.4), is located on the eastern bank of the Anacostia River, well outside the condo-conversion center of

Figure 5.2 Garden Towers in Washington, DC. (Photo by the author.)

Figure 5.3 Cathedral Court in Washington, DC. (Photo by the author.)

gravity. The property contains several rows of garden-style apartments centered around grassy courtyards. The property was built after World War II and designed for middle-class black families. By the 1980s, the property's socioeconomic profile was decidedly lower income. Mayfair is the largest property in my sample, with 469 units.

The fourth property, Kennedy Street (Figure 5.5), contains two low-rise (and adjoined) buildings with 54 units between them. Like Mayfair's resi-

Figure 5.4 Mayfair Mansions in Washington, DC. (Photo by the author.)

Figure 5.5 Kennedy Street in Washington, DC. (Photo by the author.)

dents, Kennedy Street's tenants are almost entirely low income. The property is, however, about half a mile from the Fort Totten Metro stop, which has seen some gentrification in the area immediately surrounding the Metro station.

Town Center, the fifth property (Figure 5.6), was designed by the renowned modernist architect I. M. Pei in the mid-1960s. It contains two nine-story towers with a surface parking lot between them. Each building has 128 units. Located in the city's southwest quadrant, the buildings

Figure 5.6 Town Center in Washington, DC. (Photo by the author.)

were constructed during a period of city-sponsored urban renewal and slum clearance. Town Center did not have historic designation at the time of its TOPA process but subsequently received it in the summer of 2013 (Neibauer 2013).

The sixth building in my sample is the Squire (a pseudonym), a midcentury, mid-rise building located near Cathedral Court. It is also in a wealthy part of town. The tenants' association president requested anonymity to participate in this project. To protect his identity, I do not provide a picture of his building.

The Harvard/Summit is the seventh property in my sample (Figure 5.7). As my label for this property suggests, it contains two buildings, one on Harvard Street and the other on Summit Street.[3] Both buildings are low rise, but the building on Harvard Street is substantially smaller than the one on Summit Street. The property, which has 85 units, is located north of Adams Morgan and west of Columbia Heights, well within the condo center of gravity.

Representing the TOPA Universe

I constructed this sample to represent the diversity of the city's TOPA conversion landscape. In particular, it accounts for four types of variation within

---

3. The sign in front of the Harvard was put up after conversion, but at the time of conversion, neither property had an official name.

Figure 5.7 Harvard/Summit in Washington, DC. (Photo by the author.)

the universe of tenant-led conversions. First, the sample includes properties spread across the city's two main geographic divides—Rock Creek Park and the Anacostia River. Recall that wealth tends to decrease as one moves from west to east in the city. Two properties (Cathedral Court and the Squire) are located west of the park, four properties (Kennedy Street, Town Center, Garden Towers, and Harvard/Summit) are located between the park and the river, and one property (Mayfair Mansions) is located east of the river.

Second, the sample includes socioeconomic diversity (see Table 5.1). Two of the properties (Cathedral Court and the Squire) are located in largely white, wealthy parts of the city. Four properties (Town Center, Kennedy Street, Garden Towers, and Harvard/Summit) are located in gentrifying parts of the city. And one property (Mayfair Mansions) is located in an area with a predominantly low-income, minority population and little gentrification.

Third, the sample captures variability in outcomes. Two of the properties (Cathedral Court and Town Center) converted to condominium, three (Garden Towers, the Squire, and Harvard/Summit) remained rental, and two (Mayfair Mansions and Kennedy Street) had unsuccessful TOPA bids, albeit in different ways.

Fourth, I selected properties of varying size. Sample properties included four buildings with fewer than one hundred units (Kennedy Street, Garden Towers, the Squire, and Harvard/Summit), two buildings with between one hundred and three hundred units (Cathedral Court and Town Center), and one with more than four hundred units (Mayfair Mansions). All of these properties are larger (by total number of units) than the median converted property in the city's data set (four units).[4] However, as I discovered during my research, buildings with small numbers of units were not usually converted with tenant involvement. It is, for example, usually easier to clear a four-unit building of tenants than it is to empty one with fifty or one hundred units. Moreover, even in small buildings where tenants do invoke their TOPA rights, it can be difficult to acquire a development partner because profit margins are often too small to attract one.

In addition to this sample, I employ a shadow case to test my findings by putting them into wider relief. In particular, I examine a 2004 portfolio sale of eleven buildings by a local landlord (the Bernstein family), who failed to issue tenants a TOPA notice after contracting the sale. The Bernsteins structured the sale of their properties using what was known at the time as a 95/5 transfer. In these transactions, a landlord sells 95 percent of the property to a buyer and keeps a 5 percent interest. At the time, TOPA regulators recognized only a 100 percent transfer of property as a sale for TOPA purposes. They also granted informal TOPA waivers for landlords selling properties using 95/5 transfers. After the Bernstein sale, six of the properties sued to have their TOPA rights reinstated. This shadow case is included to highlight the external factors that can derail tenants' ability to invoke their TOPA rights.

Measuring Displacement

Given the data constraints discussed at the start of this chapter, I measure displacement using a combination of quantitative and qualitative data. Most of my data were collected through interviews. I interviewed at least one tenant leader in each sample property and consulted several of them on multiple occasions.[5] I also followed up with all sample leaders via e-mail or phone for updates and fact-checking questions. During the course of these interviews, I asked tenant leaders to provide me with descriptive statistics about their properties. I began by getting basic details, including the number of units

---

4. As I note in Chapter 1, I requested data on condo conversions from the city's Department of Consumer and Regulatory Affairs in the summer of 2007. This data set included the names of buildings that had successfully applied to convert to condominium as well as their location and size (by number of units).
5. Although I initially set out to interview more people in each building, I quickly learned that in most buildings it was the tenants' association board, and often one or two people on it, who really knew the particulars of how the process worked. Tony Proscio quotes a community activist, Martha Davis, who found a similar pattern: "In most cases, maybe you end up with a majority of people pretty much understanding what's going on, a few people who never really pay any attention and just want to go about their business, and then a few leaders who really get deeply involved" (2012, 134).

in each property as well as the proportion of studio, one-, two-, and three-bedroom units per property. I also asked tenant leaders to estimate their properties' demographic characteristics. Given that some properties were quite large, I usually began by asking tenant leaders to describe their buildings' demographics in terms of age, race, and income. As I discovered, most had difficulty providing firm percentages, even when I confined my request to two or three categories (e.g., white, black, and Hispanic).

I also asked tenants to estimate the number of tenants who stayed put during the TOPA process, as well as the number who left. In the process of asking this question, I discovered that these two figures did not always equal the total number of units in a given property. One reason for the discrepancy is that landlords often stop re-renting vacated units in the months preceding a sale. Even landlords willing to abide by the TOPA law often try to reduce the number of tenants before a sale because potential buyers prefer as many empty units as possible. From a buyer's perspective empty units are attractive because they do not contain potentially stubborn tenants or require future buyouts. There was also standard tenant attrition during the TOPA process. Although none of the tenant leaders I interviewed collected data on why tenants left mid-process, they all suggested people left for varying reasons, including frustration or anxiety with the process, new jobs, or changing family circumstances (marriage, divorce, pregnancy).

Finally, I also asked tenants to provide me information on the buyout process. In particular, I was interested to know what buyout amounts were, how amounts were set, whether amounts varied over time, and how many units were bought out. Although most tenants had trouble recounting their buildings' demographic profiles, they were confident about buyout numbers, assuring me that any errors were minimal (i.e., off by not more than one or two tenants).

I also used more standard qualitative measures for tracking displacement. Specifically, I tailored my interview questionnaire to follow the TOPA process. I broke my interview questions down linearly, trying to cover each section of the process as it occurred. My goal was to identify processes (e.g., finding a third-party developer) or actors (e.g., a landlord or city officials) that would make the TOPA process more difficult for tenants to successfully complete. I also took note of how buildings changed through the process. I did so by looking at not only how many tenants stayed put but what happened to units that were empty or bought out. This allowed me to assess the degree and nature of displacement.

Given the contentious nature of debates around displacement, I reiterate here how I define the term and how I measure it. As I note in Chapter 1, direct displacement is too narrow a measure to capture the ways that gentrification contracts housing options for poor and working-class people, making it difficult for many to move within the city and ultimately forcing some to leave it. While contraction in housing options may seem beyond the scope of displacement, the lack of flexibility in the housing market can have an immediate effect on residents who need to move but want to stay in the city. Indeed, people often move because they have to. They need to upsize after having a baby or downsize after a divorce. They may lose a job or get a new one in a different part of the city. The constriction of options in a tight housing market means that even if an individual chooses to move rather than be directly displaced, his or her inability to find similarly priced housing in nearby neighborhoods is a form of displacement.

To that end, I rely here on a typology of displacement developed by Peter Marcuse (1985), who lays out three types of displacement. The first is direct displacement, which occurs when a tenant is forced to leave his or her housing because of physical and/or economic reasons. Marcuse describes turning off the heat as a cause of physical direct displacement and a landlord raising the rent as a cause of economic direct displacement.

The second is displacement pressure. This form of displacement describes people who choose to move because their neighborhoods cease to work for them. Although there is nominally choice behind such moves, they are often severely circumscribed ones. Marcuse (1985) describes a number of scenarios for illustration. When a low-cost grocery store is replaced by a more expensive one, residents must travel farther afield for their groceries (e.g., the closure of the Food Rite Metro Supermarket on P Street and the subsequent reopening of the Whole Foods Market discussed in Chapter 1). As new, wealthier residents opt for cabs or Zipcars instead of public transportation, bus routes may be closed or rerouted. Likewise, if a health clinic is moved to make way for luxury apartments, families without cars may find access to doctors difficult. As Marcuse explains, "Families living under these circumstances may move as soon as they can, rather than wait for the inevitable; nonetheless they are displaced" (1985, 207).

The final type is exclusionary displacement. Since I use this measure here, I quote Marcuse's definition verbatim:

> Exclusionary displacement from gentrification occurs when any household is not permitted to move into a dwelling, by a change in conditions that affects the dwelling or its immediate surroundings, and that: 1) is beyond the household's reasonable ability to control or prevent; 2) occurs despite the household's being able to meet all previously imposed conditions of occupancy; 3) differs significantly and in a spatially concentrated fashion from changes in the housing market as a whole; and 4) makes occupancy by that household impossible, hazardous, or unaffordable. (1985, 207)

Marcuse also issues some important rules regarding the measurement of exclusionary displacement. He cautions, for example, that "to avoid double-counting, a unit from which there has been direct displacement should not be counted again in estimating exclusionary displacement" (1985, 206n). I heed this advice here. I do not count units bought out during the TOPA process as cases of direct displacement, but I do consider them as potential cases of exclusionary displacement. Indeed, though people leave when they take a buyout, they do so in a context where staying put is an option. Thus, the coercion associated with direct displacement is not present. However, if these willingly vacated units are then changed in a way that would prevent similar renters from leasing them (i.e., converted to market-rate condos or subjected to a sharp rent increase), we can count these units as subject to exclusionary displacement.

Marcuse does, however, provide scholars with some operational flexibility. He notes that scholars may define the boundaries of the housing market differently depending on what they are studying. As he explains, the factor or factors underlying gentrification "should dictate the choice of 'market' for analytic purposes" (1985, 207). Here, I use the city as a whole to describe the market. Although DC is part of a wider metropolitan area, its separate political structure and distinct experience with the control board mean that the decisions that framed its gentrification were unique to it. Likewise, relying on a smaller geographic area, like the old central city, would be counterproductive because gentrification has expanded beyond these confines. The gentrified U Street corridor, for example, bleeds north into gentrified Columbia Heights, which is itself contiguous to gentrifying Petworth. Gentrifying U Street also bleeds south into Logan Circle.

Marcuse is equally flexible with definitions of "significant," telling readers that significance can be measured in multiple ways, including but not limited to statistical measures. Here, I cannot use a statistical measure of significance given the lack of city data on TOPA conversions. Instead, I measure the significance of TOPA's displacement mitigation with more mundane yardsticks. I assess the number who stay put, for example, by comparing it to the de facto goal of most developers interested in buying rental properties in the District—100 percent displacement of existing residents. Likewise, I assess the number of units that are put out of reach through the buyout process by comparing them to the number of units that would be put out of reach if tenants refused to use buyouts or otherwise ensured their affordability post-buyout.

Assessing Local Autonomy

I use a combination of measures to assess TOPA's capacity to deliver the city's tenants autonomy over their living quarters. For the most part, these measures are the same as those used by James DeFilippis in his book *Unmaking Goliath* (2004). However, my last measure is specific to the TOPA process.

The first measure I use to assess TOPA's capacity to deliver local autonomy is social justice. Specifically, I assess the degree to which social justice infuses the way tenants take up their TOPA rights. At the front end of the process, refusing a sale can indicate that a sense of social justice is in play. As I note in Chapter 4, tenants have a fairly short window to refuse a sale (between thirty and forty-five days). Although most of the legwork (i.e., forming a tenants' association, finding a lawyer, and getting tenants on board to refuse the sale) is done by a handful of tenants, their willingness to do this work suggests they will work toward a common good. As the process progresses, tenant leaders can also embrace social justice by choosing a final outcome that avoids displacing any tenant who wants to stay put. In a building with mostly low-income tenants, for example, a social-justice ethos would translate into choosing to remain rental even if converting to condo is financially possible and attractive for some tenants.

My second measure is collectivity. As DeFilippis (2004) notes, collective decision making is an important element of local autonomy because urban residents increasingly find themselves at the mercy of individuals—a landlord, a developer, an investor—whose interests rarely align with theirs. Collective decision making ensures that the process is democratized, that those who live in the city have the final say over changes in their building, neighborhood, or wider community. As I note in Chapter 4, TOPA is collective, at least in the first instance, because the right of refusal is accorded to tenants' associations rather than individual tenants. However, there are multiple decisions that tenants make after refusing a sale that can be assessed for evidence of collective input. One of the first decisions tenants have to make is whether they want to stay rental or convert to condos or co-ops. They also have to choose a development partner and the concessions they are willing to make in the process. The outcomes of each of these decisions do not, of course, have to have 100 percent support. Full agreement would be a nearly impossible bar to clear in a city with long-standing race and class divides, as well as in buildings where residents are spread across the life course (e.g., young singles, parents of minor children, and retirees). However, there must be a sense that tenant leaders make a good-faith effort to determine what their fellow tenants want and to find an outcome that meets the interests of the largest number of tenants. Collective thinking also means that tenant leaders would try to accommodate minority interests if doing so would not jeopardize the majority.

The third metric I use is also employed by DeFilippis (2004). Local autonomy initiatives must improve the lives of the people participating in them. I measure improvement in two ways. During DC's bleakest years, the city's housing stock experienced major disinvestment. Roofs were patched rather than replaced, decaying joists were left to rot, mold was untreated, and rodent infestations were allowed to fester. In this context improvement is measured in material terms, by the degree to which tenants use the TOPA process to repair their neglected living spaces. Second, I look at the degree to which buyouts—money third-party developers give to tenants to leave their units and renounce their TOPA claim to it—help tenants. This entails looking at the amount and uses of buyouts. Although there is no agreed-on floor above which a buyout amount can be judged as good, most of the tenant leaders I spoke with assessed buyout amounts with reference to moving costs. That is, if a buyout amount was less than or not substantially higher than the cost of finding another apartment, it was considered insufficient. Conversely, if a buyout amount allowed a tenant to pay off an outstanding debt or to make an investment with "dividends" (e.g., to pay college tuition or have enough for a mortgage down payment), it was usually defined as good.

My final metric is related to TOPA's effect on future tenants in the city. This is an abstract measure specific to the TOPA process. As I explain in the next chapter, buyouts are an integral part of the horse trading that goes on between tenants and their third-party developers. Developers often insist on buyouts in negotiations because it frees up units that can be sold or rented at market (rather than insider) rates. The ability of TOPA to ensure that particular buildings can serve as bulwarks against the luxurification that accompanies gentrification requires paying attention to what happens to bought-out units. If units are reserved for investors rather than residents,[6] or if they are priced in ways that exclude low- and even middle-income tenants, then TOPA's ability to provide local autonomy over the long haul can be called into question.

In the next section of the book, I use these metrics to assess the experiences of my seven sample properties. In Chapter 6 I outline the process and discuss each property's experience at way stations along it. I then provide a detailed analysis of the two low-income properties in my sample in Chapter 7. I give these two properties extra attention because both had failed TOPA processes. In Chapter 8, I examine my shadow case, following the tenants who filed a lawsuit to have their TOPA rights reinstated.

---

6. See Appendix 2 for a discussion of condos as investment vehicles rather than housing.

6

Displacement Mitigation and Its Limits

When RHCSA became law in 1980, its architects had two key objectives in mind. The first was to mitigate displacement. The second was to preserve affordable housing in the District. As previously noted, these two goals are potentially in conflict because conversions can reduce the number of units available for rent and inflate housing costs in an area. The bill's architects, however, expressed little concern about such outcomes. They believed the limits placed on conversions in the first part of the statute, CRHCC, would curb the pace and thus total number of conversions. They also assumed that nonprofit groups would step in to help tenants preserve their buildings as affordable rentals.

Despite these assumptions, TOPA's ability to mitigate displacement and ensure affordability has proven difficult. The built-in protections supporters assumed would prevent such conflicts proved insufficient to the task. As a result, while TOPA has had a measure of success in meeting its first goal, it has largely failed at addressing its second one. A portion of tenants in each sample property, for example, were able to stay put by invoking their TOPA rights—an average of 50.1 percent of tenants per property. However, in buildings that converted to condo, bought-out units were not only taken out of the city's rental inventory but also sold at market rates, which were well out of the range of low-income families during the study period. Moreover, while insider prices can preserve affordability for tenant purchasers, these prices apply only to them. Indeed, when tenant purchasers sell their units at a later date, they usually list them at market rates, further solidifying the gentrification of the property. Even in buildings that remained rental, affordability was weakened. Though the city's rent-control statute should protect against steep rent hikes in buildings staying rental, third-party developers have discovered a loophole in the statute that allows them to raise rents in bought-out units at higher-than-permitted rates.

In this chapter I provide a detailed account of these successes and failures and specify the processes that underpin both. The remainder of the chapter covers TOPA's positive performance mitigating direct displacement and reviews its negative contribution to exclusionary displacement and thus affordability. I also highlight the processes that permit success and failure. I conclude by commenting on what these findings can tell us about the theoretical debates discussed in Chapter 1.

TOPA's Positives

Direct Displacement Mitigation

The data I collected from tenant leaders in my seven sample properties suggest that TOPA does indeed mitigate direct displacement. The portion of units where residents stayed put ranged from 12.8 to 100 percent (Table 6.1). In buildings that converted to condo, between 12.8 and 46 percent of residents purchased their units. In buildings that remained rental, the range was greater—between 29.2 and 100 percent. For the sample as a whole, the average percentage of units preserved by property was 50.1; the median was 45.2.

Although these numbers are not as high as many advocates would like, they should not be dismissed for several reasons. Primary among them is that 707 households were able to stay put with the help of TOPA during the early 2000s real estate boom—a process that put great pressure on the city's low-income population (Reed 2012). Moreover, the number of individuals staying put is probably larger, given that many households contain multiple residents. If we use the 2000 census data on the average household size in DC (2.16 people; see U.S. Census Bureau 2001, 1034), for example, an estimated 1,527 people in these seven buildings used TOPA to stay put. These tenants were not only spared the difficulties and indignities of displacement; they were also given the opportunity to experience the improvements that come to gentrified neighborhoods, including increased safety, better city services, and more retail.[1]

---

1. New retail in gentrifying areas is often economically out of reach for low-income residents, but many of the city's new grocery stores are an exception. Although high-end grocery stores have moved to the District, so have discount chains like Giant and Safeway. Giant,

TABLE 6.1   NUMBER AND PERCENTAGE OF TENANTS WHO STAYED PUT AT SAMPLE PROPERTIES

Property	Outcome	Units per building	Number who stayed put	Percentage who stayed put
Garden Towers	Remained rental	73	33	45.2
Cathedral Court	Converted to condo	177	55	31.1
Mayfair Mansions	Buyer's attempt to purchase failed; tenants negotiated rental terms with buyer	469	469	100
Kennedy Street	Converted to half condo, half co-op	54	25	46.3
Town Center	Converted to condo	256	33	12.8
The Squire	Remained rental	65	19	29.2
Harvard/Summit	Remained rental	85	73	85.9

These numbers must also be put into wider context. As I note briefly in Chapter 1, when developers buy apartment buildings in DC, they usually prefer them to be empty. For a developer interested in condo conversion, empty units can be sold at market rates while those with tenants may be subjected to discounts (i.e., insider pricing) during a TOPA negotiation. A similar logic holds for developers who plan to keep their newly acquired buildings rental. Given the city's current popularity, most developers want to upgrade their buildings for the luxury market, and tenants who stay put (and are protected by rent control) limit the profit from "luxurification." Although rent control can be subverted, as I demonstrate later in the chapter, it often takes time and entails a good bit of legal wrangling.

Developers also prefer empty buildings because the city waives its condo-conversion fee on buildings that are empty at the time of conversion. Fees can be steep. The *Washington Post* found that the average conversion fee is $180,000 but can go as high as $1 million (Cenziper and Cohen 2008).

Developers also worry that incumbent tenants are more likely to cause trouble than new ones. This view prevails even in properties where incumbent tenants could absorb rent increases and would thus approximate, in socioeconomic terms, the luxury tenant most developers hope to attract. In situ tenants, especially long-term ones, can have a sense of proprietorship over their buildings. They are likely to know a building's trouble spots and demand repairs. And they are more likely to recognize cosmetic patches on problems in need of more substantial repair. Developers are also leery of

---

for example, has opened new stores in Columbia Heights (2005) and the H Street corridor (2013).

incumbent tenants because it is more difficult and costly to renovate a building around them than to overhaul one without them.

Not surprisingly, landlords who want to sell their buildings are keenly aware that their buyer base prefers empty buildings and do their best to oblige them, often with unsavory, if not downright illegal tactics. For example, in a 2008 exposé, the *Washington Post* documented dozens of cases of landlords threatening thousands of tenants in an effort to push them out. One landlord, Pamela Coleman, a doctor in the city, had her property manager send out a notice to tenants informing them that "next year, it will be a miracle if you all have heat and water" (Cenziper and Cohen 2008, A1).

In short, the goal of landlords selling their properties and the developers buying them is 100 percent displacement. In this context, even the lowest figures in the sample data set are meaningful. They demonstrate that TOPA can and does work in the favor of tenants, who usually lose out to developers in the competition for space in gentrifying cities.

It is worth acknowledging here that one of my sample buildings, Mayfair Mansions, is an outlier in terms of displacement mitigation, with 100 percent of its residents staying put during the TOPA process. Shirley Lawson, the tenant leader I interviewed, explained why: her association refused to put buyouts on the negotiating table with potential third-party partners. As she put it:

> We would not do that. We were adamant about that. Nobody— nobody—was removed from this property, and I'm very proud of that. Because I had heard so many horror stories about how people were promised one thing, and they left the property and was never able to return, you know. [Our lawyer] helped us with that. He put that in place for us, you know, that nobody would be displaced from this property.[2]

Another potential reason is that the property is located east of the Anacostia River in an area of the city that has seen limited gentrification. It is, of course, difficult to know which of these explanations is more important for understanding the property's 100 percent displacement mitigation. Many properties in now firmly gentrified parts of the city were once geographically marginal as well, but it is also true that gentrification remains sporadic east of the Anacostia River. However, even if we ascribe the property's location, rather than its tenants' refusal to accept buyouts, as the major factor behind its 100 percent displacement mitigation, Mayfair's tenants were able

---

2. For a list of interviewees and interview dates, see Appendix 3.

to use the TOPA process to their advantage in other tenant-friendly ways, as I demonstrate next.

Enhanced Bargaining Power

Tenants in my sample were also able to use the TOPA process to negotiate improvements to their living space. To understand how TOPA does this, we should recall how the bill empowers tenants. Although RHCSA was designed to prevent displacement, the vehicle by which it did so—the right of first refusal and tenants' ability to assign that right to a third party—has placed bargaining front and center in the process. In practice the TOPA process has become an exercise in horse trading between tenants and potential developers. Eric Rome, one of the tenant lawyers consulted for this project, explained it to tenants in the Harvard/Summit property this way: "The goal is to get developers to play 'Can you top this?' You're basically getting them to leapfrog over each other" for your business.[3]

As Rome's comments suggest, most of the bargaining occurs when tenants are choosing a development partner. Tenants find developers in a number of ways. Some consult nonprofits and tenant-advocacy groups. In other cases, developers hear about sales from the industry grapevine and reach out to tenants first. Tenant lawyers can also put out feelers to developers who might be interested in partnering with the tenants they represent. In fact, a key part of a tenants' association lawyer's job is to populate the negotiating table.

Once the table is populated, the process unfolds with a call for proposals and a date by which they should be sent to the tenants' association attorney. In the interim, interested developers can request tours of the building. Much of the city's apartment stock was built prior to World War II, so developers often want a sense of how a building's electrical, plumbing, and heating/cooling systems are holding up. They also want to know if there are threats to a building's structural integrity, such as mold, decaying joists, or termite infestations.

Once a proposal is submitted, tenants usually schedule a meeting with the prospective developer to discuss credentials (e.g., prior conversion/renovation experience) and, most important, specific plans for the building. Once all interested developers have made presentations, tenant leaders schedule a meeting of the whole association to hash out what they have heard and to develop a list of what they do and do not like about each proposal.

---

3. Rome made this comment at a Harvard/Summit tenants' association meeting on February 24, 2013, that I attended at the invitation of the tenants' association board.

At this point, the serious negotiation begins. Usually, the tenants' association's lawyer will contact developers with counterproposals, which are typically requests for better terms. Often these requests are couched in terms of "Can you top this?" That is, a tenants' association typically informs a given developer that a competitor is offering tenants something his or her group is not. Developers are then given a time frame in which to respond. Although the process can be free flowing—that is, proposals can be updated multiple times—it is limited by the time constraints built into the TOPA statute. Most tenants' associations have two or three formal rounds of proposals, as well as more informal rounds of horse trading in the days before a final decision is made.

Although tenants can negotiate on anything they choose, most negotiations focus on two priorities—insider pricing and quality-of-life improvements.[4] Of these, pricing is probably the most important issue, in a bread-and-butter sense, for tenants. However, the tenant leaders in my sample were also exasperated with the state of their often-disinvested buildings and anxious to improve them.

Insider Prices

In the context of TOPA, an insider price is a below-market price. A unit purchased through the TOPA process, for example, could cost $15,000 less than a similar unit in the same neighborhood. There is, of course, real and relative variation in insider pricing. Not surprisingly, insider prices in low-income areas are usually thousands of dollars lower than they are in wealthy neighborhoods. However, the rate of discount can also vary. They can be substantially below market, very near it, or somewhere in between.

Insider prices are also subject to the developer's bottom line. That is, they cannot be less than the actual cost of the unit, a figure that accounts for the final sale price (per unit) plus the cost of estimated repairs to the property as a whole. If the costs are higher than market rates, developers will not convert. There must also, of course, be room for profit.

Two buildings in my sample converted to condominium—Cathedral Court and Town Center. Both negotiated for insider pricing, but the process and final prices were quite different.

---

4. Bargaining for insider prices does not affect TOPA properties that remain rental since the District's rent-control legislation already protects the rents of those staying put. Blake Biles, one of the attorneys consulted for this research, told me, however, that it is not uncommon for tenants to have no idea city law protects them from steep rent increases during a change in landlords. As he explained, residents frequently tell him, "'Gee, I thought I had to leave because it's a sale,' or 'I thought I had to take this money [buyout],' or 'I don't really have a choice.'"

When Cathedral Court's tenants assigned its right of refusal to Tenacity, a local developer, it did not know in advance what its insider prices would be. As Stephen Goewey, the tenants' association cofounder and later president, told me, "We negotiated it [insider pricing] as part of a bigger package." When I asked him what that meant, he replied:

> Let's start at the beginning, when we were trying to buy the building. We, the [tenant] board and Tenacity, came up with some big ballpark numbers. Sixteen million for the buildings and about ten million in other expenses. This [ten million] included payouts to people to leave [buyouts], Tenacity's fee, capital improvements like new windows, boilers, etcetera. Then we had a grand total of twenty-six million for everything.

The $26 million would be covered through the sale of Cathedral Court's 177 units. The question, then, was how to apportion the $26 million between the units people staying put would buy and the bought-out units developers would own and later sell. In its negotiation with Tenacity, Cathedral Court's tenants' association stipulated that the tenant board, not Tenacity, would decide how to spread costs across the 177 units. As Goewey told me in an interview, "It [price setting] was totally up to us."

When Cathedral Court's tenants' association was deciding on a formula for pricing units, two issues took center stage—ensuring affordability for middle-income residents who wanted to stay put and accounting for variation within units. Although the first is a bread-and-butter issue, it was not a particularly contentious one. As I have noted elsewhere, my building was not a typical TOPA conversion. Most conversions occurred in neighborhoods east of Rock Creek Park. In 2000 these neighborhoods had large minority populations and below-average incomes. In contrast, my building was located west of the park in one of the city's wealthiest neighborhoods. Tenants in my building were overwhelmingly white and tended to work in professional jobs. As Matthew Tibbs, the association's cofounder and later treasurer, observed, "We all had pretty good jobs. We all made good money. We all had average or above-average credit."

To be sure, there were a few outliers, including a number of elderly or near-elderly people on the property. Many had moved to the neighborhood decades ago and, because of the city's rent-control statutes, paid rents well below market rate at the time. Goewey described one such resident: "It [our property] was a slum back in the day. I mean, like, it was rent controlled. I forgot what Lydia was paying, but she was paying like $400 a month."[5]

---

5. "Lydia" is a pseudonym.

At the time, Lydia lived in a studio apartment, and her rent was well below the market rate for a studio.[6] Fortunately for Cathedral Court's leaders, most residents like Lydia were elderly and, as such, protected by law. Indeed, RHCSA protects elderly residents from displacement even when a building converts to condo. Usually, the converter assumes ownership of the unit and is required to rent it to the elderly resident.

Given my building demographic, and the fact that most tenants who were vulnerable to displacement were already protected, my tenants' association's leaders did not worry about whether low-income people would be forced out. As Tibbs explained, "It really wasn't that much of an issue for us." Instead, Cathedral Court's tenants focused on making sure that insider prices were affordable to our property's lowest income brackets—the middle- and moderate-income professionals in the building. And they assessed affordability by calculating whether such tenants would be able to qualify for hypothetical mortgage amounts. The following exchange I had with Goewey and Tibbs illustrates their thought process:

> Goewey: You were one of the edge cases.
> Gallaher: What do you mean "edge cases"?
> Goewey: Well, like, we wanted to make sure that every single person qualifies for a loan. And it was like Example A, college professor,[7] making this much a year, wants to buy this unit. Like, can this happen with this income?
> Tibbs: Or, you know, 'cause at the time there were plenty of teachers there. Here's a DC or private-school teacher who's making X.
> Gallaher: Like Mary?
> Tibbs: Yeah, Mary, or Susan at the time,[8] and—oh, crap, I can't think [of the others]. There were a bunch of teachers in the buildings at the time. And it was like, can they afford it?

Although I am friends with my tenant leaders, I did not know they had used me as a test case for setting insider prices. I pressed for details.

> Gallaher: So when you were doing these test cases, what did you do? Because obviously you didn't have my credit report and stuff like that.

---

6. The census reports that the median gross rent in DC in 2000 was $618, a 50 percent increase from Lydia's then-current rent (Bonnette 2003).
7. Although starting academic salaries are well above the mean in many parts of the country, they tend to hover around the mean in DC because of the large concentration of highly paid professionals (e.g., doctors, lobbyists, lawyers) in the city.
8. "Mary" and "Susan" are pseudonyms.

Goewey: No, but we would jump into [a scenario], you know: At this income, what can they afford? What were the payments? How would that work with an ARM [adjustable-rate mortgage]? What would the monthly payments be?

Tibbs: You know, if our insider prices are in the 140s and the 160s, and somebody's making 50K a year,[9] can they afford to buy a $150,000 one-bedroom unit?

The tenant leaders in my building also pushed our developers to ensure that any tenant who wanted to get a loan could get one. At the time, a confluence of factors were working to encourage so-called B lending (i.e., subprime mortgages). This was certainly true in our conversion. Our development partner, Tenacity, had its own mortgage company, which offered subprime mortgages to tenants who could not qualify for so-called A loans. They also offered attractive teaser rates for interest on ARMs.

Although we now know that loosening credit standards was a big factor in fueling the housing bubble and that subprime mortgage providers contributed to the bubble's collapse by offloading the risk to other investors, it is important to situate this demand in the context in which it was made. In 2003 real estate prices were just beginning to rise. Optimism, rather than pessimism, ruled the day. My tenants' association leaders looked at B lending as a way to ensure that any tenant who wanted to stay put could get a loan to do so. As Goewey explained it, "We wanted to make clear to them [Tenacity] that every single person could qualify."

The second issue of concern for Cathedral Court as it set insider prices was to account for differences within units. While board members agreed that a two-bedroom should cost more than a one-bedroom, there was no consensus on how much greater the price should be. There was also concern that pricing reflect variation within units with the same number of bedrooms. Some one-bedrooms on the property were, for example, quite small, at just over five hundred square feet. Others were nearly seven hundred square feet.

The board kept two considerations in mind as it worked out how to account for such differences. The first was a concern to offload more of the costs (of the $26 million) onto developer-held units and wealthier residents in the building. Goewey noted, for example, that the association considered

---

9. When Cathedral Court converted in 2003, $50,000 was somewhat above the city's median household income of $42,597. These data are based on a three-year estimate (2001–2003) and were dynamically generated from the U.S. Census Bureau's American FactFinder website (http://factfinder2.census.gov).

making two-bedrooms significantly more expensive than one-bedrooms because they reasoned wealthier tenants lived in them:

> So, if we make two-bedrooms more expensive, on the grounds that those people have better income to afford one, then tenants with lower incomes in one-bedrooms will pay less. We also thought about basement units. Since Tenacity owned most of those, we didn't want to price those as low as they could have gone for.

The second consideration was more practical: How should the association account for the presence or absence of certain features like balconies and second bathrooms? As Goewey recounted:

> We had a lot of arguments. For example, should a second bathroom raise the cost? And how much does it really cost—the extra pipe for a second bathroom? Probably not much. A balcony? Well, that is a limited common element, so that will cost the association. A patio? Not much maintenance there.

Goewey told me that the association eventually asked Tenacity for help with benchmarking the cost of such features. He explained:

> We did a survey of condos in the neighborhood. Fitz [the developer's marketing specialist] actually did it for us. He asked real estate professionals how much things added to an overall price. What costs what. Fitz gave us the results, but he also gave us his opinion.

The information helped the association leaders learn how features, such as balconies, second bathrooms, and floor levels, were priced on the open market.

In the end, my tenants' association set insider prices that were below market rate, but not substantially so. Tibbs estimated, for example, that the average insider price for a one-bedroom condo ($155,000) was about $50,000 less than the first round of bought-out units our third-party developer sold. The difference put our insider prices about 24 percent below market value. However, the difference grew substantially with later rounds. As Tibbs recalled:

> Once we go into phase two and three with other outsider buyers coming in, suddenly the values of your condo [shoot up]. If I paid $186,000,[10] which is what I paid, suddenly, three months later, units in my building were selling for $270,000.

---

10. Tibbs's one-bedroom was priced above average because he purchased developer-offered upgrades, which were rolled into the unit price.

By 2009, when I conducted the interview with Goewey and Tibbs, they suggested that the price differential was nearly $100,000. Both marveled at the magnitude of change over the seven-year period. As Tibbs explained, again with reference to his personal situation, "At the time I just couldn't believe that I was going to pay $186,000 for a one-bedroom condo. Now, even in the lowest part of the market, you can't find a one-bedroom condo for $186,000!" Even with procedural hiccups, Goewey noted, "we all made out pretty well."

When I asked Goewey and Tibbs whether they received any pushback from the developer, Tenacity, both responded no. A key reason was timing. Our property converted to condo in 2003, just as the housing market was taking off in DC. In this context, the main source of profit margin for Tenacity was in the bought-out units. And the price for getting access to those units and being able to sell them in a booming real estate market was giving their tenant partners what they wanted. As Tibbs explained:

> They kind of realized that $5,000 on an insider price didn't matter to them. It mattered to me, it mattered to you, but to them, they didn't matter because they were going to sell [the bought-out units] for $250,000. So if they made 35K or 30K [in profit from tenant-purchased units], they were like, "We don't care."

The promise of steep profits also limited tenant complaints. Although some tenants did complain that insider prices were not as low as they had hoped, Tenacity consistently reminded tenants interested in purchasing that they would be building equity, and quickly, given the state of the market. And, as Tibbs noted, they were right: "It was an implied guarantee. But they were like, 'Never have we done this and had our tenants not make 100K.' And as it turned out, we made 100K overnight. I mean, everybody did, I would say, in equity."

Negotiation for insider pricing played out quite differently in Town Center. Like Cathedral Court, Town Center converted during the real estate boom, when housing prices were rising rapidly. However, the similarities stop there. Three differences stand out.

First, unlike Cathedral Court, Town Center's tenants' association had a higher concentration of racial minorities and people with low incomes. As Afifa Klouj, the president of the tenants' association, explained:

> I'd say about 85 percent or something were African Americans. Maybe even the same proportion of moderate to low income—mostly low-income people. We had several households also who are

Section 8. We have—I think we had about eight to ten households that were Section 8. We had more elderly residents.

The differing demographics mean that Klouj and her fellow board members were focused more intently than Cathedral Court was on ensuring insider prices were substantially below market. Without deeply discounted prices, few in-place residents could buy their units. As Klouj succinctly explained, "When we negotiated the contract and the prices, it was with the understanding that prices had to be low enough for the majority of us to afford to buy."

A second difference is that Town Center negotiated its insider prices upfront, before it assigned its right of refusal to a third party (recall that Cathedral Court negotiated the right to set prices after purchase but within the constraints imposed by the $26 million price). The process began when the association (via its lawyer) solicited proposals from developers. Klouj told me that they laid out their general conditions vis-à-vis pricing in their initial discussions with developers:

We had called several developers to send us proposals. We talked to them about, you know, coming and touring the property. And we told them, you know, what it is roughly that we wanted. And the kind of price range we are looking for because of our income. You know, the majority, the average income of our tenants. And we had, I think, about nine or eight developers who sent us proposals.

As a result, when proposals started arriving, they had proposed insider prices already included in them.

After reviewing all of the proposals, the association settled on two that seemed feasible. One was from Tenacity, the developer with which my association partnered. The other was from the Bernstein Group. The difference came down to a debate over quality versus price. Klouj liked Tenacity because its prices were lower. Other board members were attracted to what they saw as the higher quality of the Bernstein Group's previous conversions. I asked Klouj how her board came to a decision. She replied:

He [the association's lawyer] gave us guidelines on how to select, and he also sort of, like, made us focus. So he was very good at, sort of, organizing our thought process on how we were going to select. You know, he got us, like, selection criteria that we should look at. And then we had, like, a long meeting where we went through it one by one.

Although the selection process helped the association clarify its goals, the divide between those supporting Tenacity and those supporting the Bernstein Group persisted. The group's lawyer, Rick Eisen, suggested that the association employ the "Can you top this?" strategy described by Eric Rome. As Klouj explained:

> What we did was we came to a compromise. We said, "Okay, many of us like Tenacity, some of us like the quality and stuff of Bernstein, but Bernstein is more expensive, and you know, for many of us it's unaffordable." So what we did is we went back to Bernstein and we said, "Okay, here are the prices we got from Tenacity. If you match them, we'll select you. If you don't match them, we'll go with Tenacity." They [Bernstein] matched them.

The third key difference was in the differential between insider prices and market rates. Unlike Cathedral Court's insider prices, which were lower than market rates, but not substantially so, Town Center's rates were considerably lower than prices on the open market. When I asked Klouj what the difference was, she replied, "At the time [of negotiation] maybe 50 percent. By the time we bought, it was much more than that. I mean, it was like, I think I paid maybe 40 percent of the market price. No, maybe more. But it's definitely less than 50 percent by the time we bought." In fact, Town's Center's insider prices were so low that a few residents bought their apartments with the plan of immediately flipping them. The deeply discounted insider prices meant that buying and flipping promised greater profit than the already lucrative buyout, which was one of the sample's most generous. Klouj described one such person:

> One person who listed their apartment the next day after they closed, or the next couple of days, put it *so* below market price. They just wanted to cash out and get out, because this person who did this, they got the large two-bedroom apartment on the top floor. It's a corner apartment, a beautiful two-bedroom. They bought it for $143,000, and the market price is about $500,000. So they can put it for $400,000 and still make $250,000 and cash out and get out.

Klouj said the developers intervened immediately:

> But the developer stopped them and threatened to sue, because we had a clause [in the contract] that you can't compete within the first year. We're doing this not for you to do an investment; it's for you to

have a house, to have a home. So if you want to stay, it's because you want to live there.

Town Center's insider prices were more deeply discounted than those at Cathedral Court for two reasons. First, its tenants' association made substantially discounted insider prices a priority. It used its negotiating power to drive the price down, both in the initial stage, when it signaled acceptable price ranges to interested developers, and in the final stage, when it told the Bernstein Group it would select the group only if it matched Tenacity's lower prices. The second reason is idiosyncratic to the Town Center property and thus not likely to occur elsewhere in the city. Town Center's two buildings were built on land leased from the city. Thus, when the tenants' association was looking for a development partner, it needed one willing to engage in two separate transactions—first, buying the building (via the tenants' transferred right of first refusal) and, second, negotiating to purchase the land from the city. Klouj and her fellow tenant leaders were told by multiple groups that "the city's not going to sell [the land] to you." When I asked why, Klouj explained that the land was managed by the National Capital Redevelopment Corporation (NCRC), a public-private partnership that seemed interested in developing the land on its own. As she explained, "I believe NCRC, they wanted the land to develop it themselves, because they wanted to prove themselves in the market that they can do development."[11]

Klouj told me that other developers were also vying for the land. They wanted to tear down the buildings and develop the property more densely than its current configuration:

> We had surface parking lots, which is, you know—in that location, you really don't want that. You want the parking down, you know, underground, and you want to use the surface to build buildings. And you have also a large courtyard in between the buildings.

In short, access to the land was not a foregone conclusion, and the process of converting could happen only after the land was purchased.[12] Although Town Center was eventually able to work out a deal with the city, the process delayed the conversion by nearly eighteen months. And during that period,

---

11. The NCRC was shut down in 2007 after the city council passed legislation to absorb it into the Office of the Deputy Mayor for Planning and Economic Development (DePillis 2011a).
12. Technically, a developer could convert the buildings without holding ownership of the land, but most saw it as a major hurdle.

the market rate for condos continued to increase, further widening the gap between the association's insider prices and market rates.

Quality-of-Life Improvements
Another positive aspect of the TOPA process is that residents can use it to negotiate for improvements to their buildings. Some improvements are structural, such as replacing decaying joists or remediating mold. Others are related to safety—for example, new security systems to keep burglars at bay. Still other improvements can be classified as amenities, such as fresh paint and new furniture in common areas. So, too, are bike rooms and storage lockers. The tenants in my sample negotiated for all of these things and more.

Usually, buildings that end up in the TOPA process have experienced significant disinvestment. In a profile of UIP, a developer specializing in TOPA conversions, the *Washington City Paper* described its typical acquisition as "dumpy, mid-century brick buildings subject to rent control, which landlords usually treat like an imposition on their constitutional rights" (De-Pillis 2012c). Although only some of the buildings in my sample were "mid-century brick," tenant leaders universally described their buildings (presale) with words suggestive of disinvestment. David Laichena, president of the Kennedy Street tenants' association, noted, for example, that his landlord had "kind of let it [the property] go." At Cathedral Court, Matthew Tibbs told me that the buildings on the property "were in pretty bad shape." Stephen Goewey used an even stronger word—"slum"—to describe the state of the property. Shirley Lawson, the tenants' association president at Mayfair Mansions, observed in our interview that her property had begun to "deteriorate," because "as time went on, the landlord didn't put a lot of money into the place." At Town Center, Klouj told me that her landlord had stopped putting money into the property because he wanted to tear it down:

> He stopped renting, and you know, the buildings started going down. He wasn't, you know, paying too much attention to maintenance. He didn't do any of the necessary repairs and stuff. His letter [to tenants announcing the sale] stated that he wanted to tear it down.

Genevieve Moreland, a tenant leader at the Harvard/Summit property, explained the state of her property by describing its entry system for me: "We don't have any sort of doorbell system. I mean, this is going to sound stupid, but if somebody comes to see me, they have to call me, and I have to go down and let them in. And then if I'm having a party, I have to do that, like, all night long." She also described an almost decade-long recurring leak in the ceiling of her top-floor apartment. After repeated complaints, she finally called the Housing Authority, but her landlord chose to pay a fine and discount her rent rather than make the repair.

> Moreland: I've always had problems with my ceiling and roof. I called the Housing Authority twice because they weren't doing the repairs. So I know they were fined a thousand dollars one time for not repairing my ceiling.
> Gallaher: Wow!
> Moreland: Because they just weren't doing it. So every month they would have to give me discounts on my rent because I was calling and harassing.
> Gallaher: Did they make your life miserable, or did they just give you the discount and not fix it?
> Moreland: They gave me the discount and didn't fix it. I mean, they would fix it, but then they wouldn't really fix it, you know. So they would replaster the ceiling, but if you don't fix the hole [in the roof], then it's just going to happen again.

At Garden Towers things were not as bad. As Cajia Owens, the tenants' association vice president, explained in our interview, "The building, you know, just had really good bones." However, landlord disinvestment was still a problem. Owens explained:

> They band-aided everything, you know.... The top floor—we're getting a new roof right now, because we desperately needed one. Every time it snowed, I would get—because I'm on the top—I would get water damage every time it snowed.

Given the deteriorating state of the buildings in my sample, it is not surprising that tenant leaders in all of them negotiated for structural improvements. And fortunately for tenants, developers were usually willing to oblige them. Tenants have obvious reasons for wanting repairs. When a boiler breaks down in winter, for example, tenants have to lug out space heaters or burrow under blankets. But developers also want repairs. Most are trying to attract a higher-income clientele, and advertising recent investment is often an attractive selling point for buyers or renters selecting between old and new build developments. This is not to suggest, of course, that tenants and developers always agreed on the scope of repairs. They did not. Yet they were on the same page about most repairs.

In Cathedral Court, tenant leaders negotiated with Tenacity for a number of important structural repairs to the building. Each building on the property got new plumbing and electrical upgrades. The electrical upgrade was particularly welcome. One building on the property had such low voltage per unit that tenants routinely complained that they could not run a microwave and a hairdryer at the same time. New boilers were also installed in several buildings. And every window in the property was replaced with double-paned, insulated windows. Heat now stays in, and noise stays (mostly) out. My unit faces the street, and before our new windows arrived, I could hear the final destination announcement of the bus stopping in front of the building next door, even with all my windows closed.

The Harvard/Summit tenants also negotiated for structural upgrades to their buildings. Moreland noted that their development partner agreed to modernize the property's electrical systems. "We still have fuses; they blow all the time," she said. They have also agreed to install an electronic entry system, which would allow tenants to buzz up visitors and ensure better security since fewer tenants would prop doors open for expected visitors.

Tenants also used the TOPA process to negotiate for nonstructural improvements. The Garden Towers tenants' association used the "Can you top this?" strategy to get a rooftop deck. The process began when the association put out a call for proposals. During its tours, association leaders not only introduced developers to the property but also encouraged developers to include as many amenities as possible in their proposals. Owens and her fellow leaders then used the amenities listed in the first batch of proposals to up the ante for other developers interested in submitting proposals. As she explained:

> So we were kind of playing off of them on that. Like the rooftop deck. I was going to demand that that was something we'd like. And they were like, "Okay, sure." And we'd go [to the other developer], 'They're going to give us a rooftop deck. What are you going to do for us? Are you going to give us a rooftop deck?"

The strategy worked. Final proposals were delivered to Garden Tower's attorney that Owens described as "outrageous.... They [the developers] use a lot of very modernized everything."

Although the quotations from Owens are focused on amenities residents wanted, she and her fellow tenant leaders also negotiated economic concessions for residents staying put. These were important, given the demographic of the building, which included a significant number of moderate- to low-income residents. Owens explained, "We also asked for certain leniencies, like if you were to lose your job, you'd have kind of a grace period of rent. It was a sixty-days' grace period of rent." She and her fellow board members also targeted improvements for particularly vulnerable residents:

We asked to have a wheelchair ramp in the back, or wherever in the building, because we have two tenants who use wheelchairs. One lives on the fifth floor. And it's really hard when they go and come to doctors. It's just an issue, and we kind of made a promise to these individuals that we'd get a wheelchair ramp.

Like Garden Towers, the Mayfair Mansions tenants' association also used the negotiation process to improve their building. In addition to general improvements to common areas, the tenants' association negotiated for improvements inside tenants' units. One request they successfully negotiated, for example, was the installation of washers and dryers in all units. And as Shirley Lawson explained, the request was as much about safety as convenience:

We had Laundromats—like two in each court [garden-style apartment buildings]. But they were very dangerous places. I mean, people were having sex in there. They were breaking into the machines. They were sleeping in the places, urinating. You didn't know what to expect because it was a secluded room; you know what I'm saying?

Lawson's tenants' association also negotiated for the installation of sprinkler systems inside units:

Two older—not elderly but older like me—sisters had gotten burned up in their apartment on Georgia Avenue somewhere in a fire. And I kept seeing these news stories about these fires. And they kept saying these people could have been saved if they'd had a sprinkler system. You know, these people could be saved. And I said, "No! We've got to have some sprinkler systems."

As Lawson's comments suggest, disinvestment often makes tenants feel unsafe. In this regard, the bargaining power afforded by TOPA has a measurable impact on people's lives. Though these sorts of changes cannot be counted in displacement mitigation figures, they are an important part of the process. They are evidence that TOPA has carved out a middle ground between the rock and hard place where most urban tenants find themselves, a space DeFilippis succinctly describes as "continued disinvestment and decline in the quality of the homes they live in, or reinvestment that results in their displacement" (2004, 89).

TOPA's Negatives

While TOPA can be credited with mitigating displacement and reversing disinvestment, its ability to protect affordable housing is minimal. Indeed, the process, as it played out during the study period (2000–2014), guarantees what Marcuse (1985) calls exclusionary displacement. That is, while some residents are able to stay put, their buildings are put out of reach for other low-income residents in the process. TOPA contributes to exclusionary displacement through two practices that have become bound up in the process—buyouts and voluntary agreements.

Buyouts

There is nothing in RHCSA that mentions buyouts. However, they have been part of the process from the beginning, according to Eric Rome, who has represented tenants invoking their TOPA rights since the law's inception, first as an employee at University Legal Services and then in private practice.[13] A buyout is a sum of money paid to a tenant to leave his or her unit and forgo any TOPA-related claim to it. Usually, a tenant signs legal documentation that states rights to the unit will be relinquished by a given date in exchange for an agreed-on sum of money. The agreement also lays out how and when the tenant will receive the buyout. Five of the seven buildings in my sample offered buyouts. The two buildings that did not—Mayfair Mansions and Kennedy Street—had a failed and delayed conversion, respectively. I discuss the particulars of these buildings and the reason for their failed or delayed conversion in the next chapter.

Buyouts are an integral part of the TOPA process. When tenants assign their third-party rights to a developer, they negotiate for insider prices in exchange for the right of developers to offer buyouts to interested tenants. The goal for developers converting to condo is to obtain as many vacant units as possible so they can sell them at market rates. The same logic applies for buildings remaining rental. As I discuss later in the chapter, despite the city's rent-control statute, developers have found loopholes that allow them to re-rent vacated units at market rates.

Of course, the process of emptying often begins before a sale has even been initiated. Landlords who want to sell their buildings know that developers want as many empty units as possible, and they often indulge them. Some landlords use distasteful, even illegal tactics to empty their buildings.

---

13. University Legal Services for the District of Columbia (ULS-DC) has been active in helping tenants in the city navigate the TOPA process. For more on the organization, see its website at http://www.uls-dc.org/About_ULS-HCP.htm.

Others simply stop re-renting units vacated through normal tenant attrition. Although none of the tenant leaders in my sample witnessed landlord bullying, several said their landlords had stopped re-renting vacated units. Lawrence Green,[14] the tenant president at the Squire, told me that his landlord stopped re-renting months before selling the building—"a lot of units were empty." Klouj noted a similar pattern at Town Center, telling me, "When we started the association, remember almost half of the units were empty because the landlord wasn't renting—he was getting ready for this." Tibbs saw the same pattern at Cathedral Court:

> Well, you know, people would move out, and Louise [the property manager] wouldn't re-rent them.[15] So it was like, "Do you have any vacancies?" "No, we don't have any vacancies." And there were ten in our building. So, you know, like, they just weren't renewing leases.

While most buildings already have a sizable number of vacant units when they are sold, developers usually try to secure even more vacancies through buyouts. Tenants interested in staying put are often willing to help them. Securing more buyouts for a development partner is seen as a way to guarantee more favorable insider prices. Tibbs noted that his tenants' association did not advertise buyouts before they were official with the hopes of increasing vacancies. As he explained, "People started moving out before they knew what was going on. But we didn't tell them, 'Hey, we're giving you a buyout soon.'" And once the tenants' association took control of the building, it replicated its prior landlord's policy. As Goewey noted, "When we took control, we renewed leases, but we didn't rent to new people." To be fair, the tenants' association had legal concerns to worry about—the association could not offer buyouts before it owned the building. However, the course of action pursued by the association, as Goewey's comments suggest, produced more vacancies.

Buyout amounts can also become a subject of negotiation when tenants are choosing a developer. And as in the process for negotiating insider prices, tenants can use the "Can you top this?" approach to secure higher amounts. This is especially true in buildings where tenants are either unable or uninterested in staying put for the long haul. In buildings choosing to stay rental, for example, those who had hoped to buy are often amenable to leaving if a buyout amount is attractive. Indeed, such a tenant could use a sizable buyout for a down payment on a condo elsewhere. Students, interns, and other temporary residents are also willing to leave if the buyout amount is greater

---

14. "Lawrence Green" is a pseudonym.
15. "Louise" is a pseudonym.

than the cost of moving. Usually, the greater the difference, the more likely such tenants are to agree to pack up early. In these and other cases, buyout amounts can be as important as insider pricing.

The Squire fit this pattern. Because it was sold during the recession, the Squire's tenants' association did not receive many proposals for condo conversion. One developer's proposal even explicitly stated that conversion was a poor option "as a result of the housing market crisis."[16] Moreover, the building's location near several universities meant it had a sizable population of transitory residents who found a buyout more appealing than staying put at rent-controlled rates. As Green explained, "There was a big group that didn't care [about staying], because once they saw the buyout was available—those are the more transient people—they liked the buyout option." Thus, the Squire's tenants' association focused their negotiation on upping the buyout amounts for the building's tenants. The following exchange from my interview with Green demonstrates the process:

> Green: We sort of did a thing that was anonymous. Like [we'd say to each developer,] "This is the other offers we're getting." Everybody got the same thing. "This is the offers we're getting." So they had to meet the other guys.
> Gallaher: Oh, so you actually—you actually passed the other offers on to them [other developers making bids]?
> Green: Anonymously, though. . . . This is the way the attorney liked it . . . to have, you know, a bidding session on its way.
> Gallaher: So he was updating the process without, you know, sharing? Keeping confidentiality?
> Green: We had a fair process that would result in higher offers from all of them.
> Gallaher: So how many times did you guys go through that process?
> Green: It was three.

The process became so competitive that Green told me bidding continued after the deadline for the final offers had passed. Two developers competing for the building, for example, put in new offers with higher buyout amounts after the final deadline for best and final offers had passed. In one of them, the new buyout amount was $15,000 higher than the amount in the original best and final offer. As Green noted, "They cheated the process, you know?" Despite the double-dealing, Green and his fellow board members thought that they could not ignore the improved offers: "As a board, we're

---

16. This quotation is taken from a "best and final offer" delivered to the president of the Squire on September 30, 2011. I do not name the developer here at Green's request.

not prepared to turn down a big, better offer. That would be malpractice." Instead, Green and the rest of the board used the competition to improve the final deal.

There are, of course, natural checks to the buyout bidding process. The Harvard/Summit property is a case in point. The property contains two sets of buildings—one on Harvard Street and the other on Summit Street. The Harvard buildings contain fewer units (twenty-four) than those on Summit Street (sixty-one). In both of the first-round proposals Harvard/Summit's tenants received, developers proposed demolishing the buildings on Harvard Street and replacing them with a larger, one hundred–unit structure. Both developers also offered substantial buyouts to sweeten the deal—between $21,000 and $69,000. This presented a potential problem for the tenants' association. To ensure that all tenants wanting to stay put could do so, the Summit property would need to secure at least as many buyouts as there were Harvard Street tenants interested in staying put. This was a plausible goal. As Moreland noted, "Probably enough people would have [left] because of the buyouts. Like, they offered me—I think it was $22,000 or $24,000 if I would move out of my apartment. So I think enough people would have taken those amounts." However, the tenants' association discovered that it could not require Harvard residents to move to the Summit side of the property if sufficient space opened up there. That is, they would have to ensure that Harvard tenants interested in staying put were willing to do so at one of the Summit buildings. Moreland explained:

> Eric [Rome] explained to us that while the right of assignment is with the tenants' association, the right of occupancy is with the individual unit holder. So if one person on Harvard Street said, "I'm not moving," the deal would fall apart. Because they are allowed to say, "I'm not moving," and we can't make them move out.

As a result, the Harvard/Summit tenants' association had to select a developer willing to propose a plan B in case any tenants on Harvard Street refused to leave their units. One developer did offer a contingency plan—to keep the buildings on Harvard Street intact—but it came with significantly lower buyouts. As Moreland noted, "The buyouts were small. I think $1,000 to maybe $9,000 or $10,000. Mine was like $7,000." When I asked why the buyout amount dropped so substantially for plan B, she explained:

> Because they really see the value in tearing down the building. They were going to put a building of over one hundred units where there's only twenty-four now. So, for them, that was the value. And they

were willing to share some of the value with the tenants, no matter which building you lived in, because of that.

After the Harvard/Summit tenants' association selected their development partner, they had to develop a method for tenants to select between plan A (demolition on Harvard Street) and plan B (the status quo). The method they selected—that only tenants on Harvard Street could vote on which plan to accept—virtually guaranteed smaller buyouts. Although some tenants on Summit Street were angry at the method chosen, Moreland explained that she and her fellow board members did not think it would be fair to let Summit tenants decide the fate of those living in the Harvard. At the end of the process two Harvard residents opted not to move. The decision meant much smaller buyouts.

As the discussion on buyouts up to this point suggests, there were different approaches to setting buyout amounts. In my sample, four different mechanisms were used. The first set a standard rate based on the number of bedrooms in a unit, with two-bedroom apartments receiving larger buyouts than one-bedrooms and one-bedrooms receiving more than studios. Cathedral Court and Garden Towers used this approach. A second approach was to give all units the same buyout amount, regardless of variation in apartment size. The Squire used this method. The third way was based on the length of a tenant's tenure, with amounts increasing with each year of tenancy. Town Center's buyouts were organized using this method. The final way involved mixing two or more of these criteria. Harvard/Summit's buyouts, for example, were based on the size of the unit and the number of years the tenant had been in it.

Several buildings also increased buyout amounts as more residents agreed to take them. This approach was always used in conjunction with one of the other methods. That is, initial rates are set by one of these criteria but increase as more people accept them. In Garden Towers, for example, buyout amounts were set based on the number of bedrooms per unit, but the amounts increased when the number of residents taking buyouts met given thresholds. As Owens explained, "It was like zero to six [units], we'll give this much . . . from seven to fifteen units, this much." Town Center did something similar. Although its tenants' association set buyout amounts based on length of tenure, it also conducted several rounds of buyouts. Klouj estimates her association went through three or four rounds of buyouts. And with each round, amounts increased.

Although my sample is small, there is a great deal of variation in buyout amounts—between $1,000 and $65,000 (Table 6.2). When I asked Eric Rome what accounted for the variation, he pointed to four variables that help

DISPLACEMENT MITIGATION AND ITS LIMITS

TABLE 6.2 BUYOUT AMOUNTS BY PROPERTY

Property	Buyout amounts
Garden Towers	One-bedroom: $20,000
	Two-bedroom: $21,500
Cathedral Court	Studio: $7,500
	One-bedroom: $10,000
	Two-bedroom: $12,000
Mayfair Mansions	—
Kennedy Street	—
Town Center	Phase 1: $22,000–$30,000
	Final phase: $40,000–$65,000
The Squire	$45,000
Harvard/Summit	$1,000–$10,000

explain buyout amounts. The first three have to do with building economics. As he explained:

> So the buyouts are a product of how much a developer can make over and above what they are paying on the unit. So what goes into that? The purchase price on the building; what the—if you are converting to condominiums—what the insider purchase price is versus what you could sell it for on the market; and the third factor: if you are going to keep the building rental, what's the spread between what most tenants are paying and the market rent, and how long is it going to take for you to recoup that?

However, Rome noted that tenants still had a lot of leeway to negotiate because of the final, fourth variable.

> Rome: And, uh, then there's the fourth, kind of wild card [variable]. It's like, how much extra are you [the developer] going to throw at this just to get the deal? You know?
> Gallaher: And this is where your negotiating skills come in?
> Rome: Right.
> Gallaher: And where you have the most leeway?
> Rome: Right, particularly if I have people bidding against each other.

There was also a lot of variation in the numbers of tenants per property taking buyouts. Table 6.3 lists estimates of the number of tenants taking buyouts in each property. Although these are estimates, the likelihood of errors is minimal. As I note in the previous chapter, tenant leaders uniformly

TABLE 6.3 NUMBER AND PERCENTAGE OF BUYOUTS, PRESALE VACANCIES, AND TOTAL UNITS SUBJECT TO PRICE INCREASES AT SAMPLE PROPERTIES

Property	Total number of units	Number and percentage of units taking buyouts	Number and percentage of units vacated presale	Total number and percentage of units subject to price increases
Garden Towers	73	37/50.7%	3/8.12%	40/54.79%
Cathedral Court	177	58/32.8%	64/36.16%	122/68.93%
Mayfair Mansions	469	0	0	0
Kennedy Street	54	0	—	0
Town Center	256	113/44.0%	110/42.97%	223/87.11%
The Squire	65	40/61.5%	6/15.00%	46/70.77%
Harvard/Summit	85	12/14.1%	0	12/14.10%

Note: The Kennedy tenants' association president did not know how many units were vacant in his building at the time of sale. Despite this lack of data, I feel comfortable reporting that no units were subject to market rents based on the building's current status, which I detail in Chapter 9.

expressed confidence that the numbers of buyouts in their properties were accurate, off by not more than one or two units. I also include an estimate of the number of units vacated before conversion in Table 6.3. I calculated this figure by adding the number of tenants staying put with those taking buyouts and subtracting that sum from the total number of units per building.

As Table 6.3 demonstrates, a total of 260 units (22 percent of total units) were bought out in the study sample. The buyout rate is higher, however, if we include only the buildings that offered buyouts. Among the five buildings offering buyouts, 39.6 percent of units were bought out, although the range is quite large, between 14.1 percent and 61.5 percent. The number of units vacated presale in the sample is 183 total units, with a range at the building level from 0 to 43 percent (this range does not include data from Kennedy Street because its tenants' association president did not know how many units were vacant at the time of the initial sale). If we add units vacated presale with bought-out units, we can also arrive at an estimated figure for the number of units subject to price increases in the sample—443 units or 37.6 percent of total sample units and 67.5 percent of units in buildings with buyouts (again, Kennedy Street is not included in this calculation).

In the next section, I trace what happens to the prices in units that are bought out during a TOPA process. Before doing so, however, I discuss the decision-making process tenants use when deciding to allow buyouts and the tangible and real benefits that can accrue to those who take them.

When a TOPA process starts, two groups usually congeal quickly—those who want to stay and those who want a buyout. Those who want to stay are often settled in their neighborhoods and do not want to move. Those interested in buyouts are more transient, albeit in different ways. Some are newcomers with little attachment to a particular neighborhood. Others are temporary residents, such as interns or students. Still others have unstable work histories or family relationships and thus a track record of frequent moves. For such transients, a buyout, even a fairly low-priced one, is tantamount to free money—a payment to do something they were likely to do anyway. There can also be people somewhere in the middle, who can go either way. Usually, a sizable enough buyout can entice them to leave. There is, of course, no one threshold amount. It varies by individual and often depends on a host of factors, including the state of one's finances, the stability of one's job, and where one is in the life course, among other considerations.

When my association announced buyout figures, I asked my tenants' association president, Stephen Goewey, "Why would anyone stay?" I had already decided to stay put—I loved my neighborhood and my apartment—but I worried I was making the wrong decision. I had limited savings at the time, and $10,000 seemed like a nice cushion for my bank account. Goewey's response suggested that "free money" was not always free: "By the time you pay taxes on that, you'll have less than seven thousand, and you'll eat through that in no time trying to find a new place to live." He also reminded me how much money I could make if I decided to keep my unit and flip it a year or two later. Green (the Squire's tenant leader) made a similar point in our interview: "If your rent was really low, then the buyout doesn't help you much. So you'll have to find another apartment. You'll be paying market rent. Your buyout'll disappear in a year or something."

However, for other residents, a buyout can be worth it. It can, in fact, be a life-changing event. Green told me, for example, that the Squire buyout was enough for a "down payment for a house." When I asked him if he planned to use it that way, he told me, "I thought about it! But politics is not the most stable gig." How then, I asked, would he use it? "It's gonna be very good. I'm gonna pay off my student loans. I'll be debt free. I would never have been able to do that without it! . . . I mean, with my loans gone—its huge!" Green described what another tenant planned to do with her buyout:

> One lady's gonna move back to the Philippines and buy a house with her husband. . . . She's been here forever. Her husband is sick, so he flew back to the Philippines. She's gonna move back with him. She's got all this cash now to buy a house in the Philippines—no problem!

Another Squire resident I interviewed—Steve Jones[17]—told me he felt incredibly "lucky" to get the buyout. When I asked him why, he told me he had over $200,000 in student loan debt—incurred for college and the law school

---

17. "Steve Jones" is a pseudonym.

from which he was about to graduate. When I asked him what he would do with his money, he told me, "I'm going to use the $45,000 to pay bills down and take a bar prep course." He also shared with me that he felt the money gave him more flexibility in his job search. In particular, he could expand his search beyond corporate firms: "With nonprofit work, you could never pay it [his student loan debt] back."

None of this is to suggest, of course, that the process of accepting buyouts was conflict free. It was not, as I demonstrate later in the chapter. However, Green thought that the overwhelming majority of tenants in his building were happy to get such a substantial sum of money:

> Green: I mean, I get e-mails for—like, thanking me! [*Laughing*] I don't know.
> Gallaher: [*Laughing*] You don't know what to say?
> Green: I'm like, hey, don't worry about it. I'm getting something good out of this, too.

Voluntary Agreements

Once bought-out and prevacated units are in a developer's possession, they are renovated and prepared for market, either as condos or rentals. In five of the seven buildings in my sample, this process involved an increase in the housing costs associated with the unit. This is not surprising in buildings converting to condo, where developers were, until the 2008 recession, responding to a hot condo market. However, the city's rent-control statute should have protected against steep increases in bought-out units in buildings remaining rental. Unfortunately, developers have found a legal end run around rent control. To understand how they did so, we must first look at the city's rent-control statute.

In DC, rents can be raised in two ways—under standard (or automatic) rules and through petition (Department of Housing and Community Development 2013). Standard rules govern rent increases for existing tenants and vacated units. For existing tenants, landlords may increase rent by the increase in the consumer price index plus 2 percent, but not to exceed 10 percent. In recent years most increases have ranged between 4 and 5 percent (Weiner 2014). Rental increases for vacated units are usually capped at 10 percent of the previous occupants' rents, although exceptions of up to 30 percent may be granted in special cases.

Landlords may also petition to raise rents under five "special" categories—hardship, capital improvement, substantial rehabilitation, services and facilities, or voluntary agreement with 70 percent of tenants. The first three petition categories involve a landlord demonstrating that significant repair work is necessary and these costs necessitate greater increases than standard rules permit. The fourth category is designed to cover additional costs associated with the provision of new services (e.g., building-wide cable) or facilities (e.g., a new pool). The final category, a voluntary agreement petition, requires a landlord to get 70 percent of tenants to agree to higher-than-allowed rent increases. Once an agreement is signed, it goes to the city's rent-control administrator for final approval. According to Lydia DePillis (2012a), most agreements are approved after minor changes. After an agreement is put into force, all tenants are subject to it, even if they voted against it.

Historically, voluntary agreements were not associated with the TOPA process. A 1995 guide to rent control published by the District of Columbia Bar Association, for example, notes that landlords usually initiate voluntary agreement petitions "to avoid hardship and capital improvement petitions" (1995, 15). A perusal of the guidelines for these petitions helps explain why—both require substantial documentation. The guide also suggests landlords can use voluntary agreements "to resolve contested cases concerning building-wide issues" (15), such as when a heating or cooling system's problems stem in part from poor tenant upkeep. Although the guide has a section on condo conversions, it makes no mention of voluntary agreements in the context of TOPA.

Since the guidebook was published in 1995, however, the voluntary agreement has become a staple of the TOPA process in buildings that remain rental. Although the city does not publish rents at the building level, it is likely that all of the buildings in my sample had a substantial number of units renting at below-market rates. Before the 2000s real estate boom, for example, five of my seven sample properties (Garden Towers, Mayfair Mansions, Kennedy Street, Town Center, and Harvard/Summit) were located in areas with lower-than-average incomes and higher-than-average poverty (see Tables 2.1 and 2.2). Even in the two properties west of Rock Creek (Cathedral Court and the Squire), there were likely sizable numbers of units being rented at below-market rates. Tenant leaders at both buildings told me, for example, that they knew of several longtime tenants living in their properties at the time of conversion. While such tenants may have started out paying market rents, yearly caps meant their rents usually fell below market rates over time.

The question, of course, is why TOPA developers choose to use voluntary agreements rather than submit petitions for hardship, capital improvement, or substantial rehabilitation. When a building changes hands, even through the TOPA process, there is almost always an inspection, which details the problems with a building's structure and systems. Thus, a document trail demonstrating a need for substantial repairs has already been created. Moreover, it is historically rare for tenants to willingly agree to higher-than-normal rent increases. After years of disinvestment, few tenants are willing cut a landlord (new or old) much slack.

According to DePillis (2012a), developers working with TOPA properties at one time used document-heavy petition categories to raise rents because they figured it would be difficult to win tenants' support for voluntary increases. However, they discovered that tenants would push back anyway, filing legal challenges that cost money and time. Eventually, developers working with TOPA properties started turning to voluntary agreements to raise rents above existing caps. And they discovered that TOPA tenants would often sign them. Two reasons explain why. The first is that tenants staying put through a TOPA process negotiate to keep their rents, and future hikes, within the rent-control statute's existing limits while they live in their unit. As DePillis (2012a) explains, the tenants who will see rent increases (i.e., those who will rent bought-out units) "aren't around yet to protest." A second reason is that many developers make finalizing third-party agreements (and benefits like building repairs, buyouts, etc.) contingent on them.

In my sample, three of the buildings that remained rental agreed to voluntary agreements as part of the contracts they signed with third-party developers.[18] In the interest of space, I focus only on the process in the Squire and Harvard/Summit properties, but the process was the same at Garden Towers.

The similarities in these buildings' experiences suggest voluntary agreements have become a routine part of the TOPA process. Green from the Squire told me, for example, that a voluntary agreement was part of every proposal its tenants' association received. Moreover, as our conversation suggests, Lawrence described the agreements as nonnegotiable:

> Green: That's part of every deal.
> Gallaher: Yeah?
> Green: That's part of every deal. That's how they make their money back.
> Gallaher: So that was something that happened during the offers, like it was something—
> Green: It's always—it's part of every offer.
> Gallaher: Okay. Was there ever any talk with developers about changing that or getting rid of it? Or were they adamant about that?
> Green: Yeah, pretty much, they're adamant about it.

---

18. In the next chapter I explain why Mayfair Mansions and Kennedy Street did not negotiate voluntary agreements.

I asked Green if there was any opposition to the inclusion of the voluntary agreement among members of his tenants' association. He described a fellow board member who "didn't like what was going on, so she quit the board." "She's uncomfortable with the 70 percent voluntary agreement part," he told me. According to Green, the woman was lodging an official complaint with the city's rent administrator with the hope of having it overturned: "She's gonna contest it." He also told me that this tenant was even refusing to accept the small sum of money that the tenants' association had negotiated for tenants staying put (as this woman was) to compensate for the hassles they would face living through a building renovation. She was, however, the only tenant to protest the agreement.[19]

The Harvard/Summit property also had a voluntary agreement structured into the agreement with their third-party developer. Although my first interview with Genevieve Moreland occurred before her tenants' association had finalized its third-party agreement, she told me that their lawyer, Eric Rome, had informed her board that it would be difficult to strike a deal without one. As she put it, "We will have to do it, but we haven't done it yet." I asked her if there was any opposition among board members to having one. Her reply suggested unease rather than outright opposition: "I think as a board we are sort of—not opposed to it, but we would like to see some units maintain their lower rent value."

Moreland also told me that she and another member of the board reached out to their preferred developer to see if there was any wiggle room in the voluntary agreement. Although the developer was willing to be flexible, Moreland suggested he was amenable only to small concessions. And to Moreland, the concessions seemed more like bargaining chips than real compromise. As she explained:

> We asked UIP [the development partner Harvard/Summit eventually chose] directly, and they said that a lot of times the housing council [rent control administrator], or whatever the name is, will come back and say, "Okay, this is fine, but you need to keep this one, and this one, and this one at lower rent." So if we do that for them, it might help them with the housing council.

When I checked back with Moreland at the end of the process, she told me that her tenants' association had negotiated for below-market rents in slightly fewer than ten units. However, the negotiation was general rather than based on actual figures. Indeed, Moreland saw the buildings' new rents

---

19. Eric Rome, the Squire's attorney, told me that the tenant eventually changed her mind about going to the city's rent administrator.

only after they had formally assigned their rights to UIP. "We [the board] think they are really high," she told me, adding, "maybe over market." There was, however, little room to negotiate at that point. Moreland explained that if the board had failed to get the requisite signatures, "then they wouldn't have done any of the work they said they were going to do [in the initial third-party agreement]."

As Moreland's comments suggest, some tenant lawyers encourage their tenants to accept voluntary agreements. These lawyers also tend to bristle at the suggestion that there's anything wrong with the agreements. In a *Washington City Paper* article criticizing the growing use of voluntary agreements, for example, Eric Rome offered a pugnacious retort to those criticizing the agreements, suggesting that opponents think the city's poor should be satisfied with crumbling buildings. As he told DePillis, "People who are sitting in an ivory tower are saying that it's okay to keep these people in a permanent underclass" (2012a).

Although Rome's comments can be read as confrontational, they are not surprising given his role. His job is to get the best deal for the people he is representing—incumbent tenants. And tenants are more likely to get a better deal if they accept voluntary agreements. Although Rome tells tenants that voluntary agreements are unavoidable, he does negotiate to protect tenants' buyouts should the city's rent administrator reject the agreement. Green at the Squire told me, for example, that other TOPA buildings had contracts in which buyouts were "contingent upon the DC rent administrator approving the 70 percent voluntary agreement. So our attorney—that wasn't part of ours [agreement]. So all we had to do was execute [sign the agreement]."

While a voluntary agreement may guarantee tenants get a deal that allows them to stay in place, it does little to address TOPA's second key goal—ensuring an affordable rental housing stock. To demonstrate this, I use a three-step process to gauge the affordability of housing costs in the 443 units that were either bought out through the TOPA process or vacated presale.[20] I begin by creating an estimate of new (i.e., post-buyout) monthly housing costs. I then estimate the income thresholds necessary to afford them. Finally, I compare income threshold figures with poverty thresholds for one- and two-person households. I do this at the *building* level for three properties—Garden Towers, Cathedral Court, and Town Center.[21] I then do the same comparison at the *unit* level for the Harvard/Summit property. I

---

20. Recall that 28 percent of these units were vacated presale rather than through buyouts.
21. I do not include the Squire in this analysis because it was undergoing major renovations and was not yet renting units at the time of writing. I do not include Mayfair Mansions or Kennedy Street in this discussion because they did not offer buyouts.

TABLE 6.4   AFFORDABILITY OF POSTSALE HOUSING COSTS AT SAMPLE PROPERTIES, BUILDING LEVEL

Property	Monthly housing cost (rent or mortgage for a one-bedroom)	Annual income threshold necessary to sustainably cover housing cost	Income threshold compared to poverty threshold ($10,956) for one-person household	Income threshold compared to poverty threshold ($14,787) for two-person household
Garden Towers	$1,800.00	$72,000.00	6.5 times greater	4.9 times greater
Cathedral Court	$1,496.29 ($309,000 sales price)	$59,851.00	5.5 times greater	4.0 times greater
Town Center	$1,302.59 ($269,000 sales price)	$52,103.60	4.7 times greater	3.5 times greater

was able to do a unit analysis for Harvard/Summit because Moreland shared the new rents negotiated in her association's voluntary agreement with me. Table 6.4 displays the building-level comparison, and Table 6.5 shows the unit-level comparison.

In Table 6.4 I estimate monthly housing costs in two ways. In buildings remaining rental I use advertised rents. In cases where rents were not advertised, I called property managers. In buildings converting to condo, I determined housing costs by consulting a local real estate search engine to find one-bedroom listings.[22] In buildings where more than one one-bedroom unit was for sale, I averaged sales prices. I then put these figures into a mortgage calculator to derive an estimated monthly mortgage payment.[23] For my unit-level analysis, in Table 6.5, I used the rents listed in the voluntary agreement.

To avoid potential bias, I use conservative estimates for both tables—that is, housing costs are not likely go below my estimates and may very well go above them in some situations. I do not, for example, include the costs of utilities for rental units, even though most apartment dwellers pay at least some utilities on their own. Likewise, I assume a 20 percent down payment and no private mortgage insurance (PMI) when estimating monthly housing costs for condos, even though many first-time home buyers put less down and as a result pay PMI. The second column in Tables 6.4 and 6.5 lists these estimated monthly housing costs.

The third column in each table lists the income threshold necessary to sustainably cover monthly housing costs. I determine income thresholds

---

22. I used the Frankly Realtors site, at http://www.frankly.com.
23. To calculate annual mortgage payments, I used the online mortgage calculator at http://www.mortgagecalculator.org.

TABLE 6.5   AFFORDABILITY OF POSTSALE HOUSING COSTS AT HARVARD/SUMMIT PROPERTY, UNIT LEVEL

Unit	Monthly housing cost established by voluntary agreement ($)	Annual income threshold necessary to sustainably cover housing cost ($)	Income threshold compared to poverty threshold ($10,956) for one-person household (times greater)	Income threshold compared to poverty threshold ($14,787) for two-person household (times greater)
1	2,475	99,000	9.0	6.7
2	2,535	101,400	9.3	6.9
3	2,535	101,400	9.3	6.9
4	2,475	99,000	9.0	6.7
5	2,475	99,000	9.0	6.7
6	2,535	101,400	9.3	6.9
7	2,415	96,600	8.8	6.5
8	2,646	105,840	9.7	7.2
9	2,409	96,360	8.8	6.5
10	2,535	101,400	9.3	6.9
11	2,405	96,200	8.8	6.5
12	2,250	90,000	8.2	6.1
13	2,633	105,320	9.6	7.1
14	2,469	98,760	9.0	6.7
15	2,438	97,520	8.9	6.6
16	2,503	100,120	9.1	6.8
17	2,475	99,000	9.0	6.7
18	2,475	99,000	9.0	6.7
19	2,475	99,000	9.0	6.7
20	2,475	99,000	9.0	6.7
21	2,250	90,000	8.2	6.1
22	2,371	94,840	8.7	6.4
23	2,410	96,400	8.8	6.5
24	2,475	99,000	9.0	6.7
25	2,272	90,880	8.3	6.1
26	2,535	101,400	9.3	6.9
27	2,250	90,000	8.2	6.1
28	2,475	99,000	9.0	6.7
29	2,475	99,000	9.0	6.7
30	2,475	99,000	9.0	6.7
31	2,475	99,000	9.0	6.7
32	2,469	98,760	9.0	6.7
33	2,475	99,000	9.0	6.7
34	2,699	107,960	9.9	7.3
35	2,600	104,000	9.5	7.0
36	2,280	91,200	8.3	6.2
37	2,730	109,200	10.0	7.4
38	2,600	104,000	9.5	7.0
39	2,535	101,400	9.3	6.9
40	3,080	123,200	11.2	8.3
41	3,264	130,560	11.9	8.8
42	3,080	123,200	11.2	8.3
43	3,080	123,200	11.2	8.3

TABLE 6.5 (Continued)

Unit	Monthly housing cost established by voluntary agreement ($)	Annual income threshold necessary to sustainably cover housing cost ($)	Income threshold compared to poverty threshold ($10,956) for one-person household (times greater)	Income threshold compared to poverty threshold ($14,787) for two-person household (times greater)
44	3,080	123,200	11.2	8.3
45	3,231	129,240	11.8	8.7
46	2,535	101,400	9.3	6.9
47	2,475	99,000	9.0	6.7
48	2,503	100,120	9.1	6.8
49	2,535	101,400	9.3	6.9
50	2,535	101,400	9.3	6.9
51	2,475	99,000	9.0	6.7
52	2,600	104,000	9.5	7.0
53	2,250	90,000	8.2	6.1
54	2,490	99,600	9.1	6.7
55	2,475	99,000	9.0	6.7
56	2,475	99,000	9.0	6.7
57	2,713	108,520	9.9	7.3
58	2,270	90,800	8.3	6.1
59	2,665	106,600	9.7	7.2
60	2,413	96,520	8.8	6.5
61	2,699	107,960	9.9	7.3
62	2,467	98,680	9.0	6.7
63	2,475	99,000	9.0	6.7
64	2,475	99,000	9.0	6.7
65	2,665	106,600	9.7	7.2
66	2,405	96,200	8.8	6.5
67	2,341	93,640	8.5	6.3
68	2,514	100,560	9.2	6.8
69	2,496	99,840	9.1	6.8
70	2,600	104,000	9.5	7.0
71	2,326	93,040	8.5	6.3
72	2,535	101,400	9.3	6.9
73	2,192	87,680	8.0	5.9
74	3,041	121,640	11.1	8.2
75	2,475	99,000	9.0	6.7
76	2,250	90,000	8.2	6.1
77	2,475	99,000	9.0	6.7
78	1,870	74,800	6.8	5.1
79	1,870	74,800	6.8	5.1
80	2,167	86,680	7.9	5.9
81	1,901	76,040	6.9	5.1
82	2,250	90,000	8.2	6.1
83	2,475	99,000	9.0	6.7
84	2,558	102,320	9.3	6.9
85	1,870	74,800	6.8	5.1

by assuming that housing costs are 30 percent of gross income. Of course, many people in expensive housing markets like DC's pay far more than 30 percent of their income for housing. However, the U.S. government currently sets government-subsidized rents at 30 percent of income because anything higher is regarded as potentially destabilizing, especially for those with low and moderate incomes, who have less give in their budgets and often cut back on essentials, such as heating or cooling and food, when housing costs exceed 30 percent.

The fourth and fifth columns in Tables 6.4 and 6.5 compare income thresholds to the poverty threshold for one-person and two-person households in the district.[24] In 2010, these figures were $10,956 and $14,787, respectively. I use poverty thresholds as a basis for comparison here because I want to assess the degree to which TOPA addresses the needs of those whose only tenure option is to rent. Poverty thresholds are, of course, conservative benchmarks for capturing the incomes of those who can only rent. Many households with incomes above these thresholds would fit into this category. Unfortunately, there is no standard figure we can use to mark the cutoff between those with and without tenure options. However, readers should keep two comparisons in mind when looking at these figures. The first is the difference between the income thresholds and the city's median household income—$65,830.[25] The second is the difference between the median household income and poverty thresholds.

In my building-level analysis (Table 6.4), two patterns emerge. First, none of the market-rate units are accessible to low-income tenants. Even in the lowest-priced unit (a Town Center condo selling for $269,000), an individual resident needs to make an income nearly 5 times greater than the poverty level to afford the housing costs. And this does not account for a 20 percent down payment, which many banks currently require for affordable borrowing. On the high end, an individual would need an income 6.5 times the poverty threshold to sustainably meet housing costs. In short, while TOPA mitigates direct displacement, it also contributes to exclusionary displacement.

Second, buildings that convert to condos have lower housing costs than those remaining rental. This is surprising because most scholars assume that moving from rental to ownership is why housing costs increase and displacement ensues. A number of reasons help explain why bought-out units in conversions have lower housing costs than those in buildings remaining rental.

---

24. This figure includes households with one adult and one child.
25. The city's median household income is a five-year estimate from the American Community Survey (2008–2013) and was dynamically generated from the American FactFinder website.

After the recession in 2008, for example, the condo market softened as credit dried up and underwriting standards were strengthened. The condo market has rebounded, but converted buildings must now compete with newly built condos constructed during the boom. These buildings tend to have more and better amenities, meaning units in condo conversions typically sell at lower price points. Of course, condos in converted properties are a bargain only in a relative sense. Their costs remain out of reach for low-income tenants. And new, stricter lending standards mean that even thrifty low- and moderate-income tenants are often locked out of credit markets.

The unit-level analysis (Table 6.5) provides a similar picture of exclusionary displacement. Before I expand on the patterns that demonstrate it, however, it is worth noting that even though Table 6.5 includes a rental amount for every unit on the property, only twelve units were vacated through buyouts, so the rents listed for the units where tenants are staying put is the amount the landlord can charge once the unit is vacated.

The first notable pattern is that all of the income thresholds in Table 6.5 are larger than the city's median household income (2008–2012). The difference is also quite substantial. Indeed, the average difference is +$33,981, which is 52 percent greater than the city's median household income.

This sort of spread is also apparent when we look at the difference between preconversion rents and those allowed under the new voluntary agreement. The mean increase is 58.2 percent ($803.76), and the median is 30 percent ($600). These increases are between 6.5 and 13 times greater than the typical rent increase allowed under standard or automatic rules. Recall that recent rent increases in rent-controlled units have ranged between 4 and 5 percent (Weiner 2014). Indeed, 61 percent of units (fifty-two) are subject to hikes greater than 30 percent, 14 percent (twelve) are subject to increases exceeding 100 percent, and 3.5 percent (three) can be raised over 200 percent.

A second pattern concerns the affordability of rents listed in the voluntary agreement. None of them are affordable for working-class or low-income residents. Indeed, the cheapest rents on the list will require an income that is 6.8 times greater than the poverty threshold for a single-person household and 5.1 times the threshold for a two-person household. Not surprisingly, higher-priced units require substantially more—11.8 and 8.8 times the poverty threshold for a single- and two-person household, respectively.

Finally, these numbers suggest that UIP's promise to the Harvard/Summit tenants to keep ten units at affordable rates was an artifice. The property's lowest new rent, $1,870, requires an income threshold of $74,800—an amount that is almost $9,000 larger than the city's median household income. These are not low-income salaries.

Theoretical Implications

The empirical material presented in this chapter has important theoretical implications for our earlier discussions about the role of condos in gentrification, the capacity for local autonomy in globalized times, and questions about how to best measure displacement.

The data presented here demonstrate that condo conversion is not a singular process. In particular, my data contradict two assumptions in the literature. The first is that condo conversion always hurts in situ tenants. When conversion is placed in tenant hands, they can benefit from the process. The second is that right-to-buy schemes are a form of enclosure because they undermine renting. In my sample, the majority of tenants' associations actually used TOPA to stay rental. None of this is to suggest, of course, that these problems do not exist in other contexts. They are certainly still applicable in many cases. However, my findings do suggest that presumably neoliberal processes are often malleable and can be used to meet decidedly nonneoliberal ends.

In a similar fashion, TOPA demonstrates that market-oriented solutions can deliver tenants some control over the gentrification process. As I note in Chapter 5, there are four metrics to assess the capacity of a program like TOPA to deliver local residents autonomy over their housing. The first of these—social justice—was in evidence in all of the buildings in my sample. Though none of the tenant leaders I interviewed described his or her actions in the language of social justice, all undertook actions that were suggestive of it. All the tenant leaders in my sample acted to protect their fellow tenants, especially vulnerable ones. Most important, tenant leaders strove to ensure that any tenant who wanted to stay put could do so. Tenant leaders in Town Center, for example, made sure unit prices were affordable for their lowest-income tenants. Likewise, tenant leaders in Harvard/Summit accepted a low buyout amount so that tenants in the Harvard property would not have to leave their building to make way for a demolition. Tenant leaders in both Mayfair Mansions and Kennedy Street refused to accept buyouts because they worried it would lead to mass displacement. In short, tenants used TOPA to help each other rather than meet solely individual needs.

The way tenants used TOPA also demonstrated collective decision making. All the tenant leaders I interviewed held dozens of meetings to secure their fellow tenants' views on key decisions during the process. Tenants had a say on key decisions, such as choosing third-party developers, setting insider prices, and accepting or rejecting buyouts. In short, though a tenant board in each property ultimately made key decisions, they used a consultative and consensus-driven approach to do so.

Finally, all the tenants in my sample used the TOPA process to improve their circumstances. Every single property negotiated and secured common-element improvements in their building, such as new windows, repaired roofs, upgraded wiring, and improved safety features. Tenants were also able to negotiate for in-unit improvements. Mayfair Mansions got new sprinklers and washer/dryer units for every apartment. Tenants also sought and won improvements especially for vulnerable residents, as the Garden Towers tenants' association did when it had a wheelchair ramp installed in its back entrance.

The only area in which TOPA failed to ensure local control concerned the fate of bought-out units. Indeed, the key weakness in the TOPA stature is a trade-off that has become integral to it—voluntary agreements. When residents agree (however unhappily) to accept voluntary agreements in order to secure a third-party developer, they foster exclusionary displacement and ultimately help solidify gentrification. Voluntary agreements represent a fundamental weakness in the program because they mean that local autonomy is ultimately fleeting.

Finally, the data here demonstrate why it is so important to use multiple metrics to measure displacement. Specifically, if I had confined myself to a direct displacement measure, I would have reported that zero displacement had occurred in my sample properties. That is, because people leave by choice when staying put is a viable option, none of my sample buildings experienced direct displacement. I could even echo Hamnett and Whitelegg's view and contend that TOPA conversions occur on a "clean social slate" (2007, 106). However, the exclusionary displacement measure impelled me to make a second-round assessment by looking at whether units vacated during the process could be rented by similar residents. In this sense, all of TOPA's bought-out units were subject to exclusionary displacement. This is a troubling finding for DC at this moment. Not only is the population growing, but the new residents coming into the city are also often wealthier than those already here. Given that new developments are targeted almost exclusively toward these new residents, it is no cliché to say that every unit counts for low-income people who need to move but want to stay in the city.

7

Markets, Politics, and Other Obstacles to Low-Income Home Ownership

For low-income tenants, TOPA can be a double-edged sword. It offers an outcome it cannot guarantee. Blake Biles, one of the attorneys consulted for this project, crystallized this point for me in our first interview. When I asked him whether he thought TOPA was doing "what it is supposed to do," Biles replied yes and then offered a caveat: "But TOPA doesn't say the owner has to take what you can afford."[1]

Although all of the buildings in my sample had some low-income residents, only two were exclusively so—Mayfair Mansions and Kennedy Street. In both cases, tenants invoked their TOPA rights. And in both cases tenants experienced what I classify here as failed TOPA processes. That is, tenants were either prevented from buying their units or delayed from doing so for years. In this chapter I detail the experiences of tenants in both buildings. Before proceeding to their specific experiences, however, I start with a general overview of the types of problems all low-income tenants' associations face in navigating the TOPA process.

Problems Big and Small

As I note elsewhere in this book, once tenants invoke their right of first refusal, they have 120 days to secure financing to match the initial sale price

---

1. For a list of interviewees and dates of the interviews, see Appendix 3.

(Reed 2013a). In buildings where most residents are middle income, this process is usually done in partnership with a for-profit developer. Although the process can hit bumps in the road, they are usually not related to financing. Developers in the TOPA business typically have little trouble acquiring construction loans, and most middle-class tenants are able to qualify for mortgages. Those who cannot are accommodated with discounted insider prices (e.g., Town Center) or attractive buyouts.

For various reasons, the process plays out differently in low-income buildings. In particular, tenants in low-income buildings are more likely to work with nonprofit developers and to secure financing through city programs.[2] Several reasons explain the difference. Primary among them is the city's well-established network of organizations devoted to helping the city's low-income tenants. Nonprofits often seek out low-income tenants in buildings contracted for sale and direct them to resources the city provides for those who want to invoke their TOPA rights.

A second reason is that low-income tenants often find it difficult to find for-profit developers willing to work with them. Cultural differences probably keep some for-profit developers at bay, although few would admit as much. It is also not uncommon to find that buildings with large numbers of low-income residents have been subjected to greater disinvestment than those with middle-class tenants. Developers are often wary of the greater upfront costs these buildings require and the smaller profit margins they entail. Others stay away from low-income buildings if they are outside current gentrification hot spots, where risks are presumed to be greater.

It is also worth nothing that the for-profit developers who do work with low-income tenants sometimes leave disgruntled residents in their wake. When I interviewed George Rothman, a nonprofit developer, he described the tactics some for-profits use with low-income tenants as "unconscionable." When I asked him to explain, he mentioned a local developer that had started including "guaranteed financing" in its proposals:[3]

> I started hearing that if a tenant group went along with their proposal, they would guarantee a mortgage. Sure, they guarantee them, but they didn't guarantee them an interest rate. For them it's "So,

---

2. The city has a number of programs to help tenants purchase homes. The First Right Purchase Program can be used by low-income tenants' associations invoking their right of first refusal. Individuals (working within or outside the TOPA process) can also use the Home Purchase Assistance Program. The First Right Purchase Program is largely funded through the city's Housing Production Trust Fund (Reed 2013a), while the Home Purchase Assistance Program receives most of its funds from the U.S. Department of Housing and Urban Development (Falcon 2012).
3. At the request of Rothman I do not name the developer.

what's the big deal? People get hurt." Right? You go in and say, "Yes, you qualify for this unit," and then give them a 12 percent [interest] rate. Either they are stretched, or they leave before settlement.

Unfortunately, developers can often turn a profit using this tactic. Tenants who drop out just before settlement, for example, open up a unit that can be sold at market rates. And because such tenants planned to buy, they would have already forfeited their rights to buyouts, which are negotiated and distributed before conversion begins. News of these tactics can spread, however, and make attracting future low-income business more difficult for the developers that use them.

The great recession that began in 2008 is another reason low-income residents tend to work with nonprofits and seek city financing. The recession radically restructured the U.S. housing market. Borrowing got harder, especially for low-income applicants. To be sure, in the decade before the recession, borrowing had become too easy. As the Consumer Financial Protection Bureau (2013) observes, there was a "gradual deterioration in underwriting standards" in the years leading up to the recession. Many consumers were able to acquire loans without verifying their income (Shiller 2008). Others were given mortgages with so-called teaser interest rates, which made monthly payments affordable until higher rates kicked in a year or two into the mortgage (Gramlich 2008). Still others received interest-only loans, which lowered monthly payments but kept home owners from building equity. Banks also began relaxing down payment standards (Holt 2009), with some permitting borrowers to place zero down.[4]

Although these new loan products, often called subprime loans, were easy to obtain and thus very attractive for borrowers traditionally locked out of credit markets, they were also more costly in real and relative terms (Furman Center for Real Estate and Urban Policy 2010; Shiller 2008). Interest rates were usually higher on subprimes, and practices such as paying off interest but no principle meant borrowers were not building wealth (Shiller 2008). Moreover, because many loans were unsustainable for borrowers, the positive aspect of subprime lending—opening credit markets to historically underserved populations—was often undone by foreclosure.

The 2010 Dodd-Frank Wall Street Reform and Consumer Protection Act stopped many of the most egregious practices by banks, essentially forcing lenders to readopt more rigorous underwriting procedures. These standards were also imposed on Fannie Mae and Freddie Mac, government-sponsored

---

4. Historically, down payments functioned to give buyers "skin in the game." People with equity in their homes are less likely to walk away from them when money gets tight.

enterprises that facilitate lending by buying mortgages in the secondary mortgage market.[5] In response, banks did two things. First, they reduced the number of loans they originated. Between 2005 and 2010 mortgage originations, as measured in total dollars, were cut nearly in half (U.S. Census Bureau 2012, 743). Second, banks shifted the types of loans they originated. Most stopped originating subprime mortgages (Furman Center for Real Estate and Urban Policy 2010). In their place, banks offered conventional loans, which have more rigorous underwriting standards, or government-backed mortgages, which are sponsored by one of four agencies—the Federal Housing Administration (FHA), the Rural Housing Service (RHS), the Veterans Administration (VA), or the Farm Service Agency (FSA). In urban settings government-backed loans are usually guaranteed by FHA.

These shifts in the mortgage market have made home ownership particularly difficult for low- and moderate-income residents. Most low-income people do not qualify for conventional mortgages, which usually require at least a 10 percent down payment (some banks require as much as 20 percent). Indeed, subprime mortgages—many of which required minimal or even no down payment—were targeted to low-income people precisely because most could not meet the down payment standards of conventional loans. While government-backed loans are more accessible than conventional loans—FHA, for example, requires only a 3 percent down payment—they still require standards that would disqualify many low-income people (e.g., those with undocumented income or little savings).

New underwriting standards, which affect government-sponsored loans as well as conventional mortgages sold to Fannie Mae or Freddie Mac, also restricted lending in the condo market. After 2008, conforming loans for condos (those that conform to Fannie/Freddie/FHA standards) required the buyer and the association to win FHA approval. Condo associations eligible for FHA financing had to demonstrate that a majority of units were owner occupied and that floor space devoted to retail and other nonresidential uses did not exceed 25 percent of the total, among numerous other regulations (Harney 2012). Although FHA relaxed some standards in 2012, condo associations must still meet rigorous requirements to qualify for FHA approval (Freedman 2012). The goal behind tighter underwriting for condo associations was to reduce speculation in the condo market (Harney 2008). Condo

---

5. In June 2008 Fannie Mae and Freddie Mac were put under government conservatorship after it was discovered that many of the loans in their portfolios were "toxic" (i.e., subprime loans in or near default). After significant restructuring, both institutions continue to facilitate lending by buying loans in the secondary mortgage market, a process that gives banks more capital for further lending.

complexes with large numbers of investors had high numbers of default after the 2008 recession (Agarwal et al. 2014).[6]

In DC, these new requirements also dampened developer interest in condo conversion. I witnessed this trend firsthand when I began researching the Squire, which was contracted for sale in 2010. When the Squire's tenants' association was soliciting bids from potential development partners, it asked that solicitations include a hybrid option—a condo conversion that could accommodate a significant number of renters. According to Green, the president of the tenants' association, a hybrid option was a compromise.[7] It would provide something for people interested in buying while also accommodating those who wanted to stay but could not afford to buy. However, only one of the Squire's four offers even included a condo option. And one of the remaining three proposals offered a lengthy explanation for why the hybrid option was *not* workable. In that proposal, the developers pointed out two obstacles to condo conversion.[8] The first was tighter underwriting by Fannie Mae and Freddie Mac, which buy many of the loans originated by private banks:

> In order to qualify for what is termed a Conforming Loan, a condominium building must meet certain criteria. What that means is that, in order for a traditional lender (Bank of America, Wells Fargo, Capital One, etc.) to provide a loan, they will require that the condominium building is approved by Fannie Mae and/or Freddie Mac, meaning that it must conform to their standards. If it does not conform, then Fannie Mae and Freddie Mac will not insure the loan and these lenders will not lend against the building.

The developer then listed some of Fannie and Freddie's new standards,[9] which would make a hybrid scenario unworkable, including that "at least

---

6. During the 2008 recession subprime defaults often contributed to a downward spiral in condo associations. When owners in default stopped paying their condo fees, for example, associations had less money on hand to pay their bills. In turn, an association's poor finances kept potential buyers at bay, a situation that further hurt existing owners who needed to sell. During the recession many owners were not in a position to wait out the market because they had lost their jobs. When these owners could not find buyers, many were forced to default, further weakening their association's finances.
7. Association attorneys generally encourage developers to offer proposals that cover the range of tenant interests. Eric Rome told me he routinely does this with interested developers, even when the option is favored by only a minority of residents. More options create more leverage against potential competitors and can provide insight into a developer's interests and constraints.
8. I do not name the company that wrote this proposal at Green's request.
9. The proposal was prepared before FHA relaxed its underwriting standards for condos, so some of the conditions listed in the developer's memo no longer apply.

51–70% of units must be sold to Owner Occupants" and "at least 51% of the units must be pre-sold prior to any settlement occurring."

The developer's second argument followed from the first. Without approval from Fannie Mae or Freddie Mac, potential buyers would have to rely on portfolio lenders willing to make nonconforming loans.[10]

> A Non-Conforming Loan is viewed as a much riskier investment for a bank, and so, with their increased risk, a Portfolio Lender will require much stricter lending criteria to help keep them insulated. The most stringent requirement, and that which has the largest impact, is that they WILL require a 20% down payment, whereas a Conforming Loan can be secured for as little as 5% down (Wells Fargo currently has a 3.5% program).
>
> The critical issue with this has to do with what that does to your pool of potential purchasers. As an example, under this "Hybrid" condominium scenario, a probably first-time homebuyer looking to purchase a 1-bedroom unit for $350,000 will need to have $70,000 of cash available in order to close. The reality is that there aren't many first-time homebuyers with that amount of cash available. As a result, the potential purchaser that has toured your unit, and loves the building, won't be able to qualify, and so he/she will move on to shop elsewhere. Your pool of potential purchasers becomes drastically reduced as a result—and the value of the building suffers. Your units will remain on the market longer, and will sell for less. The building will have empty units that are having a tough time being sold. This vacancy in units will increase the risk of default on loans and offer the potential for condominium fees not being paid. Foreclosures may follow, and the Association may not be able to pay bills, make repairs, or provide general upkeep.

I also encountered postrecession developer aversion to condo conversion in 2013 at the Harvard/Summit property. There, aversion was fueled not only by tighter underwriting standards but also by excess inventory. In the run-up to the recession developers had gone on a condo building spree. When the economy faltered, developers found themselves in a bind. They could not find buyers for new units, and projects already under construction were slated to expand an already bloated inventory, further depressing prices. The backlog of condos made conversion an unattractive option for many developers. Eric Rome told me in the summer of 2013, "Everyone out there

---

10. Portfolio lenders keep the loans they originate rather than sell them on the secondary mortgage market.

now thinks the condo market is glutted, and smart investors are pursuing long-term rentals. . . . So the smart money—the smart developers are putting their money in long-term rental housing these days." At Harvard/Summit the glut in DC's condo market meant that even though its third-party developer was willing to offer a conversion option, it was not an attractive one. Genevieve Moreland at Harvard/Summit told me, for example, that the insider prices the developer offered did not appear to be discounted at all. As she explained, referencing her own unit:

> Moreland: They sent around a list of what they called insider pricing. I thought the pricing was really high. I can't remember exactly what my pricing was, but it was over $400,000 to buy the unit. . . . I would need to put down around $29,000, and then I'd be paying $1,000 more per month than I'm paying in rent. So, to me, that didn't seem like a great deal.
> Gallaher: Well, I'm surprised that $400,000 would be an insider price. I mean, how much does a one-bedroom in this neighborhood sell for?
> Moreland: I looked. It depends on how much work you are willing to do on a place, but you can find one-bedrooms for under $300,000. It might not be as big as mine, but you can definitely find something that is not $400,000.
> Gallaher: So you didn't think that was an insider price really?
> Moreland: No.[11]

The offer also proposed to convert only one building on the property, meaning that just a fraction of units would even be available for purchase. Moreover, the building proposed for conversion was attached to buildings slated to remain rental—a situation Moreland felt was less than ideal:

> To me it doesn't seem like a great idea to be buying a condo in a building that's attached to all of this rental property. You'd be sort of self-managing in terms of your own trash and water, and because they are upgrading the electric, they would switch them out to their own electric grid. All of that stuff. So you'd be in charge of all of that. But you'd still have shared expenses with the rental building, like landscaping, or what if the roof needed to be replaced? Things like that.

---

11. Eric Rome told me that he thought the prices were below market but not by much.

Finally, the proposed developer's plan put responsibility for selling market-rate units onto tenant purchasers' shoulders. As Moreland explained:

> They told us that one whole address would have to convert to condos, . . . and let's say there were nine units in the address that was going to convert, and only four people wanted to buy; then those four people would be responsible for finding buyers for the other five [units]. [The developer] wouldn't do it.

In short, the developer was unwilling to assume the normal risks associated with a conversion project but would allow tenants to shoulder them if they so chose.

Given the long-standing problems low-income people face getting credit, as well as the additional burdens caused by the recession, it is not surprising that low-income tenants in the TOPA process often choose to work with nonprofits when they seek to convert their buildings. Unfortunately, the nonprofit route offers no panacea. In particular, low-income tenants tend to face two problems. The first is mismanagement by those meant to help them. In the two properties discussed in this chapter, management breakdowns occurred in both the nonprofits brought in to assist and the city agency overseeing them.

Although the issues related to nonprofits are usually idiosyncratic, the problems with the city are long-standing. In the next chapter I trace problems in the agency responsible for managing the TOPA process until 2007— the Department of Consumer and Regulatory Affairs (DCRA). At times, these problems threatened to undermine the entire law. Unfortunately, DHCD, the agency currently in charge of TOPA, seems to suffer from some of the same management lapses.[12] In a 2012 audit on the collection of condo-conversion fees, for example, the District's Inspector General's Office found that each agency lacked "adequate management controls" to collect the fees owed it or to ensure that the TOPA process was run effectively (Willoughby 2012).[13] Specifically, the audit revealed that the city had failed to collect nearly $32 million in fees owed to it during the audit period.

Politics in the Wilson Building, where the mayor's office is located, also get in the way. The lack of professionalism in many city agencies means that city statutes are interpreted differently depending on who occupies the mayor's office. After the 2004 mayoral election, for example, the city tightened its loan criteria for low-income residents seeking loans for TOPA purchases.

---

12. Problems in DHCD's management of TOPA are especially troubling because the TOPA portfolio was expressly moved to DHCD so that it would be properly managed.
13. The audit period, 2004–2010, meant both agencies' performance was evaluated.

As a result, many low-income buildings midway through the TOPA process saw their plans upended. Some were even forced into foreclosure (DePillis 2010a).

I now turn to the problems Mayfair Mansions and Kennedy Street faced taking the nonprofit/city financing route. I begin with Mayfair Mansions, where tenants grappled with an inexperienced nonprofit developer and unpredictable funding from DHCD. I conclude with Kennedy Street, where the recession played a greater role in the building's problems converting in a timely manner.

Mayfair Mansions

Mayfair Mansions was built in the 1940s. Although the complex is not architecturally unique—seventeen garden apartment buildings with grassy common areas in between—it has an important place in the city's history. Developed by two prominent African American leaders, Mayfair was designed for the city's working- and middle-class black population, whose housing options were limited at the time (Fitzpatrick and Goodwin 2001). White landlords often refused to rent to black people, and available rentals were clustered in densely populated parts of the city. Mayfair, however, was open to black residents and located in a relatively sylvan urban setting. In an era of segregation, it provided a rare opportunity for black people to live in a pleasant, low-density residential environment inside the city.

By the time Mayfair's owner issued a TOPA notice in 2005, the complex had lost some of its luster. The civil rights movement, the 1968 Martin Luther King Jr. riots, and suburban opportunity spurred black middle-class flight from the area. During the 1970s and 1980s the complex fell into disrepair. By 1989 a DC branch of the Nation of Islam was patrolling the complex in an effort to keep drug dealers off the grounds (Page 1989).

Shortly after issuing a TOPA notice, Mayfair's owner called a meeting with tenants. It was an unusual move. Most landlords cease direct communication with tenants after issuing TOPA notices. Property managers and lawyers take over communication to protect the landlord from accusations of meddling in the TOPA process. The owner's goal for the meeting seems to have been preemption; he hoped to placate nervous tenants, thereby discouraging them from refusing the contracted sale he had negotiated. As Shirley Lawson, president of the Mayfair Mansions tenants' association, observed:

> And we go to the meeting. And we're very afraid. Because we've just gotten this certified letter saying that he's going to sell for $40 million. I couldn't even count that high. You know, I actually had to look at the zeros to make sure, you know. So, of course, you know, we're

like, "What are we going to do?" So in his best grandfatherly voice—
and you'll maybe understand somewhere down the line why I make
these inflections—he says, "Everything's going to be fine." He says—
he tells us, basically, utopia. "Oh, you're going to get a renovation;
you'll get some new paint. You're going to get some new windows.
You're going to get new appliances."

Lawson told me that many residents were suspicious. They started peppering the owner and the representative of the contracted buyer with questions:

And I can remember poor Drew [the buyer's representative]—we had him twisting in the wind. Because something strange happened at that meeting. A few of the plantation people rose up. Me. And I said, "Well, that sounds like utopia, and we know there's no such thing as utopia. Am I missing something?" And he looked at me with the grin of a shark. And he said, "No, I don't think you're missing anything."

Although the meeting was advertised for tenants, representatives from the city's nonprofit sector were also on hand. Lawson told me, for example, that she was approached during the meeting by an employee of the Marshall Heights Community Development Organization. "I don't know how she ended up at the meeting," Lawson said, but she was not surprised the woman approached her. "In the mid-eighties I had worked for Marshall Heights. I was their first community education specialist."

Marshall Heights wanted to arrange another meeting with the tenants, and Lawson agreed to help organize it. She ran into obstacles almost immediately. First, she had to find a meeting space. As Lawson explained, they could not hold a meeting on-site because "the owner was not being cooperative towards us at all." She also had trouble advertising the meeting: "We didn't have access to the [other] buildings." With Marshall Heights' help, they found a local church willing to host the meeting. And Lawson enlisted her grandsons for help with advertising:

So we had to put them [meeting announcements] on the front doors. And it was so funny when you saw the fliers. Some were, like, down there, and some were up there, and some were down there [*gesturing*]. And the people was like, "Well, what's with that?" I had to give my grandchildren a couple of dollars to put the fliers up.

In preparation for the meeting Marshall Heights also invited ULS, another nonprofit, to attend. ULS offers legal advice to low-income people unable to afford it. In the District, ULS has been active in educating tenants about their TOPA rights.

The goal of the meeting was simple—to inform tenants how the TOPA process works. Indeed, though a TOPA notice from a landlord is a vital part of the process (the right of first refusal is triggered by a TOPA notice), it does not lay out the specific steps tenants must take to buy their buildings. That is where nonprofits like Marshall Heights and ULS play an important role, especially for low-income tenants with limited resources and connections. As Lawson explained, "They passed out this beautiful, nice, informative little yellow sheet that had shown how the path to, you know, purchase—how it works."

The first step was to form a tenants' association. Although there was already one in place, Marshall Heights and ULS suggested the group form a new one and include "2005" in the name. When I asked why tenants needed a new group and a new name, Lawson explained that it was to protect them from landlord interference:

> That's how we ended up with the name Mayfair Mansions 2005 Tenant Association. And people, you know—when it got to be 2006, they were like, "Oh, no, you have the wrong name." No, that's our name. Because the management office, they were not pleased, of course, and they pitted some tenants against us. And he [a Marshall Heights employee] said to put that 2005 in there. It would protect us in case they tried to establish another tenants' association, you know, parallel to ours.

I asked Lawson how another tenants' association would affect the process, and we had the following exchange:

> Gallaher: If they tried to establish another tenant association, it would be to try to vote against you?
> Lawson: Exactly. To try to disrupt. Which, eventually, this guy—it was a guy; I won't use his name, but he told me, eventually, that he had been sent to tear up the tenant association and run me off.
> Gallaher: And this was another tenant?
> Lawson: Yes.
> Gallaher: Wow!
> Lawson: And that man—
> Gallaher: I guess he didn't know you very well, did he?
> Lawson: No, but he did get to know me. But that man had been the bane of my existence for the whole five years that I was the tenant association president.

MARKETS, POLITICS, AND OTHER OBSTACLES

Lawson and her fellow tenant board members also had trouble with their original lawyer.[14] When I asked her what the troubles were about, she replied, "This man was so unsettling to me." In fact, during our interview she twice used the phrase "snake oil salesman" to describe him. It turned out that she was suspicious of his motives:

> He got ahold of this other guy that worked for this big real estate concern. I'm sorry I can't remember these names now. But the guy— now, let me explain this right, now. The guy worked for this big real estate firm, but he was working independently and using the real estate firm's letterhead. Okay. Between him and the lawyer, I think they were going to buy this property.

Once the lawyer started showing Lawson and her fellow tenant board leaders his plans, she grew even more worried:

> So we were meeting in his office, and he had his green chalkboard, and he was showing us how they were going to, uh—his plan was to turn all these places into condominiums. And I could grasp that. But the thing that stuck out for me was that with his plan, it meant none of us were going to be able to live here. . . . He was showing us how this was going to break down and how we could pay. You know, the majority of us out here are on Section 8. You know? And we couldn't pay. And all of that said to me was, we ain't coming back [with this plan].

While the condo-conversion process tends to spur economic anxiety for most people, it also produces cultural anxiety in the city's low-income black neighborhoods. As I explain in Chapter 3, some African Americans in DC view gentrification as part of a sinister plan on the part of white people to move them out of the city.

After the meeting with their lawyer, Lawson and a fellow board member consulted contacts at ULS and Marshall Heights. ULS suggested that they find another lawyer, and Marshall Heights helped the association write a letter of termination for the current one. Mayfair Mansions' tenants' association then started shopping for legal representation. ULS recommended Rick Eisen (whom I also interviewed for this book).

> Lawson: Well, we got to Rick, and Rick says, "I don't want to do it."
> Gallaher: Really?

---

14. At Lawson's request, I do not use the lawyer's name here.

Lawson: Yes. He says, "I don't want to do it." And we just begged. "Come on, Rick, please. Mr. Eisen, please, we need a lawyer."

Gallaher: Did he say why he didn't want to do it?

Lawson: He said because he didn't want to infringe on what his colleague had started. You know, in the community—the lawyer community or whatever, you know. And we begged—I begged—and you know, then he gave us some strict rules. He said, "Now, you have to try to work it out with your lawyer. Do this and do that, and if you don't [work it out], then I'll, you know, try to do it."

Lawson and her fellow board members followed Eisen's advice and tried to work things out with their initial lawyer. After those attempts failed, Eisen signed on as the association's attorney. His first move was to start a search for a loan to cover the association's earnest money deposit, which would secure the tenants' bid on the property. Usually, tenants' associations will take out short-term loans while finalizing the search for a developer. The loan is then paid back by the developer.

Once a short-term loan was secured, Mayfair's tenants had to decide which path they wanted to take (remain rental or convert) and which developer would be their partner. Lawson told me that most people wanted to stay rental, but a sizable minority were interested in converting to condominium. As a result, the association decided to set aside five of the complex's seventeen buildings for a condo-conversion project and retain the remaining twelve as rentals. After consulting with multiple developers, including the company that contracted the original sale with the complex's landlord, Mayfair's tenants chose to partner with two nonprofits—Marshall Heights, with which it had existing connections, and Community Preservation and Development Corporation (CPDC). The plan called for Marshall to manage the condominium conversion and CPDC to renovate the rentals. The city sealed the deal by offering the two companies a $24.1 million construction loan (Shaun 2010; DePillis 2010b).[15]

In Chapter 6 I describe Lawson and her fellow board members' successes at negotiating improvements to their buildings during the process of selecting a third-party developer. They were able to bargain for several improvements to the buildings, including fresh paint, new windows, in-unit washer/dryers, sprinkler systems, and other structural and systemwide repair work. None of this is to say, of course, that the renovations were easy to live through. Because Lawson and her peers on the board were adamant

---

15. Shaun (2010) reports the construction loan was for $24.2 million. DePillis (2010b) lists the loan amount at $24.1 million.

about avoiding buyouts, most people had to live through at least a portion of the renovations in their own units. Lawson recounted one Thanksgiving dinner as particularly stressful:

> I almost had a nervous breakdown. I mean, for Thanksgiving I went and bought a frying pan. I cooked my whole Thanksgiving dinner out of a pot and a pan. I mean, because everything was packed up. Oh, my God, they took so long, I mean, to renovate.

When repair work was more substantial, tenants were briefly moved to empty apartments in the complex.[16] Lawson explained:

> They moved us [residents in her building] to the last apartments that were to be renovated, which was right across the court, right in front of us here. And they kept rotating us like that, right. Because we weren't going; we weren't leaving our property.

The difficulties aside, Lawson thinks the pain of the renovations was worth it. In particular, she was proud of her success getting washer/dryer units for each apartment. For her, the fight was as much about dignity as it was about being able to do laundry safely. She recounted the patronizing response she first received when she mentioned washers and dryers to CPDC representatives: "They patted me on my head [and said], 'Do you know how much something like that would cost, Ms. Lawson? Do you know how much?'" In response, Lawson gathered her fellow board members and set up a meeting at DHCD to argue their case to CPDC's lender:

> Lawson: Well, we said, we want to meet with DHCD. So all of us put on our little church hats—not really, but we had our church-hat attitudes—and we went to meet with DHCD. And there, I put down my first impassioned plea to them. . . . And I just asked them, you know, because the under-feeling in the room was that—and nobody ever said it—"how dare these poor people ask for washers and dryers?"
> Gallaher: Like you-were-getting-above-your-station kind of attitude?
> Lawson: Exactly, exactly. And I think that made me even angrier. And I asked each one of them, "Do you have a washer and dryer?" And, of course, they did. And I said, "Are you telling me

---

16. Although Mayfair's original owner had not stopped renting apartments in advance of his sale (as other owners in my sample had done), normal attrition meant there were still some empty units available for temporary reshuffling.

our children deserve to be dirty because we are poor?" And, you know, it went in that genre. And at the end we got the washers and dryers. We have washers and dryers in every unit.

Unfortunately, Mayfair's condo conversion was not successfully executed. In June 2010, the five buildings slated for condo conversion went into foreclosure proceedings. The city initiated the process to secure the $7 million still outstanding from its initial short-term loan (DePillis 2010b). Why the conversion failed is subject to debate. In a *Washington City Paper* article about the unsuccessful conversion Marshall Heights's interim CEO is quoted as blaming the market: "By the time we reached early 2008, the market just fell out of the bottom, and so many people who at one time had qualified for a mortgage, those people were no longer qualified to purchase" (DePillis 2010b).

Lawson thinks the market had little to do with the conversion's failure. Instead, she blames Marshall Heights and DHCD. Although she did not want to buy a condo herself, her role as Mayfair's tenants' association president meant she kept up with the conversion process. To her, management of the project seemed off from the beginning. She recalls, for example, that Eisen had expressed skepticism about Marshall Heights: "Because Rick was saying, 'Oh, no, Marshall Heights don't have that kind of money, Shirley.' But they swore that they could do the condos, which were five buildings." She also observed that Marshall Heights had a lot of "management turnover" during the process. As a result, it never seemed to her that the organization had a clear plan for bringing the condo conversion to fruition. As she explained, "They paid people to do telephone surveys. They ran us crazy and worried us to death. And the whole process was so convoluted. People didn't understand it, and people wanted no part of it." At times, Marshall Heights even seemed incompetent. Lawson recounted, "They never actually knew—and you're the first person I'm making a public statement to about this—they never actually knew what they were doing."

In her *Washington City Paper* article on the failed conversion, Lydia DePillis (2010b) also suggests Marshall's disorganization stemmed from inexperience. Marshall had never done a big condo conversion before it took on Mayfair Mansions. And for a company with little conversion experience, the development was fairly large—five buildings. In particular, the organization's inexperience likely contributed to its inability to secure a secondary construction loan to get the project off the ground.

Marshall Heights also had difficulty getting tenants through the homebuyer process. Here, however, the preponderance of the blame rests with DHCD. Like other nonprofits, Marshall required people interested in buying their apartments to take a home-buyer education course. However, the low-income nature of the building meant most residents could buy only with a significant subsidy. Initially, DHCD offered to help Mayfair's tenants through its Home Purchase Assistance Program, which "provides interest-free loans and closing cost assistance to qualified applicants" (Department of Housing and Community Development 2014). Midway through the process, however, DHCD scaled back on the amount of money individual tenants could borrow. In my interview with Lawson, she could not remember how much promised loan amounts were cut but told me the amount was significant. DePillis (2010b) reports that the reduction was over 40 percent—from $70,000 to $40,000 per home buyer. It was enough to put ownership out of reach for many tenants hoping to buy.

The issue of timing is also important and demonstrates the difficulty in apportioning blame between Marshall Heights and the city. In many ways a deal like this requires synergy to succeed. All parties have to be working smoothly and in concert with one another to reach a common goal. It may well be the case, for example, that Marshall Heights's inability to get a loan was primarily a result of the recession. However, if the city had not reduced its financial assistance to Mayfair's tenants, the company may well have had an easier time getting a construction loan before the recession. Likewise, if Marshall had developed a better plan and been more organized, the city may have been less inclined to scale back the amount of money it was willing to lend tenants working through the TOPA process. In short, if the process had been better coordinated, the conversion could have gone through before the recession hit. Indeed, Mayfair's initial sale occurred in 2005, well before the recession began and during the height of the city's real estate boom, when financing was relatively easy to secure.

Although Rick Eisen put more of the blame on DHCD than on Marshall Heights, he told the *Washington City Paper* that the recession was *not* to blame:

> Nothing ever made any sense. They never ended up getting enough qualified buyers because the program was so complicated and confusing that of the people who were interested and qualified, nothing was happening, so they gave up. The bad economy, frankly, was an excuse. (DePillis 2010b)

In my interview with Lawson, she told me that Eisen's comments made her happy:

> The lie that they like to tell people is "Well, you know, the housing bubble burst." No, it did not. And that quote that Rick put in that article—that was my truth, and I had to drop him a line and tell him

thank you for getting my truth out there because that's—no, no! We were running ahead of the curve.

Eisen also called into question the city's decision to foreclose. In her *Washington City Paper* article about the foreclosure, DePillis (2010b) reports that CPDC approached the city after Marshall Heights indicated it was going to default and offered to renovate the five buildings slated for conversion and run them as rentals. Its plan would have averted foreclosure. However, CPDC told DePillis that the city seemed focused on getting another local developer, Forrester Construction, to complete the project, even though CPDC had completed its work at the property on time and within budget. When the city failed to strike a deal with Forrester, it sold the property at a foreclosure auction. There it was purchased by a company co-owned by Forrester and another local developer with city contracts. Eisen told the *Washington City Paper*, "Why it was necessary to bring in a whole new cast of characters to reinvent the wheel, I don't understand. It doesn't make sense to me" (DePillis 2010b).

There was one bright spot in the conversion imbroglio's finale. Mayfair's new owners agreed to renovate the five buildings slated for conversion and keep them as rentals. And because Lawson and her fellow board members had refused buyouts, most of the original residents who had wanted to buy were still living on-site in the units they had planned to buy. Though some people left, they did so of their own accord. In short, home ownership may not have panned out, but no one was displaced.

Kennedy Street

Kennedy Street is a small, two-building complex. At the time the property was sold in 2005, each building contained twenty-seven units, primarily one-bedrooms and efficiencies. The complex lies about a mile from the Maryland border in a quiet residential neighborhood. Until recently, the majority of the housing stock comprised stand-alone houses, with an occasional low-rise apartment building tucked between them or situated on the area's main thoroughfares, North Capital Street and New Hampshire Avenue.

Like Mayfair Mansions, Kennedy Street was almost entirely low income. David Laichena, president of the tenants' association, estimated in our interview that at least ten of the incumbent residents at the time of the sale were elderly people on fixed incomes. There were also approximately eight immigrant families in the building, including Laichena.

The building's makeup influenced how the tenants' association decided to approach the TOPA process. Laichena told me he sat down with tenants in his building and discovered that a full condo conversion would be difficult.

MARKETS, POLITICS, AND OTHER OBSTACLES

He told me, "You have to have a human face. And then, to me, as the president of the board, I sat with them, and I questioned their income statements and sat down, and the majority of them could not qualify for nothing." Kennedy Street did, however, receive several offers from potential development partners. One, based in Philadelphia, offered a condo-conversion scenario. As Laichena explained:

> He was a developer from Philadelphia. . . . He wanted to buy the buildings and then wanted to buy us out. We could not continue as tenants, or if you want to buy your unit, then he was telling you to buy as is. You know, get someone to appraise, and then whatever the bank approves for you, you buy.

Laichena and his fellow board members declined to take the offer. Like Lawson at Mayfair Mansions, Laichena was sensitive to the issue of displacement. As he told me, if the association went condo, "most of the tenants would have been displaced."

There were, however, some people in the complex, including Laichena, who were interested in buying their units. Laichena told me that the neighborhood was changing for the better. The first draw, he noted, was proximity to the Metro: "You can walk to Fort Totten Metro station—a ten- or fifteen-minute walk." He also noted other improvements:

> There are a lot of activities which are not decent activities around the neighborhood, although it has improved a lot. I've been there for the last, I think, eleven years, and since I came there, it has developed a lot because they have built a school, a charter school, just next to [local business]. There is a gas station that just came. And then there is another building across from [local business] that, you know, turned, and now they have a brand-new condo. It was empty, with squatters.

To accommodate those interested in buying condos, Kennedy Street's tenants' association decided on a dual-form model. They would turn one of the buildings into an LEC and the other into a condo.[17] The co-op, which the tenants named Unity Co-op, would own both buildings. As Laichena put it, "The co-op side was selling the condo side." The idea would also help low-income tenants stay in place and improve their apartments. Indeed, the

---

17. Recall that LECs restrict the profit a purchaser can make when reselling a unit. The goal is to provide housing opportunities for low-income residents while preserving affordability for the next owner (Huron 2012).

proceeds from the condo sales were supposed to finance the co-op renovation, permit insider prices, and pay down a significant portion of the original loan.

It is also worth noting that neither building was fully rented, so no one would be displaced by converting one of the buildings to condo. As occurred in many buildings, Kennedy Street's owner had stopped re-renting units in advance of the initial contracted sale. And a few in situ residents were interested in buying condos, which relieved pressure to make sure all those interested in staying put could take a unit on the co-op side.

To finance the deal, Kennedy Street's tenants' association also did something no other association in my sample did—they did not work with a third-party developer. Instead, they purchased the buildings on their own, through loans. At the time, the idea was plausible. That is, the building's low-income tenants could meet their loan obligations, despite their limited means, because they had an asset to sell.

To realize their plan, Kennedy Street's residents worked with Mi Casa, a nonprofit organization that helps tenants navigate the TOPA process. Laichena explained that Mi Casa played a role similar to that of a third-party developer: "They are the ones that ran the day-to-day operations [for us]." With Mi Casa's help, Unity Co-op was able to apply for and receive a short-term loan (two years) from a local lender, Adams Bank. This allowed the residents to refuse the contracted sale and buy the buildings.

Mi Casa also helped Unity find long-term financing. In August 2008, Unity received a long-term loan from Mercy Loan Fund, a subsidiary of Mercy Housing, a national nonprofit that advocates for affordable housing in communities across the country.[18] The loan provided money for acquisition (Unity Co-op was able to pay off its original loan with Adams Bank) and construction (most notably to renovate the condo side of the property and ready its units for sale).

Unfortunately, the conversion project got off the ground just as the recession was beginning. Unity received its loan in August 2008. Only four months earlier the investment firm Bear Stearns collapsed, sending Wall Street into a downward spiral. Despite the grim financial picture, Unity continued apace with its plans, using the loan to renovate the building slated for condo conversion and prepare it for sale. Sixteen months later, renovations, which included upgrades to the building's electric, plumbing, and mechanical systems as well as fresh paint and new appliances in individual units, were completed.

When I first interviewed David Laichena in late September 2010, however, none of the units had been sold. When I asked why, he pointed to the

---

18. For more information on Mercy, see its website at https://www.mercyhousing.org/about.

recession: "The market crashed, and then we were underwater like anybody else." Unity was having trouble finding buyers for its condos and as a response was forced to lower its prices. Laichena explained, "It *was* $190,000 for a one-bedroom; it is almost $170,000 now, because we went down again." Not surprisingly, the association's dire finances drew the attention of its lender. Worried about the association's ability to meet its obligations, Mercy placed new restrictions on Unity. Specifically, Laichena told me that Mercy would not permit interested buyers to go to settlement until Unity had twelve buyers under presettlement contract:

> We haven't sold [any units] because the condition of the people who loan us money to buy, the mortgage owners. They are giving us a condition that we have to be able to sell twelve to close the first deal. . . . We kind of got that target. We are missing maybe one. But we have to have twelve to close. Twelve contracts approved with underlying letters and everything from the bank.

It seemed an onerous requirement, so I asked Laichena what Mercy's reasoning was.

> Laichena: It's this lady. She's a little bit tough. Her name is Jennifer. I don't know why. The way she writes stuff. And, of course, we cannot push on her because she is—she is a senior loan officer that makes these decisions. And I think, one, they don't want to lose money. And they don't want this building sitting there for long. So she thinks, I think, that that's the best way to expedite it. You know, especially [to get] insiders to buy.
> Gallaher: Oh, so she's encouraging—she basically wants you guys [tenants] to buy condos [instead of co-ops]?
> Laichena: She's pushing. Yes.

Given the low-income nature of the building's tenants and the high rate of attrition during the process, it seemed a counterproductive move on Mercy's part. I queried Rick Eisen, Unity's attorney, to see if he had any more insight into Mercy's motives. He explained:

> Mercy's reasoning in requiring a minimum of twelve settlements before allowing the first one was that it wanted to keep open the possibility that it could sell the entire building to one investor or investor group who might want to operate it as rental, and that would be much more difficult if a few of the units were owned by owner-occupants and Mercy could only sell, say, seventeen or eighteen units

to an investor. Once the settlements met a minimum threshold—twelve in this case— then Mercy was willing to give up the idea of selling all twenty-two units in bulk to one investor.[19]

It was not, Eisen explained to me, a "realistic" requirement. And it left Unity and Mercy in a standoff of sorts. Laichena told me, for example, that Mercy was threatening to foreclose on the building. After four years, and little to show for it, Laichena was fed up: "I told Eisen to tell them, 'Go ahead.'" Laichena's exasperation was fed by a sense that foreclosure would be just as bad for Mercy as it would be Unity's tenant purchasers. He noted, for example, that foreclosing on the building would not help Mercy recover its money because the building's value had decreased substantially since the recession. He also noted that foreclosure would hurt other nonprofits who had loaned Unity smaller amounts of money and could pursue Mercy for repayment in court:

> If they were smart, they would not have done that because it could be a disaster for everybody. We would be affected; even people around us—Mi Casa, Weber [smaller creditors on the project]—they would also lose their payments. You know, the ones that accrued or [were] not paid yet. Everybody would be affected, but they [Mercy] would lose most. This is a nonprofit organization. This is a group of nuns, and they don't want their name out there being sued or whatever.

After I spoke with Laichena in the fall of 2010, Unity's consultant, Mi Casa, stepped in to help Unity avoid foreclosure. Specifically, Mi Casa helped broker a forbearance agreement with Mercy lending. Under the terms of the agreement, Mi Casa was able to separate the loan into two separate loans, one for the co-op and one for the condo. The goal was, as Mi Casa explains in a project narrative for the local Advisory Neighborhood Commission, "minimizing the risk to the Co-op and allowing them to renovate their building as originally planned" (Advisory Neighborhood Commission 4B 2011). And to facilitate the co-op's progress, Mi Casa applied for and won several grants to help Unity pay down a portion of its co-op loan and begin renovations on that side of the property. Mi Casa also stabilized the condo side of the project. At the time, the building was fully renovated but empty. Given the weak condo market, however, Mi Casa decided to rent the units rather than sell

---

19. During the renovation several efficiency apartments were combined with one-bedroom units to create two-bedroom apartments, reducing the total number of units from twenty-seven to twenty-two.

them to low-income families. Juan Pablo Vacatello, who manages the building for Mi Casa, explained in our interview, "We run it as a rental building, and fourteen [units] are being leased as a master lease to Latin American Youth Center for three different programs. Six units are being rented."

The rents are also affordable. Vacatello told me, for example, that a one-bedroom rents for $847 and a two-bedroom for $1,200. These prices were nearly 25 percent below the average DC rents for one- and two-bedroom apartments at the time. In 2010, for example, the median rent for a one-bedroom apartment was $1,100 (Reed 2012).

While Unity Co-op avoided the worst-case scenario—foreclosure—its experience is less a cause for celebration than a sigh of relief. Although no one was displaced from the building (through direct or exclusionary means), many of the people who could have benefited from the process left the building rather than deal with the uncertainty brought on by the recession and the threat of foreclosure. Laichena told me, "We lost almost a quarter of us, because right now we are around twenty-five." Academics do not have a category for such people caught up in inefficient programs meant to protect them from gentrification, but one is surely needed since many in situ residents end up leaving when they would prefer to stay.

What Sort of Vehicle Is TOPA for Low-Income Tenant Empowerment?

What do the experiences with Mayfair and Kennedy Street tell us about TOPA as a vehicle for low-income tenants to gain some control over processes of gentrification? The evidence is mixed. On a positive note, both tenants' associations were able to avoid contributing to exclusionary displacement by refusing to use buyouts. This is no small feat in a context where buyouts are a common part of the TOPA process.

However, the effort for low-income tenants to become home owners was fraught with far more difficulty than it had to be. Unity Co-op was able to stave off foreclosure and continue as an LEC, but it will have a rough road ahead of it. The current owners are low income and pay mortgage amounts that are well below market value. Vacatello told me that the insider pricing at Unity amounts to monthly payments of between $500 and $1,000. Whether these payments will suffice to continue paying down the loan and maintaining the building is an open question.

Moreover, the unpredictability in the process begs the question, Can TOPA work for most low-income tenants? The process depends not only on decent market conditions but also on efficient behavior from entities presumably committed to helping low-income tenants use the TOPA process.

As DePillis observes about Mayfair's experience, "Affordable development deals don't happen at bureaucratic speed, and there's little room for that kind of error" (2010b).

Finally, if TOPA is to serve as a vehicle for local autonomy, it must work for people of all income levels. Indeed, if TOPA becomes the sole province of middle-income and even wealthy tenants, it will lack the vital element of social justice that allows us to distinguish between exclusive forms of local autonomy (e.g., a gated community) and ones aimed at leveling gentrification's playing field. To be fair, the DC Fiscal Policy Institute found mostly positive results in its study of DC programs designed to help tenants invoke their TOPA rights (Reed 2013a). However, the experiences of tenants at both Mayfair Mansions and Kennedy Street suggest there is still room for improvement.

8

"95/5"

The TOPA Sidestep

Although tenants often fail to invoke their TOPA rights, landlords view the statute as a major hindrance to their business. As I note in Chapter 4, a local real estate columnist for the *Washington Post* once observed that most landlords think TOPA is "nothing more than 'tenant blackmail'" (Kass 2004). More recently, local real estate attorney Mark Griffin argued that the city's tenant-friendly posture "discourage[s] good landlords from operating in DC" (quoted in Baschuk 2010). In the legal case I detail in this chapter, attorney Richard Luchs even argued that TOPA was unconstitutional.

Given these views, it is not surprising that landlords and the developers who want to buy their properties have sought to sidestep the TOPA process with the help of experienced real estate attorneys. In this chapter I look at one mechanism by which landlords and developers have done so—the 95/5 transfer. In a 95/5 transfer, a landlord transfers 95 percent of his or her property to a buyer and retains a 5 percent share. Until late 2005 the TOPA statute defined a sale as a 100 percent transfer of property, so a landlord could sidestep the TOPA requirement that tenants be given a TOPA notice by using a 95/5 transfer. In particular, I trace one local landlord's 2004 sale of eleven buildings through a 95/5 transfer and the legal fallout that ensued. I begin, however, by contextualizing landlord efforts to circumvent TOPA, defining 95/5 transfers, and discussing their use in the early 2000s.

Context

Although landlords and their lawyers frequently argue against TOPA on philosophical grounds, they also have financial reasons for wanting to sidestep TOPA. Many landlords, for example, fear that the time granted for tenants to claim their TOPA rights and find a development partner can upend an otherwise guaranteed sale. As *Washington City Paper* journalist Ryan Grim explains:

> While it may seem that building owners wouldn't care whether their money came from PN Hoffman [a local developer] or from a group of tenants, the reality is quite different. The law grants tenants time to form an association, vote on proposals, and seek financing—a process that can take up to 660 days, according to Raenelle Zapata, a former rent administrator at the DCRA. As tenants go about weighing their options, various calamities can ruin the building's marketability, including a simple cooling of the real-estate market. (2006b)

The primary way landlords try to sidestep TOPA is by emptying their buildings before making a sale. As I note in Chapter 6, landlords selling empty buildings are exempt from issuing TOPA notices or paying the city's condo-conversion fee, which can be quite hefty.[1] Although landlords sometimes resort to illegal means to empty a building (e.g., by harassing their tenants or shutting off key services), there are plenty of legal ways to clear a building. A landlord can, for example, decline to re-rent units vacated by normal attrition or offer tenants cash to leave. As Blake Biles, the lead attorney on the legal case covered here, noted in our first interview:

> Tenants have the right to organize and do what they want to do, and owners do as well. And I represent tenants, and I'm a zealous advocate for them, but if you want to avoid giving TOPA notices, one way to do it is to have an empty building. Okay? There's nobody living there, so you don't have to give notice to anybody. It is totally legal for you to buy people out who're living there and try to get everybody to leave. That's legal. This is America.[2]

Emptying a building can be challenging, however. Tenants often refuse to leave. In a gentrifying city, leaving an apartment in a downtown neighborhood can be financially unwise, especially for low-income tenants. As

---

1. Debbie Cenziper and Sarah Cohen (2008) estimate that the average fee is $180,000.
2. For a list of interviewees and interview dates, see Appendix 3.

Biles observed, cash offers from landlords are not always sufficient enticement. Using a hypothetical example of a $10,000 cash payment to leave, he explained why most tenants will choose to stay:

> Now, there's this view, if you don't work with lower-income people, that that's a lot of money for those people, you know? But the fact is, it's taxable. Usually, they're living in rent-controlled property. When you look where they're living, they're usually living there for a reason. It's cheap. And with cheap comes—their experience has been crappy, but it's cheap. It's near local transportation, it's in the city, they can get their kids into schools, and so for all those reasons, they're livable.

Even in cases where landlords cross the line and start shutting off services, many residents will continue to stay put. The *Washington Post* exposé discussed in Chapter 6, for example, describes a family willing to hang on despite dangerous living conditions:

> At 7436 Georgia Ave. NW., LaTreaviette Prailow and her husband lived for months without heat, huddling under blankets to stay warm. The heating unit caught fire in December 2006. It wasn't fixed until more than nine months later. Still, Prailow wants to stay because she fears that she won't find another affordable apartment close to public transportation, which her husband uses to get to his housekeeping job at George Washington University. (Cenziper and Cohen 2008, A1)

Given the constraints that accompany the emptying strategy, it is perhaps not surprising that landlords also seek other ways to avoid having to deal with TOPA's provisions. During the recent real estate boom, one such mechanism was the 95/5 transfer.

Sale or Scam? 95/5 Transfers

In the context of TOPA, the sale of a residential property is a trigger event. When a building is contracted for sale, the landlord is required to issue a TOPA notice, which informs tenants of the contract and their right to refuse the sale and make the purchase instead. This event sets in motion a series of actions tenants must take to buy their buildings, as well as numerous deadlines.[3]

---

3. For the steps tenants must take to assert TOPA rights, see the flowchart provided by the Office of the Tenant Advocate at http://ota.dc.gov/sites/default/files/dc/sites/ota/publication/attachments/TOPA2_-_5_or_More_Units.pdf.

A 95/5 transfer is designed to get around the provision in RHCSA that requires landlords to alert tenants that a building has been contracted for sale. Usually, in a 95/5 transfer a landlord agrees to sell 95 percent of a property to a given buyer. The remaining 5 percent is retained by the landlord or sold to a holding company controlled by the landlord or an associate. After a relatively short period of time, a year or two, the remaining 5 percent is sold to the initial buyer. During the height of the early 2000s real estate boom, many real estate attorneys in the city argued that 95/5 transfers were not subject to TOPA requirements because the statute specified a sale as a 100 percent transfer.

Although 95/5 transfers would be classified as sale by any standard meaning of the word, the statute's definition of a sale has been subject to political wrangling almost since its inception. In 1983, when TOPA was first reauthorized, for example, a proposed amendment was introduced to eliminate a potential ambiguity in the legislation about *what* constituted a property sale. In particular, the amendment's authors were worried that companies set up to hold property could be sold, in whole or part, without triggering TOPA rights, since it was the company rather than a given property that was being sold (Proscio 2012; Grim 2006a). The amendment proposed to close that loophole by replacing the term "sale" with the phrase "majority transfer" to ensure such transactions were included in the definition. As Ryan Grim explains, "Without the change, an owner could sell a company that owned a property and claim he hadn't actually sold the property" (2006a). The amendment failed in part because Mayor Marion Barry opposed it. According to Grim (2006a), Barry argued that the amendment was unnecessary since few properties were sold this way, and it would in any case be difficult to enforce. The real estate market for multifamily buildings in DC was fairly stagnant in the late 1980s and early 1990s, but Grim suggests that even then, "properties began to trickle through the loophole" (2006a).

In 1994, the amendment was again brought before the council. This time it passed, but not before it was altered in an important way. Specifically, while the language including the sale of holding companies in the definition was retained in the newer version of the amendment, the term "majority transfer" was deleted and the phrase "100 percent transfer" inserted in its place (Grim 2006a). In essence, the language specifying that the sale of a holding company constituted a sale for TOPA purposes no longer mattered because a landlord could simply get around the requirement to alert tenants by selling just shy of 100 percent of his property.

With any legislation, of course, there is room for interpretation. The bureaucracy in charge of regulating a given law often has a good bit of leeway in how it carries out the task. In the case of TOPA, regulators could have viewed the 1994 amendment as contradicting the purpose of TOPA and thus granted exceptions only for properties for which there was evidence a landlord was truly maintaining some control over a share of the property (e.g., with the creation of a joint board of directors). Or regulators could have accepted the amendment's seeming numerical specificity and enforced it literally.

For the early part of my study period, TOPA was under the regulatory aegis of DCRA, and during this time it chose to regulate the statute literally. It did so primarily through an unofficial practice that evolved into a routine part of the sales process by the early 2000s, when the real estate boom began. At some point in the late 1980s or early 1990s—no one seems to agree on exactly when—DCRA officials started offering landlords draft opinions on whether a scheduled residential real estate transaction constituted a sale (Grim 2006a, 2006b; Weiss 2005a, 2005b).

During the real estate boom in the early 2000s, DCRA routinely interpreted planned 95/5 transfers as *not* constituting sales. Landlords receiving these letters would then feel free to contract a sale without alerting tenants. Without TOPA notices, most tenants discovered their buildings had been sold only after the actual sale had gone through and well after they could invoke their right of first refusal. It is estimated that DCRA signed at least 105 such letters between 1999 and 2005 (Grim 2006a).

Given that DCRA's practice of issuing opinion letters was informal and at odds with the statute's ethos, it is worth asking who was responsible for implementing the practice. Indeed, there is nothing in the original legislation or implementation documents that describes, let alone requires, such letters. Rather, they appear to have emerged over time and taken on formal weight as a result of their government imprimatur.

In January 2005 Jim Graham, a city councilmember representing Ward 1, took a stab at answering this question when he took over the committee in charge of DCRA oversight. Graham was far different from Sharon Ambrose, his predecessor in the chair's seat. While Ambrose was regarded as a landlord- and developer-friendly politician, Graham was viewed as an "old school liberal" more friendly to tenants (Grim 2006a, 2006b).

Graham found an agency at odds with its principal task (Sinzinger 2005). The deviation was particularly noticeable in the agency's offices devoted to housing issues, including rent control, inspections, and the TOPA process. Two months into his tenure, Graham scheduled a hearing on DCRA's housing portfolio and called as witnesses the agency's acting head and a number of high-level employees. A portion of the hearing was devoted to the proliferation of 95/5 transfers and the draft opinion letters making them possible. When queried about the opinion letters, however, DCRA's leaders testified they had never seen any of the letters in question.

In response, Graham reconvened the hearing a few weeks later and called as witnesses employees responsible for the day-to-day management of TOPA—two supervisors (James Aldridge and Raenelle Zapata), one frontline employee (Linda Harried), and a clerical assistant (Darney Dorsey).[4]

Once the panel of witnesses was seated, Graham directed all of his questions to Linda Harried. Although Harried was not a supervisor—her job title was housing regulation officer—her signature appeared on almost all of the opinion letters DCRA had issued to landlords. Graham began by noting that one local attorney seemed to have requested the majority of recent opinion letters. Pointing to a copy of a request sent to Harried's office, Graham observed:

> Richard W. Luchs, esquire. Isn't that interesting? His name keeps appearing over and over and over again. Richard W. Luchs, esquire, Greenstein, DeLorme, and Luchs, P.C., Suite 900, 1620 L Street NW, Washington, DC 20036. Again, nearly 50 percent of the letters that we know of—and again, many of them have been purged—are presented by this law firm, by Richard Luchs.

Graham asked Harried if she had a process in place for assessing the requests by attorneys such as Luchs.

> Graham: In sixty some letters you have changed not a word. I mean, is this a real process?
> Harried: Absolutely a real process.
> Graham: Did it ever—as you were signing, signing, signing, signing, did you ever think there are tenants that are losing their valuable rights and that they're not being notified of this? Did you ever suggest, well, maybe we ought to let the tenants know that I'm about to approve a letter which has as its practical and definite impact that their right—their opportunity—to purchase is extinguished? Did it ever enter your mind to say to Mr. Aldridge, or to the general council of DCRA, or to Ms. Zapata that, you know, maybe we ought to let the tenants know about this?
> Harried: It absolutely did not, and it did not because—
> Graham: It absolutely did not?
> Harried: Did not. Because I did not feel I was taking their right from them. In accordance with the law, 100 percent of the property must be sold to one entity, or there is no offer of sale. And quite frankly, this issue has come up before. Legislation has been pro-

---

4. A video recording of the March 4, 2005, hearing is available from DC's Office of Cable Television at http://dccarchive.oct.dc.gov/services/on_demand_video/on_demand_march_2005_week_1.shtm.

posed before to eliminate it or to alter it. Legislation has never passed....

Graham: But—but you've testified that you made only minor changes [to the letters]. We've indicated to you that we can't find any changes at all. That you have signed letter after letter without independent investigation, without checking with lawyers who knew the field. Uh, this seems like a routine approval.

Harried responded forcefully in the negative—"not at all, not at all"—but her subsequent explanation suggested otherwise.

Graham: It doesn't seem like a routine approval to you?
Harried: Not at all. And let me reiterate what I said a minute ago, that some of those letters that came from whatever law firm was submitting were taken from what I had previously written. They wrote back to me a suggested response that I had given them previously.
Graham: Did you ever draft a letter from scratch relating to these exemptions?
Harried: I actually did not, because the letters were already being done ... since around '87.

The next councilmember to pose questions was Kwame Brown. While Graham focused his attention on Harried, Brown turned to her supervisors, Aldridge and Zapata. In a back and forth with Zapata, for example, Brown asked if she had ever seen any of the opinion letters Harried had signed.

Brown: Ms. Zapata, did you have any idea of these letters? Have you ever seen one of these letters?
Zapata: Not that I can recall offhand, no.
Brown: Did you know that these letters were even being sent out?
Zapata: I most certainly do. It's been a topic of discussion. I've testified on them for the last three years.
Brown: So you know the letters are being sent out, but you've never seen one of the letters that you've testified on?
Zapata: I've—not that I can recall.
Brown: So how do you testify on letters you've never even seen?
Zapata: I testify on the legislation ... surrounding the 95/5 transactions.

During the hearing an unannounced witness, Gerl Brandon, was brought in to testify. Brandon had been a contractor under Harried's supervision before she was abruptly dismissed. In an exchange with Councilmember

Adrian Fenty, Brandon suggested that DCRA had been "captured" by those it was purportedly regulating.

> Fenty: Someone from DCRA said you were bad for business. Who said that?
> Brandon: Mr. James Aldridge and Linda Harried reported to me that Mr. Aldridge had received several visits and complaints prior to receiving a letter from Mr. Richard Luchs and a Miss Wiggins. One of the visitors, according to Miss Smith [a fellow employee], was Sean Farr; another was Mr. Mark Policy [two prominent real estate attorneys in the District]. And as clearly as I can understand, it was one of them who referred to me as being bad for business.
> Fenty: And then that was adopted by James Aldridge and Linda Harried and repeated to you?
> Brandon: Yes.
> Fenty: And that was around the time of November [2004], when a personnel action was taken against you?
> Brandon: Yes.

Brandon also testified that she had seen several uncashed checks lying around the office where she worked.

> Fenty: You talked about checks being found on a desk or in an office at DCRA. Whose responsibility—whose care were these checks supposed to be in?
> Brandon: Those checks were in the care of Ms. Linda Harried.
> Fenty: And if she had been doing what was her responsibility, what would have happened with those checks?
> Brandon: Those checks should be deposited into the DC treasury for DCRA.

Councilmember Fenty also wanted to know who had written the checks. Brandon replied that the checks were mostly from developers and tenants' associations paying legally mandated condo-conversion fees.

When Councilmember Graham was given an opportunity to question Brandon, he asked what happened to the checks. Brandon's response suggests most were never deposited. In fact, check writers had to follow up with the city to have checks deposited.

> Brandon: To my knowledge, Eisen and Rome [a law firm specializing in representing tenants] was one of the few agents that

did replace expired checks that were found in the office. And Mr. Rosario with that office appeared on the seventh floor one afternoon, and he was not happy, and he lectured about the custody of these checks and how this just shouldn't happen. . . .

Graham: So we do know of at least one specific instance where the check did expire or where checks did expire?

Brandon: I believe there were about five or more.

Graham: And had Eisen and Rome been asked to bring in expired checks?

Brandon: I can't speak on that, sir. What Mr. Rosario said was that they [Eisen and Rome] found them when they were auditing their books, that the checks had not been cashed.

Graham concluded his time with Brandon by incredulously observing that DCRA was not even taking money it was legally due. Although Graham was unable to ascertain at the hearing how much money the city had lost, a subsequent audit by the city's inspector general in 2012 revealed that the city had failed to collect $32 million in conversion fees between 2004 and 2010.

When I watched Graham's hearing online for the first time, I was torn about where to place responsibility for the letters and the 95/5 process they abetted. In the press, Harried received much of the blame (Grim 2006a, 2006b; Wiess 2005a). In the *Washington City Paper*, Ryan Grim (2006a) referred to the draft letters as the "Harried letters," and coverage in the *Washington Post* tended to focus on the fact that Harried had signed most of the letters and could not recall disagreeing with any landlord's interpretation of a proposed 95/5 transfer as *not* a sale (Weiss 2005b). Harried's public testimony did little to dispel the impression. At the hearings she came across as the kind of bureaucrat people love to hate. She appears to have never considered what her actions meant for thousands of tenants across the city, and she grew defensive when pressed to explain herself.

However, it is also clear that Harried's supervisors, though detached from her day-to-day work, supported Harried's literal approach to enforcing the statute's definition of a sale. Indeed, Zapata indicated as much when she testified that the letters were consistent with the law. The mayor and city council deserve blame as well. Marion Barry, who often styled himself as a determined advocate for the city's poor (Barras 1998), refused to close the loophole in 1983. And later attempts to fix it were similarly stymied. Graham's predecessor, Councilmember Sharon Ambrose, did nothing to close the loophole during her tenure on the oversight committee, even though tenants had begun complaining about 95/5 transfers as soon as the city's real estate market began heating up and landlords started unloading properties suitable for condo conversion (Grim 2006b).

Graham's decision to "turn up the heat" on DCRA early on in his tenure paid off. The agency's director, who was regarded as landlord friendly, was replaced by someone more tenant friendly (Grim 2006b). The new director announced DCRA was putting a halt to the practice of offering draft opinion letters (Weiss 2005b). Later in 2005, Graham also introduced legislation to close the 95/5 loophole. It passed, finally bringing a key mechanism to subvert TOPA to an end.

Graham's interest in 95/5 transfers was likely sparked by the fact that many of the transfers occurred in his district, which experienced rapid gentrification during the real estate boom. However, one of the transfers in his district appears to have played an outsized role. It happened in 2004 when local landlords Harold and Maxine Bernstein decided to sell eleven of their residential apartment buildings in a so-called portfolio sale. Although 95/5 transfers were common at this point, the Bernsteins' transfer made what many considered a mockery of the process. After tenants discovered what had happened to them, they contacted Graham, who connected them with an attorney willing to represent them pro bono. The lawsuit that was eventually filed took ten years to resolve.

I turn now to this case, which serves as a shadow case on the TOPA process. It allows us to look at the results presented in Chapter 6 in broader context. Indeed, though TOPA's successes should be celebrated, they are tempered by the fact that thousands of city residents were preemptively excluded from even trying to use the process to stay in place. The 95/5 transfer is no longer legal, but it continues to cast a pall on the TOPA program because the loopholes that allowed it to happen coincided with a real estate bubble—just the point in time when TOPA could have been most effective.

A Resolution a Decade in the Making

In 2004 Howard and Maxine Bernstein put eleven of their rental properties up for sale through the brokerage firm Marcus and Millichap. The initial asking price was $88 million. Although the buildings were not adjacent to one another, all of them were centrally located in neighborhoods just north of downtown, including Mount Pleasant, Columbia Heights, and the eastern edge of Dupont Circle. According to court documents, the couple sold the buildings because they planned to move to Florida.

To recount the sale and the legal fallout that ensued, I rely on numerous sources. To establish the factual record, I used the court case *Richman Towers Tenants' Association, Inc. v. Richman Towers LLC*.[5] I also twice consulted

---

5. Nos. 08-CV-1027, 08-CV-1114, 08-CV-1340, 08-CV-1354, 08-CV-1438, 08-CV-106 (D.C. April 14, 2011).

Blake Biles, the attorney who represented the tenants' association in this case. Finally, I interviewed two tenant leaders—Cathy Schneider and John Samuels[6]—at the Barclay, one of the buildings participating in the lawsuit. Their different perspectives on how to resolve the issue highlight just how difficult undoing the damage caused by 95/5 actually was.

Shortly after listing the Bernstein properties, Marcus and Millichap contacted Carmel Partners, a national real estate firm based in San Francisco, to gauge their interest in the buildings. Carmel Partners was interested and after an inspection negotiated a purchase price of $83 million with the Bernsteins. Although all eleven buildings were sold together, the sale was structured so that each building would be considered a single-purpose entity. To avoid triggering TOPA rights, the Bernsteins also structured the sale as a 95/5 transfer (DePillis 2011b). And before the Bernsteins contracted the sale, their attorney, Richard Luchs, requested and received a draft opinion from DCRA stating that the transfer did not constitute a sale for the purposes of the TOPA statute.

The Bernsteins' eleven buildings were sold using three transactions, one occurring just before closing and two on the day of closing. All transactions were governed, however, by a Single Purchase and Sale Agreement. Prior to closing, the Bernsteins' transferred the eleven properties into individual LLCs, referred to in court documents as LLC I entities. On the day of closing, each LLC I entity transferred the deeds and 100 percent of the property to a matching subsidiary, which the court called LLC II entities. The Bernsteins were the sole owners of both the LLC I and LLC II entities. In the final transaction, the membership interests of each LLC II were transferred to two separate entities—99.99 percent to Carmel Partners and 0.01 percent to Quarry Enterprises.

Although the Bernstein sale is often held up as a quintessential example of a 95/5 transfer, it was unique in a number of ways. First, unlike characteristic 95/5 transfers, the majority portion of the transfer equaled 99.99 percent of the total property value rather than the standard 95 percent. Second, the minority share of the property, here 0.01 percent, was not transferred to an LLC owned or controlled by the Bernstein family. Instead, it was transferred to Quarry Enterprises. A man named Jim Ferris is the only person known to be associated with Quarry Enterprises. He was the Marcus and Millichap broker who had initially contacted Carmel Partners about the Bernsteins' property and, according to court records, was an acquaintance of Carmel Partners' president.

Although the Bernsteins sold their property in one day, the sale was in legal limbo for a decade as the tenants' lawsuit, and appeals to it, moved

---

6. "John Samuels" is a pseudonym, used at the interview subject's request.

through the DC court system at a glacial pace. At stake was whether the Bernsteins' 99.99/0.01 transfer constituted a sale for TOPA purposes. For their part, tenants wanted the transfer defined as a sale because their right of refusal hung in the balance. If the transfer was not a sale, tenants would forgo their right to buy the building and decide its fate. On the other side, the new owner's investment hung in the balance. If the transfer was defined as a sale, the owner could lose control of the building and potentially witness a negative return on its investment.

Getting Organized

In 95/5 transfers tenants usually discover their buildings have been sold after the fact. It was no different in the Bernsteins' eleven buildings. Samuels told me, "Our only notification was after the fact. . . . My feeling was it sort of hit us like a comet." Schneider concurred, noting, "We never got a notice from the landlord." However, unlike Samuels, Schneider had heard the building was up for sale: "I heard by rumor that it was being sold. I went to the manager, Fernando, and said, 'I heard the building's being sold.' He said, 'No, that's not true.' The next thing I know, it was sold." Tenants in the Barclay began to organize quickly. As Schneider explained, "We met right away. We started immediately. We already had a very active tenant board. I was already on the board, and we had meetings right away."

Initially, however, the various Bernstein buildings sought redress independently of one another. Indeed, before the 2004 sale, there was no connection between them. None of the buildings were located next to one another, for example, so the Bernsteins did not treat them as a single complex. There were also demographic differences among them. Most buildings had low-income tenants, but a few had middle-income tenants. In our interview, Blake Biles described the eleven buildings in the Bernstein sale as a "hodgepodge," something he observed was common in portfolio sales:

> Those eleven buildings—you can imagine once you buy portfolio buildings, you're gonna get a mix of buildings. Portfolio's anything. There're gonna be some things I'm really buying to get these five, but they're making me take these other five, so there's a mix of mid-level-income buildings and some lower-income buildings, so there's a hodgepodge.

Most buildings first responded to the sale by working through government channels. Tenants contacted their councilmember (for many, Jim Graham), the mayor, and even DCRA. They asked for the sale to be canceled and for their TOPA right to be reinstated. As Biles observed:

> After that [the sale] was all done, various tenant associations tried various ways to get the government to undo it, but they basically went and tried to go through the government, go through the executive branch, through administrators, as opposed to going to court.

Getting a lawyer, however, was no easy task. Although the Barclay was one of the portfolio's middle-income buildings, its association found the fees out of reach. Schneider noted, "The first law firm we talked to—and now I'm forgetting their name; it starts with an 'S.' They sounded like they would be expensive. We were worried about how we would afford a lawyer." As a result, Schneider recounted, the association turned to developers for help: "Tenacity was one of the firms that we interviewed. . . . Tenacity said that if we signed a contract with them, that they would hire the lawyers, and we wouldn't risk anything." The Barclay's tenants' association soured on Tenacity, however, when it discovered that the developer's pitch was unduly optimistic. As Samuels put it, "Initially, we were quite impressed. In time we came to be very unimpressed with them. I just thank God we broke off our dealings with them before we got too far into it."

The tenants had better luck approaching Jim Graham, the councilmember for Ward 1, where most of the buildings were located. Graham contacted a local law firm, Arnold and Porter, to see if anyone would take the case. Although Blake Biles did not identify Graham by name—"We were pushed by somebody: would we look at it and represent?"—Schneider was more specific. I asked her, "How did you find Blake?" She responded:

> He found us. Jim Graham got him for us. Jim contacted, because nine of the eleven buildings were in Jim's district. And so Jim asked Blake—Arnold and Porter—to represent the buildings in his district pro bono. Because he was really upset about these 95/5s. That's also why he proposed the amendment that closed the loophole on them.

The entry of Arnold and Porter on the scene in late 2006 was a fortuitous event for tenants who had hit a wall in their efforts to find redress through government channels. The statute of limitations for fighting the sale was about to expire (in early 2007). If the tenants missed that date, they would have had no legal recourse to fight the sale. Having a blue-chip law firm do the case pro bono also meant their lawyers would have plenty of resources to bring to the case. As Biles explained in our first interview:

> It's easy to do pro bono work in big law firms. Uh, I'm not diminishing the work and the time involved, but the fact is our work for commercial clients pays for this. In any department, we do a huge

amount of pro bono in tons of areas. All of that, you know, um—don't lose sight of the fact it's all funded by all the work we do for very big commercial companies.

The decision to take the case pro bono also benefited the middle-income buildings in the portfolio of eleven buildings. Indeed, had they been stand-alone sales (not a part of the eleven-building portfolio), Biles told me his firm would not likely have taken them on:

We did it on a pro bono basis because a number of buildings were low-income, gentrifying buildings, because that was part of the portfolio. And in that case we agreed also to take on ones that were not low income because normally we wouldn't take them on for pro bono cases—there's no need—but because it's exactly the same legal issue for all those, we ended up filing a lawsuit on behalf of six of them right before the statute of limitations expired.

A Lawsuit and an Appeal

Although Arnold and Porter took the case before the statute of limitations ran out, they faced a number of challenges in building cases for all eleven properties. Some buildings' tenants were too disorganized to join the suit. Schneider cited infighting as a key reason for the disorganization:

We were lucky because our tenants' association was twenty years old. The Ravenel [one of the eleven buildings], which was like our building in terms of makeup, never got it together to be a part of the lawsuit. They had real problems uniting and organizing.... The one on Columbia Road—that was a nightmare to organize. It was huge [in size]. And they ended up having two or three tenant associations, all of them competing and slandering each other. I remember the story; they ended up arguing with each other. They couldn't get it together in time to participate in the lawsuit.

Attrition was also a problem. In the nearly two and a half years between the original sale and Arnold and Porter's arrival, most buildings had experienced significant turnover. And the high rate of turnover created a problem vis-à-vis the wording in the TOPA statute. As Biles explained, TOPA requires that a tenants' association "represent more than 50 percent of the people [who] lived in the building *at the time* of the transaction." And being able to establish representation was necessary to establish that tenants had "standing" to bring the case. In the end, Biles and his team were able to collect sufficient documentation of standing from only six of the eleven buildings. As he explained, many of the buildings had a "high immigrant population—a high illegal population—and so it was very, very difficult for us, coming in two and a half years after the transaction, to document things."

For the remaining six buildings Arnold and Porter brought forward individual lawsuits in June 2007 claiming that each of the transfers amounted to a sale and that tenants' right of first refusal had been abrogated. For each case, the tenants' association was the plaintiff, and the building LLC set up by Carmel Partners was the defendant.[7] Arnold and Porter represented tenants, and Steptoe and Johnson represented Carmel Partners.[8]

The DC Superior Court ruled on all six cases using a procedure known as summary judgment, which allows a judge to make a ruling without a trial. The five judges who heard the six cases all issued judgments in favor of the owners, though the reasons varied by case. In one case the judge found that the original sale did not constitute a sale by TOPA standards.[9] In another case the tenants' association was found to lack standing to bring the case.[10] In the four remaining cases summary judgments were rendered using both criteria—that the transfer did not constitute a sale and that tenants lacked standing.[11] Although disappointing for tenants, the result was not surprising. After Arnold and Porter filed their suit, the DC Superior Court issued several rulings against other tenant challenges to 95/5 transfers.

Arnold and Porter appealed the summary judgments in a consolidated appeal, *Richman Towers Tenants' Association, Inc. v. Richman Towers LLC*. Arguments on the case were heard on January 14, 2010.

Not surprisingly, tenants and their new owners had starkly different interpretations of both the real estate transaction at the heart of the case and the TOPA statute meant to govern it. For their part, Carmel Partners made numerous arguments in favor of keeping the summary judgments intact. I highlight the three dominant ones here. The first was a novel argument not used in any of the prior 95/5 cases. Specifically, the defendants argued that the TOPA requirement that tenants receive a notice of sale applies only to buildings in which a sale will result in the demolition of the property or in a shift away from residential use. To defend this reading, Carmel's attorneys referenced the following portion of the statute:

---

7. The Bernsteins and Carmel's title insurance company were codefendants in the case.
8. Richard Luchs represented the defendants until the point of litigation.
9. Lanier Apartments Tenants' Association, Inc. v. Lanier Regal, LLC, Inc.
10. 3150 16th Street Tenants' Association v. Marconi Park II, LLC.
11. Richman Towers Tenants' Association, Inc. v. Richman Towers LLC; Barclay Tenants' Association, Inc. v. Barclay Apartments, LLC; Argonne Tenants Council, Inc. v. Park Plaza Apartments; 3312 16th Street Tenants' Association, Inc. v. Sarbin Towers, LLC.

> Before an owner of a housing accommodation may sell the accommodation, or issue a notice of intent to recover possession, or notice to vacate, for purposes of demolition or discontinuance of housing use, the owner shall give the tenant an opportunity to purchase the accommodation at a price and terms which represent a bona fide offer of sale.

The defendants argued that the placement of commas around the phrase "for the purposes of demolition or discontinuance of housing use" meant that the previous clause relating to sales was modified and restricted by it. Thus, the TOPA statute did not apply to the Bernstein transfer because the defendants, Carmel Partners, had kept all their newly acquired buildings intact and were maintaining them as rental accommodations.

In a related argument, the defendants argued that applying TOPA broadly (i.e., to all sales, not just those in which buildings were slated for demolition/discontinuation) would breach Article 1, Section 10, Clause 1 of the U.S. Constitution.[12] Specifically, they argued that a broad reading of TOPA is unconstitutional because it would be "a disguised tactic to assist in redistribution of wealth that infringes on the property rights of owners and is not centered around any legitimate public policy." Finally, with a nod to motive, the defendants argued that the Bernsteins had structured a complex sale for "their own tax and estate purposes" and not, as the various tenants' associations had argued, to avoid triggering TOPA requirements.

For their part, Arnold and Porter focused on two arguments in their appeal. The first concerned standing. In the initial case most of the buildings were found not to have statutory standing to challenge the sales because their tenants' associations were unable to demonstrate that they represented 50 percent (plus 1) of the tenants living in the building at the time of the sale. In the appeal, the associations argued that even if some of them did not possess statutory standing, all could demonstrate associational standing since individual members of the group did have a right to sue in the case (i.e., some members in the association lived in the buildings at the time of the sale).

The second argument concerned whether the Bernsteins' property transfer constituted a sale. In its initial petition Arnold and Porter had argued that 95/5 transfers were not consistent with the intent of the TOPA statute. However, the court had since rejected that argument in other challenges to 95/5, so Arnold and Porter decided to go a different route. They argued instead that the Bernstein's 95/5 transfer was fraudulent inasmuch as the transaction actually transferred 100 percent of the property to new owners

---

12. This clause is often called the "contracts clause." It limits how states may intervene in private contract negotiations, disputes, and the like.

but had concealed that fact through a complex sale structure. As Biles noted in our interview:

> We couldn't argue against the fact that courts had said [in previous rulings that] less than that [100 percent] under the old law was not a sale. Rather, we argued, uh—I would say we argued in a sense that it really was a 100 percent sale, but what they did was a sham.

Schneider explained the argument in more detail:

> Blake appeals and changes the argument. And what Blake argues is that we are not a 95/5. We are fraud. Because in our case, they sold 99.99 percent of the building. The 0.01 percent was either given to the lawyer who conducted the transaction or disappeared, but there's no record that [the original owners] kept anything. There seems to be a record that there was, in fact, discussion by Carmel Partners' lawyer [that they] could get around TOPA by doing this. But they did this so blatantly, and he said this is just fraud. And apparently, one judge listening to this just says, "So you mean they [the Bernsteins] kept a nickel?"

On April 14, 2011, the District of Columbia Court of Appeals issued a ruling on the case. The judges prefaced their decision by explaining their overall approach to the case:

> TOPA is a remedial statute, and it is to be generously construed "toward the end of strengthening the legal rights of tenants or tenant organizations to the maximum extent permitted under law." D.C.Code § 42-2405.11 (2008). . . . Moreover, we are of the opinion that TOPA, like other remedial statutory and constitutional provisions, "forecloses sophisticated as well as simple-minded modes of nullification or evasion." Goodman v. District of Columbia Rental Hous. Comm'n, 573 A.2d 1293, 1297 (D.C.1990).

The approach signaled the mostly good news the ruling would deliver to tenants. The court ruled, for example, that "the transfers constituted a sale subject to the requirements of TOPA." It justified its ruling on two grounds. First, it noted that the Bernsteins "transferred absolute title to the buildings" in the initial transaction. Indeed, the complexity of the sale notwithstanding, the three separate transfers were negotiated in a Single Purchase and Sale Agreement. Second, though the court did not use words such as "sham" or "fraud" to describe the transaction, it also rejected the defendant's assertion that the sale had been conducted for tax purposes. As it noted, "To suggest that the creation of a 0.01% interest in Quarry was designed for any other purpose than to avoid a transfer of 100% interest to a single buyer (and thus the owners hoped, to avoid the requirements of TOPA) taxes our credulity." In the factual portion of the ruling, the court of appeals also explicitly acknowledged the tenants' claim that the ownership of Quarry Enterprises was in question. It noted, for example, that

> Quarry did not have an office or an accountant, nor had it filed a tax return. It had never entered into any agreement, aside from those related to the 2004 transaction for which it was established. Quarry had never made any loans, or purchased insurance, or made cash distributions, and it had never opened or maintained a bank account. In fact, during the course of his deposition, Mr. Ferris, the only person associated with Quarry Enterprises, did not know the company's location. . . . The Witness also testified that he had never received any compensation from Quarry for any work that he had performed.

The ruling also addressed the defendants' wider argument that TOPA does not apply to tenants involved in so-called ordinary sales where a building changes hands but remains a residential property. As the court noted, the acceptance of the defendants' position depends in large part on how one interprets the placement of the commas in the statute:

> The sole ambiguity, if there is one, is whether the phrase "for demolition or discontinuance of housing use," which is set off by commas, modified the words "sell the accommodation," as well as one or both of the other two kinds of transaction to which the statute refers.

The court rejected the defendants' interpretation on three grounds. First, it noted that the defendants' "proposed construction essentially nullified the words 'sell the accommodation' and leads to irrational results." Citing existing case law, the court noted that the placement of commas cannot be used to garble, change, or otherwise misrepresent the purpose of a statute. The court also pointed to the copious records, in court and in council proceedings, about the stated and intended purposes of the law. In particular, the court observed that the council had discussed both the inclusion of the wording in question—the "for demolition or discontinuance of housing use" clause—and the eventual placement of commas around it. The court noted that during the markup of the bill, Councilmember John Ray proposed amending the statute to expand, not contract, who was covered under the

TOPA statute. The court quoted Ray's justification during the bill's markup as evidence:

> What this amendment does is to reestablish that principle [from the bill as first introduced] of allowing the tenants to not only purchase the building where the owner is putting the building up for sale, but also where the owner is planning on demolishing the building or discontinuing the use of the building as housing.

The court also observed that the council discussed why it added commas around Ray's proposed language during the same council hearing. One of Ray's colleagues was worried that the new wording could prevent an owner from returning to live in his or her own home without first offering the tenant the right to purchase the building. Commas were inserted to remove any confusion. As the court noted:

> In order to resolve any perceived ambiguity, the Council's General Counsel suggested that putting "some commas around 'or notice to vacate' might make it clearer" that the "notice of intent to recover possession" refers only to such notices issued for purposes of demolition or discontinuance of housing use.

Finally, the court rejected the defendants' argument that interpreting TOPA as applying to all property sales (rather than just those slated for demolition) would amount to an unconstitutional "redistribution of wealth." The court was unmoved, curtly noting that "these contentions are without merit." It continued:

> TOPA does strengthen the bargaining power of tenants, but even if we assume, for the sake of argument, that the effect of the statute as heretofore construed is to improve the financial condition of some less affluent citizens, and to a very limited extent to reduce the gap between rich and poor, the same might likewise be said of the graduated income tax, publicly assisted housing, Medicare, unemployment compensation, and a host of other programs. The owners have cited no authority, and we know of none, that would support a holding that TOPA is unconstitutional because it somehow "redistributes wealth."

The court also offered a more measured assessment of what TOPA does and does not do. As it explained:

> The owners also appear to attack the application of TOPA to all sales on Due Process grounds. However, notwithstanding their claim that

TOPA as heretofore construed promotes what might be characterized as a Robin Hood-style "redistribution of wealth" in disguise, the statute is not quite as revolutionary as that. TOPA requires an owner who wishes to sell a housing accommodation to provide the tenants with an opportunity to purchase that accommodation "at a price and terms which represent a *bona fide offer of sale*." D.C.Code § 42-3404.02(a). (Emphasis added.) Moreover, the closely related right of "first refusal," see § 42-3404.08, requires the tenants, in effect, to match any offer made by a third party. Thus, if the tenants elect to exercise that right, the owner will be able to sell the accommodation for the same price and on the same terms as if the sale were to a third party purchaser.

While the ruling was a victory for tenants negatively affected by 95/5 transfers, it was not a complete triumph. In four of the six buildings, the court agreed with the lower court's summary judgments that the tenants' associations did not have either statutory or associational standing to bring their cases. In the matter of statutory standing, the court noted simply that "none of the remaining four organizations provided evidence that it represented at least half of the qualifying heads of household," which, as noted previously, is defined as 50 percent (plus 1) of residents living in the building at the time of the sale. On the matter of associational standing the court noted that the decision could be overturned only "by the full court sitting en banc, and we are compelled to reject it here." This ruling meant that at the end of seven years, only two of the eleven buildings sold by the Bernsteins could have their TOPA rights restored. The two buildings with standing were the Barclay, a middle-income building, and the Lanier, a lower-income property. Space constraints prevent me from discussing each building's experience. I review the Barclay's here because it was the more contentious of the two.

A Standing Dilemma

After the ruling Arnold and Porter had two options. The first was to appeal for an en banc hearing of the appellate court to fight for the inclusion of the four buildings denied standing. Unlike a first-round appeal, where a panel of judges hears a case, an en banc hearing is held before all sitting judges on the appellate court. The second option was to continue to the next stage with just the two buildings granted standing. This created a dilemma for the pro bono team representing all six buildings. Schneider explained it this way:

> Now, the other four buildings, Blake and the law firm felt really strongly about [them] because they thought, "These are poor

buildings with people with lots of jobs that are difficult to organize," and they had taken the case pro bono to represent buildings like this, and it was really unfair of the court to deny them standing. And so they wanted to appeal the decision on standing, but that would put them at a conflict of interest with us. So they asked us to give them authority to appeal, even though it risked—we risked losing our win, losing everything.

I asked Schneider how her tenant board reacted, especially given the stakes—that after a long, belated victory, a second-round appeal could snatch it all away. Fortunately, the decision was not contentious, and it comported with what Arnold and Porter wanted to do. She explained:

We all felt strongly in favor of doing that, both because we agreed with the sentiment—we also thought the poor buildings shouldn't be the ones penalized—and because we recognized they had taken us pro bono and worked with us pro bono all these years largely because of the poor buildings. And what were we going to tell our lawyers—"No, you can only work with *us* pro bono"? So we all said yes. Without any hesitation. There was no disagreement. We all agreed right away.

Four months later the appellate court declined to hear the appeal en banc. Its decision meant the four buildings denied standing would receive no redress, but the two remaining buildings could seek a remedy. Things would get only more complicated.

Mediation

In the District of Columbia, as in many jurisdictions, mediation is often a required part of civil litigation. The idea is that two parties can, with the help of a mediator, strike a deal without a judge having to render a final judgment. In the case at hand, the mediation process began in early 2012 after the appellate court declined to hold an en banc hearing. The case was then handed off to a different judge, who contacted lawyers for both sides for possible remedies, which would be starting points for the mediation process itself.

The tenants had two options for remedy—a monetary settlement or the reinstatement of their TOPA rights. When I asked Schneider what Biles had submitted to the judge as the tenants' desired remedy, she responded:

The right to buy the building. The granting of our TOPA rights—the granting of our TOPA rights that were denied us. It's the only thing we want. We want the TOPA rights that were denied us in 2004, and we want it for the price that the building was sold for in 2004.

Although a reinstatement of TOPA rights was a significant request, especially since it could be read as "undoing" a sale,[13] the demand for the 2004 price was probably just as important when considered in the context of the DC housing market. In the eight years since the eleven buildings had been sold, the District experienced rapid gentrification.[14] The buildings were, therefore, now worth more, so tenants would have to pay a higher price for them in 2012 than they would have had to pay in 2004.

Moreover, asking for the reinstatement of TOPA rights would not preclude an eventual monetary settlement. If the tenants were allowed to seek a third-party developer at the building's 2004 price, they would likely find numerous developers interested in working with them. And in the horse trading that goes on when tenants select a third-party developer, they could negotiate for much higher buyouts and/or lower insider prices with the 2004 price than they could with the 2012 price. As Schneider put it, "If we wanted a monetary settlement at the end, we'd be getting a better one from a developer than we were going to get from Carmel Partners." Schneider and Samuels both told me that Carmel Partners had approached the tenants' association with cash offers multiple times before the en banc hearing was declined. In each case, the amounts were paltry.

Although mediation proceedings are confidential, both Schneider and Samuels told me the process failed to produce an agreement. As Schneider explained, without giving away any of the confidential aspects of the process:

> During the process we are so far apart; they separate us, and they end up having the mediator going back and forth between the two rooms.... [At the end] we're so far apart, the mediator says, "You're so far apart—miles apart. There's no chance [for reconciliation]."

Samuels had a similar recollection, although he put it more colorfully: "We got nowhere; they treated us like we were something that had come in off the street on their shoes."

---

13. When I interviewed Blake Biles, he speculated that some judges would be apprehensive to reinstate tenants' TOPA rights because it would be tantamount to undoing a real estate transaction.
14. The neighborhoods where the Barclay and Lanier were located shifted from transitional to almost fully gentrified spaces in the decade after the original sale.

In December 2012, the judge heard a final round of arguments from both sides. The parties were then left to wait for a court remedy. Whatever the outcome, it would be the final say on the matter, the denouement to a near-decade-long struggle.

Settlement

Nine months later, in August 2013 the parties were still waiting for the court to issue a remedy. And with no time limit, it was anybody's guess how long it would take. Fortuitously, for the Barclay's tenants, Carmel Partners was interested in selling the building and, like most developers, wanted to avoid a TOPA process. As a result, they were willing to negotiate seriously to settle the lawsuit and as part of that process get tenants to agree not to invoke their right of first refusal. It meant tenants had the upper hand. As Biles explained to me in our second interview, "You have leverage over them. For a big company this is a line item, one of many, many buildings in the country [they own]. So the incentive is to get it [a deal] done."

A settlement would, however, put the reinstatement of TOPA rights off the table—a fact the tenants would have to consider as they decided whether to meet with Carmel. When I asked Schneider and Samuels what they thought about the 2013 overture from Carmel, they had different opinions. Samuels was inclined to bargain for a monetary settlement. He told me that he had never been interested in buying his unit, even in 2004 when the initial sale took place: "I didn't feel particularly interested in getting a big mortgage at that time in my life—I'm seventy now and would have been sixty then." He had supported the TOPA reinstatement because he saw it as the best avenue for getting a decent monetary settlement. Now that Carmel was serious about negotiating, he was willing to listen. As he explained,

> I'd come around to the money side myself because I could see, being very selfish about it, that if we got the building, the amount of work that would be involved in finding another developer to partner with and all of that would require at least another year. We'd have to negotiate. We'd have to sell that to the rest of the people in the building, many of whom are not interested in a condo. And I just didn't want to go there.

Schneider, however, continued to support a TOPA notice as the best remedy. When I asked why, she explained, "I'm seeing it as my retirement." She told me that owning her unit would give her financial flexibility. She could sell the unit for a substantial profit, rent it and cover expenses with some cash left over, or live in it until she needed to divest. She also explained that if the tenants negotiated for a financial remedy, her building would likely stay rental and she would be forced to stay put:[15]

> Part of the problem for me is that the building—I have rent stabilization, so I pay lower rents, but if I move anywhere else in the city, . . . that goes way up. My salary has been low, so I could not even afford to rent anywhere in this city. And if it stays rental, I can't leave. And so I want the flexibility to have—to be able to live elsewhere, to have some freedom in my retirement.

When the tenants met to discuss Carmel's overture, it became clear that only a few residents were still interested in buying their units—about "three or four when it came down to it," Samuels noted. When I asked Schneider and Samuels why the numbers were so low, both pointed to the building's changing demographics. Samuels used the word "short-timers" to describe the new tenants. Schneider called them "transient," noting that "what we've tended to have is lots and lots of students and interns that double and triple up in apartments, stay a year or two, and move out."

Once the tenants agreed to negotiate with Carmel, they had to decide what their floor would be—that is, the minimum amount of money they would accept in settlement. They also had to assemble a negotiating team who would hold the line in their meeting with Carmel's representatives. Samuels, who was on the negotiating team, explained:

> We were told not to settle for less than $3.9 million. And we were not to agree to anything, but if we could get them to commit [to that amount], we were then authorized to say we'd go back to the building and see if we could get approval.

After a daylong, often tense negotiation, the Barclay tenants accepted a settlement from Carmel Partners for an amount slightly over their asking price—$4 million.[16] It was a milestone for the tenants, and many felt vindicated. Up until that point, Samuels told me, Carmel Partners' attitude had always been "We don't really think we owe you anything."

---

15. In 2013 the condo market was soft so most developers did not offer conversion options.
16. Because Carmel was selling the building, it was required to give tenants a TOPA notice. However, the agreement between the two parties stipulated that disbursement of the settlement money was contingent on tenants not invoking their TOPA rights.

Distribution

The tenants' next task was internal. They had to devise a method for dividing up the settlement money. If all fifty-six units in the building were occupied by the tenants living in the building at the time of the 2004 sale, the process would have been easy. Each household would receive just over $71,000. However, only thirteen of the original tenants remained in the building when the settlement was reached. As a result, the Barclay's tenants had to take into account three groups of tenants. The first group included tenants who were in the building in 2004 and during the settlement negotiation in 2013. The second group consisted of tenants who lived in the building in 2004 when the initial sale was conducted but had moved out before the settlement. The final group was composed of tenants who lived in the building at the time of settlement but not in 2004 when the initial sale happened.[17] To help readers follow the discussion, I refer to these groups with the shorthands "originals who stayed," "originals who left," and "new arrivals," respectively.

The second task was to actually figure out who belonged in each group. This list would serve as the universe of tenants eligible for a share of the $4 million settlement. Accounting for the originals who stayed and the new arrivals was easy—both groups lived in the building. Tracking the originals who left was more difficult. "We had a hell of a time tracing some of these people down," Samuels told me. They used three methods to find former tenants—the association's records, which were quite detailed; Google searches; and a professional search engine.

Samuels told me that in the end, the board was able to track down all but fifteen or sixteen of the forty-three originals who left. He also explained why the board spent so much time on the process: "We did a good, thorough job on this. Because we were thinking if we ever need to go into court on this, we need to be able to tell the judge on this, with an honest heart, that we did our best to find X, Y, and Z, and we just couldn't."

The second step was to divide eligible tenants into compensation categories. These categories do not match the categories of tenants mentioned previously. Rather, they account for not only where one was during the original sale and later settlement but also whether one supported the association's legal struggle.

Category 1 covers tenants who were in the building in 2004 and agreed to sign the documents Arnold and Porter compiled to demonstrate standing

---

17. Although this group of tenants did not have their TOPA rights abrogated, they were members of the tenants' association and thus party to the agreement between Carmel and the association.

in the 2007 lawsuit. Some of these tenants no longer live in the building. Category 2 captures tenants who lived in the building in 2004 but would not sign the documents Arnold and Porter compiled for standing. I asked Samuels why some tenants had refused to sign. He replied, "Maybe they thought it was hopeless. Maybe they thought that somehow—we kept explaining to them [that] we're not asking for money; we're not going to ask for money. Maybe they didn't believe that." Schneider had a similar recollection about trying to get signatures: "We went by their units over and over again, and they just wouldn't sign." As a result, she saw category 2 as the "free-rider category." She said:

> So their rights had been violated, but had they made a decision to claim those rights? By not signing, they weren't claiming those rights *and* they were putting in jeopardy the ability of those who were claiming them to be given standing at the court.

Category 3 covers tenants who moved into the building after 2004, showed their support for the tenants' association, but left before the settlement.[18] Schneider described this as a "gift category." These tenants were not legally entitled to a portion of the settlement because they had no claim to a unit (as either original or current residents). However, the tenants' association felt their help at key points along the way should be accounted for during distribution.

Category 4 was for current residents and included the long-timers in the building since 2004 as well as current leaseholders who moved in after the initial sale. Category 5 was a category devised for any tenant who did not fit into any of the other four categories. Except for category 3, categories were not mutually exclusive. So, for example, both Schneider and Samuels fit into categories 1 and 4. Table 8.1 lists compensation amounts for each category.

Although the categorization scheme was complicated, a few simple principles underpin the distribution strategy attached to it. First, the Barclay's tenant board did not treat all 2004 tenants the same. Though everyone's rights had been abrogated, the tenants' association wanted to distinguish between tenants who had signed the documents used to establish standing in the 2007 lawsuit and those who had refused to do so. As Samuels explained, signing the standing documents was "the gold standard" inasmuch as establishing standing was what had allowed the tenants to seek redress. This sentiment was reflected in the huge gap in compensation between the first two categories—$72,000 for category 1 and $1,000 for category 2. Second,

---

18. The Barclay tenants' association created a petition after 2007 to gauge internal support in the building. Tenants who signed it were eligible for category 3.

TABLE 8.1 BARCLAY TENANTS' ASSOCIATION, SETTLEMENT DISTRIBUTION PLAN

Compensation categories	Number of tenants	Compensation ($)
1	33	72,000
2	25	1,000
3	25	3,500
4	56	20,735
5	0	350

physical presence in the building at the time of settlement was given substantial weight. Thus, new arrivals were rewarded more handsomely than some original tenants (category 2) and former tenants who had helped out in important ways during the lawsuit (category 3). Tenants in category 4, for example, received $20,735, whereas categories 2 and 3 received $1,000 and $3,500, respectively. Finally, the ability to fit into more than one category underscored these principles. Original tenants who fit into categories 1 and 4 received a total compensation of $92,735.

When I discovered how the Barclay's tenant board had divided their settlement, I was surprised. I had assumed that after a decade of struggle, any remedy would be devoted primarily to the tenants whose original rights were abrogated rather than current residents. When I interviewed Samuels, I asked him what the board's rationale was: "The people in category 2 and 3, why would they get less than category 4? Was that a legal thing? Were you were worried that the people in category 4, the current residents, would kick up a fuss if they didn't get something because they were numerically strong? Or was it [that] it was harder to deal with those people no longer here?" He responded:

> Well, the people in category 4 are the people, you have to remember, who are now sitting in the building. You could certainly make a legal argument that the whole $4 million should be split among the existing tenants of the building, and those who were here prior to 2014, when the sale takes place, are not entitled to anything. It's just tough luck. And we were trying to avoid somebody doing that. So we wanted to give them some incentive to not do that, which means a substantial amount of money.

Not surprisingly, Schneider, who clashed with Samuels on numerous issues over the decade, saw things differently. "It's completely unfair," she told me. When I asked why, she explained that she felt people in category 4 were given too much money:

We didn't even have any length of time for [eligibility in] category 4. So, for instance, this just happened to me. I was at the elevator. Somebody was moving out. I said, "When did you move in?" They said, "Eight months ago." [I said,] "So you were one of the beneficiaries?" He said, "Yeah, what luck. I got the money, and now we're going!" So people moved in, took the $22,000, and they moved out. We had been in proceedings for ten years. It's not fair.

The Continuing Salience of Regulation

The question at the heart of Samuels and Schneider's disagreement—was compensation to current residents not in the building in 2004 a smart tactical move or an unfair give-away?—is important but begs a wider question. Is the city willing to defend the TOPA law rigorously and consistently? The Barclay's final outcome may have been politically expedient, but it was not optimal when considered in light of the statute's main goals.

Unfortunately, the evidence in this chapter suggests TOPA rights are protected inconsistently at best, and erratically at worst. The inconsistency is brought into sharp relief by looking at the positive results detailed in Chapter 7 and comparing them with the negative results presented in this chapter. As I note in Chapter 6, residents in 707 units were saved from displacement through the TOPA process. However, the Bernsteins' 99.99 percent/0.01 percent sale effectively denied residents in 802 units spread across eleven buildings their TOPA rights. After a decade in court, only two buildings, with fewer than 100 units combined, were compensated for their loss. That is, tenants in the remaining 700 units might as well have lived in a different city.

These results also suggest that for local autonomy to work, local leaders must be on board. Unfortunately, local elites in DC have often aligned with those who shared their class interests, supporting elites inside and outside DC at the expense of residents here. During the early part of the real estate boom, for example, high- and mid-level bureaucrats in DCRA seemed more interested in accommodating landlords and developers than the tenants they were meant to protect. Moreover, the council member in charge of DCRA oversight during the same period did nothing as hundreds of tenants saw their rights disappear through 95/5 transfers. The specter of the control board and the reasonable fear it still invokes notwithstanding, only a few elites have proven willing to question the development-at-all-costs mantra that has guided the city's approach to investment.

9

Is TOPA the Politics of Staying Put We Want?

My interest in TOPA spans more than a decade. Initially, I wanted to understand the process because I was going through it. Then I watched with curiosity as the real estate market took off. I wondered how many other tenants in the city would do what I had done—get a foot in a real estate market growing rapidly out of reach. Soon after, I heard about 95/5 transfers. I was relieved our buildings had avoided the fate of the Bernstein properties, but I was angry, too. Why do landlords have to behave so greedily, I wondered, when a payout awaited either way? Eventually, I decided to study the process systematically, as an academic.

Although it may seem strange given the duration of my interest, for most of this time I felt like the essence of TOPA was just beyond my interpretive reach. Initially, I struggled to figure out what analytic box to put TOPA in—neoliberal, Keynesian, or social justice. Midway through the process, I accepted the futility of that endeavor. TOPA was a hybrid. Its history and contemporary uses demonstrated as much.

Acknowledging TOPA's hybridity, however, made it more difficult for me to politically assess it. Indeed, though neoliberalism, Keynesianism, and social justice are empirical categories inasmuch as they describe types of solutions to urban problems, they are also political. They signal how one explains the causes of urban vulnerability and, as a result, fashions antidotes to it. To be sure, political assessment goes beyond mere classification. How one views neoliberalism, for example, depends on whether one is an advocate or critic of it. However, categorization is a crucial first step in a political assessment because it provides a mutually intelligible script across the urban analytic spectrum.

Once I realized I could not place TOPA in a single analytic box, I struggled with a new problem—how to weigh TOPA's positive outcomes against its negative ones. I knew I could not create a quantitative balance sheet because I lacked the statistical data for such an accounting. So I opted for a conceptual exercise instead. I would see how the statute's neoliberal and social-justice elements were balanced in practice. I reasoned that if one approach was dominant, I could still politically assess TOPA based on my view of the analytic category it most approximated. As I demonstrate, however, TOPA's imperatives were too entangled to determine the balance between them and often unfolded in unexpected ways.

In this chapter I discuss how I came to terms with these struggles and how I eventually made a political assessment. I begin, however, with a short review of the outcomes in my sample buildings and the shadow case detailed in the previous chapter. I then describe the limitations I encountered when using standard analytic categories to frame my analysis of TOPA. I conclude by answering the question that has animated my interest in TOPA from the beginning: Does TOPA provide a politics of staying put we can support?

TOPA's Outcomes

Displacement Mitigation

As I note in Chapter 4, TOPA has two key goals—to mitigate displacement and protect the city's affordable-housing stock. To assess how well TOPA meets its first goal, I began with a simple question: How many people in my sample stayed put through the TOPA process? My data demonstrate that a sizable number of people used TOPA to stay in place. Specifically, residents in 707 units (58 percent of total sample units) were able to stay put through the TOPA process, although there was wide variation across the sample (only 12.8 percent of tenants stayed put in Town Center while 100 percent did so at Mayfair Mansions). This percentage is lower than some low-income housing advocates would like, but it is noteworthy for two reasons.

First, the de facto goal of most developers is 100 percent displacement. Few reach it, but many aim for it (Cenziper and Cohen 2008). As I note in Chapter 6, the city waives its condo-conversion fee for developers who convert empty buildings. Landlords know about the waiver and often try to empty their buildings before initiating a sale to attract buyers. Indeed, the first part of RHCSA—CRHCC, which permits conversion only if 50 percent (plus 1) of tenants vote to approve it—was instituted because landlords and developers interested in conversion routinely forced out their in situ tenants. In short, when compared to the 100 percent displacement goal, a stay-put rate of 58 percent is a real achievement.

Second, there are real people behind these figures, and their ability to stay put obviously means something to them. They can continue to live near work or stay in the neighborhood they grew up in. They can also enjoy the improvements gentrification can bring to a neighborhood, including better safety and grocery stores. For all of them, the disruption and attendant anxiety that come with displacement are avoided.

To assess how well TOPA meets its second goal, I examined the 42 percent of units where tenants did not stay put. I knew I could not count these units as cases of direct displacement. Their occupants left in a context where staying put was a viable option. In sample buildings staying rental, for example, tenants who wanted to stay put could do so at existing rents and with rent-control protections intact. Likewise, in buildings converting to condo, tenant leaders worked hard to ensure that tenants who wanted to stay put could do so by securing insider pricing. Given that people who left were not forced to do so, I could have claimed that TOPA was an unqualified success.

I did not feel comfortable doing so, however. Because the remaining 42 percent of units in my sample were put back into circulation, it was necessary to chart what happened to their affordability afterward. It is here that an exclusionary displacement measure became so important. It allowed me to capture whether changes in these units' tenure or housing costs would exclude people who could have rented them prior to the TOPA process. When shifts in tenure and costs occur on a large-enough scale (i.e., in multiple neighborhoods), low-income tenants are not only excluded from certain units; they can also be excluded from the city. Those who need to make intracity moves (e.g., to downsize after divorce) may find few if any apartments available in their price range. Likewise, low-income youth ready to leave the nest will find it difficult to establish independent households *in* the city.

My interview data suggest that TOPA contributes to exclusionary displacement because of two practices that have evolved over time—the use of buyouts and voluntary agreements. Buyouts are used to attract potential third-party developers, who look at empty units as a source of profit. In buildings converting to condos, for example, developers want to refurbish bought-out units for the luxury condo market. In buildings remaining rental, developers also want to rent bought-out units at luxury rates. Since rent control prohibits sharp rent hikes, however, developers need a way to make buyouts worth their while. Increasingly, they rely on a historically little-used provision in the city's rent-control statute—voluntary agreements—to make buyouts work. Although most tenants will not voluntarily agree to steep rent increases, tenants in TOPA properties often accept voluntary agreements because third-party developers refuse to sign deals without them.

Taken together, these practices mean that the housing costs in bought-out units are brought up to market rates, effectively excluding low-income citizens from them. In my sample, 443 of 1,179 total units (37.5 percent) were transferred to market rate through TOPA.[1] The prices of these units range from 4.7 to 6.5 times the poverty threshold for a one-person household and from 3.5 to 4.9 times the threshold for a two-person household (see Table 6.4).

The class dynamics of exclusionary displacement are also important. Although my data do not capture class change in the city as a whole, the shifts in housing costs in my sample demonstrate clearly that many of its buildings are being remade for those with higher-than-average incomes. And as my focus on TOPA buildings suggests, that remaking is not occurring on empty or underused space (i.e., on a blank slate) but in lived in spaces.

Regulation and Oversight

The ability of TOPA to succeed is also limited by the city itself. My analysis of the Bernsteins' portfolio sale in Chapter 8 demonstrates that TOPA's displacement-mitigation numbers could have been much larger if the city had properly regulated the statute and sufficiently funded efforts by low-income tenants to use it.

During the study period covered here, two agencies regulated the TOPA process—DCRA and DHCD. DCRA's performance was so poor that in 2007 the city stripped TOPA from its portfolio and handed it to DHCD. Although DHCD's performance has been far from stellar, the most egregious violations against the spirit and letter of the TOPA law occurred when the statute was under DCRA's watch. Until mid-2005, for example, midlevel DCRA officials routinely approved 95/5 transfers without any official investigation of sales arrangements and virtually no oversight by agency supervisors or legal counsel.

The eleven properties sold by the Bernstein family in 2004 made a mockery of the idea that the agency's TOPA office was defending tenant rights. Instead, agency officials created an unofficial process that gave landlords legal cover to avoid notifying tenants of their right-to-buy. In the Bernstein

---

1. The percentage of units saved from displacement (58 percent) and the percentage brought to market rate (37.5 percent) do not equal 100 percent because of the twenty-five units in the Kennedy initially set aside for condo conversion. These units do not fit squarely in either the stay-put or exclusionary displacement categories. These units were either vacated in the presale period or via attrition during the process, but they were kept at affordable rents with the help of Mi Casa.

portfolio sale alone tenants in 802 units were denied their TOPA rights, and the city council estimates thousands more were equally disenfranchised during the early 2000s. In the Bernstein property very few tenants (approximately one hundred) were able to seek redress through the court system. Their redress was not only a decade in the making but compensatory rather than reparatory. Moreover, compensation was distributed both to tenants whose rights had been abrogated in the 2004 sale and to current residents who were not even living in a Bernstein property in 2004. Legal give and take notwithstanding, this outcome is difficult to square with the statute's intended purpose.

The city has also fallen short in how it helps low-income tenants trying to navigate the TOPA process. Although the city created the Housing Production Trust Fund to fill the gap for tenants' associations unable to secure private financing, it is not a stable source of funding. The fund's financing (a percentage of deed-recordation fees and transfer taxes on real estate sales) makes it dependent on a healthy real estate market. However, even in the flushest of times, housing advocates view the fund as insufficient to meet the need across the city (Pierre 2007).

The city has also been erratic in how it disburses money from the fund and other reserves for low-income home buyers. Tenant purchasers at Mayfair Mansions, for example, were promised one amount only to have it reduced over time. The reduction meant that many of them could no longer qualify for loans to purchase their units. A similar fate has befallen other low-income tenants trying to secure city financing to buy their buildings and apartments (DePillis 2010a).

The city has also allowed tenants to work with inexperienced nonprofit developers. By law tenants can choose their third-party partners, but the city could influence those choices with sticks and carrots. It could, for example, withhold construction loans from companies without proven track records at condo conversion. It could also provide tenants with lists of developers who have successfully completed projects. Unfortunately, the city often seems to use its sticks erratically, hurting potential tenant borrowers while failing to intervene when it could and should do so. Mayfair Mansion's development partner, Marshall Heights, had never done a large condo conversion before it signed on to help tenants buy several of the garden-style apartment buildings in the complex and convert them to condo. After several management transitions, much busywork for tenants, and months of waiting, the buildings slated for conversion were put into foreclosure proceedings, moving tenants slated for ownership back into the renter's seat they had hoped to vacate.

What are we to make of these results? In the next section I describe the difficulty I had in answering that question. Not only did TOPA's hybridity stymie my efforts; I also discovered that even when a given provision in the statute—for example, the right-to-buy—fit squarely within a given analytic category, it would often play out in unexpected ways.

Trying to Put a Round Peg in a Square Hole

The summer of 2010 was the first time someone told me that TOPA's main goal was empowerment. I was sitting across the table from Rick Eisen, a prominent tenant lawyer in the city and had just asked him if TOPA was meeting its goal in mitigating displacement. Eisen replied that the statute's real goal, and where its power lay, was in "empowering tenants."[2]

As I progressed with my research, I would hear the same sentiment from others. However, I was skeptical. The original legislation laid out a rationale for the statute that rested heavily on grappling with problems of displacement and the precipitous decline in the city's affordable-housing stock. In fact, the term "empowerment" does not even appear in the statute. The language that most closely approximates it is a phrase about improving tenants' "bargaining position" in the statute's first goal:

> Discourage the displacement of tenants through conversion or sale of rental property, and to strengthen the bargaining position of tenants towards that and without unduly interfering with the rights of property to the due process of law. (*Rental Housing* 1980, 3)

Even if we accept Eisen's interpretation, we must still ask what kind of empowerment the statute offers. Neoliberal interpretations of empowerment are quite different from those proffered under the broad rubric of social justice. Moreover, how one assesses that empowerment depends on one's political standpoint.

In neoliberal circles empowerment is often defined with reference to what it is not—dependence on government for food, shelter, and work (Hayek 1944). In the context of housing, this means that neoliberals see programs like public housing or rent control as mechanisms to rob their beneficiaries of initiative and, so disenfranchised, to chain them to government. In this interpretive context, condo conversion is a mechanism for empowerment because it gives people an opportunity to become owners, thereby cutting their dependence on landlords (and government protections like rent control) to meet a basic human need.

Not surprisingly, critics of neoliberalism view empowerment differently. Although there are a variety of alternatives to neoliberalism—anarchism,

---

2. For a list of interviewees and interview dates, see Appendix 3.

Marxism, neo-Keynesianism[3]—most advocates from these schools of thought believe empowerment comes from reclaiming the "urban commons" that have been taken from the many by neoliberal regimes and given to the few (McCarthy 2005; Lee and Webster 2006). Attempts to reclaim the urban commons are often discursively articulated, at least by academics, as a fight for the "right to the city" (Mitchell 2001, 2003; Purcell 2003). What neoliberals call empowerment is often referred to by critics as "accumulation by dispossession" because ownership is frequently accomplished by privatizing public goods (Harvey 2008; Glassman 2006; Negi and Auerbach 2009). For critics of neoliberalism, then, condo conversion is a negative phenomenon, dispossessing vulnerable residents of their housing so that those with higher incomes might buy them.

When I began my study, I assumed I would be able to classify TOPA using one of these analytic categories. In particular, I reasoned that if tenants were able to use TOPA to stay put—that is, to assert some local control over gentrification processes—I could classify it under a social-justice rubric. However, if only wealthy tenants were able to use TOPA or if most incumbent tenants could not make TOPA work for them, then the conversions that ensued would be neoliberal and something I would not support. I quickly discovered, however, that measuring success was no simple matter. Although it was relatively easy to count how many people stayed put, there was no established threshold for claiming success. Was a stay-put rate of 50 percent or greater sufficient, or did I need a supermajority to declare the statute a success? I was also unsure how to assess buyouts. If a tenants' association unanimously supported offering buyouts, should I focus on the benefits buyouts brought to incumbent tenants or the disadvantages that awaited potential future tenants trying to rent bought-out units? Early on in my research, I realized that TOPA simply would not fit into any one analytic category.

I was still reluctant, however, to abandon my theoretical guideposts. Theory is helpful precisely because it allows us to situate localized events in wider processes and, in comparing the outcomes to theoretical benchmarks, to make wider political judgments about them. To that end, I decided to engage in a conceptual exercise. I would see if I could discern a balance between the statute's neoliberal and social-justice elements. I reasoned that I could still theoretically classify TOPA if one of its imperatives was dominant and, so classified, make an overall political assessment of it. Instead, I found that TOPA's contradictory imperatives were deeply entangled. Moreover, its

---

3. Proposed solutions are also quite varied. They include organized squatting (Lehrer and Winkler 2006), market opt-outs (Huron 2012), and pragmatic defenses of welfare state safety nets (Reed 2012; Lazere and Pohlman 2008).

imperatives often unfolded in ways that defied theoretical expectation. Two examples serve to demonstrate.

TOPA: A Privatized Solution for the Collective

A key contradiction in the TOPA statute can be found in the disconnect between *how* TOPA helps and *who* it helps. Specifically, though TOPA's solution is neoliberal (ownership), it is designed to help a collective rather than individuals.

Like most municipal statute drafters, TOPA's architects never made an attempt to place their bill in wider academic debates. However, the bill can be categorized (post facto) as neoliberal in two key ways. First, the solution it provided for tenants caught up in a real estate boomlet was ownership. Instead of protecting tenants' homes from redevelopment (e.g., with a comprehensive condo-conversion ban) or investing in low-income housing (e.g., buying multifamily properties and reserving them for low-income rentals), the statute gave tenants market power. They were given the right to buy their building if and when their landlord decided to sell it. In short, TOPA allowed tenants to engage in what *Washington Post* real estate columnist Benny Kass has called "tenant capitalism" (2004).

A second and related element that gives TOPA neoliberal standing is the role of private capital in making it happen. In buildings with mixed incomes, the city plays virtually no role in the process except to manage process-related filings. Moreover, though the city provides assistance to nonprofit developers working with low-income tenants, it is usually in the form of loans rather than grants and, if necessary, can be recouped through seizure of collateral. The foreclosure of Mayfair Mansions, for example, was initiated by the city. In short, TOPA is a private solution for a public problem[4]—the restoration of the city's aging multifamily housing stock and its continued availability to low- and moderate-income city residents. As Eric Rome observed in our interview:

> The city's philosophy is, you know, we all agree we need more affordable housing, and we need more dollars poured into affordable housing. You know, that's a no-brainer. Everyone agrees. But the city's idea is to put that, you know—to put that mostly on the backs of private developers and to deny their own responsibility for that.

---

4. Although the housing stock in capitalist economies is primarily in private hands, cities have a vested interest in the social reproduction of their workforce. Cities often intervene in local housing markets to ensure sufficient supply and, in some cases, affordability.

Despite TOPA's neoliberal form, the bill's structure mirrors antineoliberal perspectives in one key way. It was structured to serve a durable, long-standing urban collective—the tenants' association. Indeed, one of the most important parts of the statute, although one little remarked on, is that the right of refusal is granted to a tenants' association rather than individual tenants. If tenants fail to form a tenants' association, register it with the city, and ultimately do what is required to refuse a sale, the original contract of sale proceeds and individual tenants within a building have no right to buy their units. Only a tenants' association can unlock the rights extended by the statute.

It is also worth noting that the neoliberal benefit TOPA provides does not operate in the ways predicted by critical scholars. That is, the collective, in this case the tenants' association, does not experience dispossession. A percentage of tenants in all of the buildings in my sample stayed put, for example, and some did so as home owners. These units became a tangible asset, a mechanism for building wealth. Indeed, even if one takes the position that the city should focus on ensuring affordability rather than home ownership for low-income residents, it is hard to see this process as a form of dispossession. The same can be said of tenants taking buyouts. Although tenants leave, there is no dispossession involved because tenants have a choice between staying put or taking a buyout. As Eric Rome told me in our interview, TOPA allows paying rent to finally pay off: "It's about transferring economic power to the tenant and to give you some power based on all the rent you've paid over the years, and the legislative history reflects that as an economic empowerment tool." In short, though TOPA is thoroughly neoliberal in its capacity to turn renters into home owners, it also works for a collective not usually the beneficiary of neoliberal policies, and in ways that counter accepted wisdom about who the market usually rewards and how.

TOPA Tenants: Divided but Not Dispossessed

A second key contradiction is that while the TOPA process ultimately divides tenants' associations (between those who stay put and those who leave), this division is not the result of a divide-and-conquer strategy meant to facilitate dispossession. The statute gives tenants' associations the power to buy their own buildings, or to select who does, and to set the terms, if not the price,[5] for doing so. For buildings that opt to stay rental, TOPA boils down to "pick[ing] your own landlord," as Rome put it. This power is one of the reasons landlords, their attorneys, and some developers despise the TOPA agreement despite its capitalist trappings. It gives power to

---

5. Recall that TOPA requires tenants to match the initial contracted sale price.

the "wrong" people in capitalism—those with little money and traditionally little bargaining power. The court battle that ensued after the Bernsteins' portfolio sale in 2004 provides a good example. Although attorneys for the initial buyer, Carmel Partners, tried to have the tenants' case dismissed on the grounds that it would amount to an unconstitutional taking, their real problem seems to have been less about taking and more about who was doing the taking. The source of their indignation was clearly signaled when, in *Richman Towers Tenants' Association, Inc. v. Richman Towers LLC*, Carmel's attorneys described TOPA as a tool for the "redistribution of wealth." Much to the chagrin of landlords and those who represent them, TOPA fundamentally opens up who can accumulate or benefit from real property–derived capital accumulation.

The primary problem for those wishing to use TOPA as a form of "resistance" is that the division of the collective prevents it from resisting displacement outside a narrow time frame and building-specific location. The key function of a tenants' association is to manage the process by which the collective will divide itself (between those staying put and those leaving) and what benefits will accrue to each side (e.g., buyout amounts, insider prices, building improvements). In buildings staying rental, for example, negotiations over buyout amounts help determine how many tenants stay put and how many leave. The same can be said of insider prices. The degree to which units are priced below market helps determine how many tenants stay and how many leave. In the end, the very right that cements collective action also leads to its fragmentation.

What all of this means for resistance is equally contradictory. While TOPA allows particular groups of tenants the power to set the terms by which they will deal with one manifestation of gentrification, it is a temporary power. As a result, TOPA is a poor springboard for future, more durable resistance.

Political Assessment

Unsatisfactory Options

Because TOPA is impervious to theoretical disambiguation, it was difficult to make a political assessment based on its fit with my (or any) preferred approach to urban problems. In the absence of a clear theoretical benchmark, I turned to a more organic array of options for evaluating TOPA, three of which I detail here.

The first is to reject TOPA on purist grounds. Given my framing—that local autonomy is preferable to neoliberal urbanism—this would mean rejecting the statute on the grounds that its neoliberal components damn the promise offered by its social-justice ethos and its collectivist components. It would also mean labeling tenants who take buyouts or consent to voluntary agreements as complicit in neoliberal practices that strip the city of affordable housing. Indeed, buyouts and voluntary agreements reproduce neoliberal norms inasmuch as individual gains undercut the collective promise of the statute. A purist response would be generally consistent with those who argue that the only way to successfully confront neoliberalism is to fully pull out of its orbit (i.e., to adopt anarchism; for more on this, see Springer 2012).

Unfortunately, scholars who have looked at instances of tenants trying to opt-out of the market in their search for housing tell a cautionary tale (DeFilippis 2004; Huron 2012). Huron's (2012) analysis of tenants using TOPA to create LECs is a case in point. The idea behind LECs is to limit equity so affordability is maintained over time. Huron's analysis shows, however, that people living in LECs cannot fully divorce themselves from the market, even when they want to. Many potential buyers still need loans to purchase shares, but banks often refuse to extend credit for property that will not appreciate. Likewise, shareholders in LECs sometimes question why they are playing by rules that few others accept and that are disadvantageous to boot. These feelings can emerge at any time but are especially common during real estate booms, when the value of neighboring properties spikes and co-op members question their decision to forgo home equity as a mechanism for building wealth.[6] There is, it turns out, no easy way to go off the neoliberal grid in an urban context.

A second response is to embrace TOPA because it is the only game in town. And because TOPA does help low-income people, it should be supported and protected (Lazere 2013; Reed 2013a). Indeed, without RHCSA, tenants would have no leverage during periods of intense gentrification. They would not, for example, be able to disrupt a contracted sale of their building or, as a result, determine (or even influence) a new landlord's plan for the building. If a new landlord wanted to convert to condominium, tenants would not have the right (per CRHCC) to veto the plan. Similarly, even if tenants supported conversion, they would have no claim to their particular unit or the opportunity to bargain for insider prices. When considered in this light, TOPA's problems carry less weight. They can be endured, tweaked, or managed because TOPA's benefits outweigh its costs.

This view is largely consistent with the approach taken by a majority of the city's low-income-housing advocates. Because TOPA is the city's main tool for dealing with displacement, most groups have focused their efforts

---

6. Some LECs in the city have transitioned back to standard co-ops so that tenants can earn more equity (Huron 2012).

on strengthening city programs that make it possible for low-income tenants to effectively use the TOPA process (Reed 2013a; Lazere 2013; Lazere and Pohlman 2008). The deputy director of the DC Fiscal Policy Institute (DCFPI), Jenny Reed, explained to me that her organization has focused most of its TOPA work on evaluating city programs that help low-income tenants better use TOPA:

> Most of the work that I have done around TOPA has actually been around DHCD's First Right Purchase Program—on the program the city has to help tenants who want to purchase their building who can't get financing on the private market on their own.

This focus makes sense. Groups that advocate for low-income citizens, and sustainable policies for them, will obviously tailor their effort to meet the needs of their target population.

The problem is that no one has been tracking how TOPA plays out in contexts where tenants partner with for-profit developers and use mechanisms like buyouts and voluntary agreements.[7] My data suggest that many of the city's low-income population live in buildings that are mixed income. In my sample, all of the buildings that worked with private developers (rather than through the city) had some low-income residents. Moreover, my data on the effects of buyouts and voluntary agreements on housing costs demonstrate that these buildings become less economically diverse post-buyout. In fact, voluntary agreements hasten these shifts since they set *all* "next-resident rents" at market rates. Even in units where tenants stay put through the TOPA process, voluntary agreements stipulate that rents can be raised beyond rent-control limits as soon as these residents leave. Given high mobility rates in cities, voluntary agreements effectively eliminate the intended drag that rent control is supposed to have on the rate and pace of rent increases.

A third response is an academic version of the colloquialism "it is what it is." In academic terms, this is an argument for recognizing the complexity that attends the translation of ideals into policy and policy into outcomes. Put another way, theoretical categories are always upended because the way policy works on the ground is subject to variables theorists can neither know nor predict. When I finished the data-collection portion of this project, my thoughts were broadly consistent with this third view. Because I was immersed in the details of the conversion process—setting insider prices,

---

7. Reed told me in our interview that her organization has just begun to look at the buyout issue. "It's actually a conversation we are having now," she told me. DCFPI's scrutiny will be much welcomed.

negotiating buyout amounts, debating voluntary agreements—it felt difficult to tie my findings back to something theoretically coherent.

All three of these views are, however, politically unsatisfactory. The first is the most ideologically consistent, but it is also utopian inasmuch as no one has figured out how to successfully pull out of neoliberal modes of production, consumption, and social reproduction. Likewise, while the optimism that surrounds TOPA is easy to understand—it *has* kept people in place—it is hard to justify in the face of evidence about how it contributes to and even hastens exclusionary displacement. It is harder still to stake a political claim on an approach that amounts to "this is better than nothing." Though the sentiment may be true, it is equally true that TOPA is probably worse than something else too. The final view is also unsatisfactory because it provides no guidance for understanding how DC's experience fits into wider urban trends.

A Way Out?

In his book *City Futures*, Edgar Pieterse (2008) describes the difficulty in pinning down what is and is not liberatory in contemporary cities. Although focused on cities in the global south, his view resonates with me. Pieterse describes the literature on cities in the global south as marked by two competing narratives. On the one hand are scholars like Mike Davis (2006), who provide "a relentless catalogue of the utterly devastating conditions that characterize the daily lives of the majority of the world's urban dwellers" (Pieterse 2008, 2). For Davis, the only response is militancy by the urban poor. On the other hand are those who display an "irrepressible optimism" (2) about the urban future in the global south. Yes, conditions are bad, they say, but policy makers just have to work harder to find technical fixes for them.

Pieterse (2008) expresses frustration with both of these frames because they seem oblivious to their failings. Militancy, for example, comes with high costs for those engaged in it. There is also no evidence the urban poor are organized enough to pull off a revolution in one city, let alone in multiple ones. Likewise, technocratic responses have been deployed for decades without stopping the depredations Davis (2006) viscerally recounts.

In response, Pieterse (2008) posits a new approach that combines what he calls "radical incrementalism" and "recursive political empowerment." According to Pieterse, radical incrementalism is based on two notions: first, that we should continue to strive for radical change and, second, that we should temper our enthusiasm for it by recognizing that change "cannot be wish[ed] into existence." In practical terms this means "bringing change into the world through more discrete avenues: surreptitious, sometimes overt, and multiple small revolutions that at unanticipated and unexpected moments galvanize into deeper ruptures that accelerate tectonic shifts" (6–7).

Recursive political empowerment serves as a corollary to radical incrementalism. It, too, is centered on two premises. The first is that making things better for "the poor and abandoned requires agency by these very same constituencies" (Pieterse 2008, 7). Second, because the poor are rarely part of cohesive collectives and rarely define themselves through the labels academics assign to them (e.g., the disenfranchised, the subaltern, the working class, etc.), empowerment is at least in the first instance individual. As Pieterse argues, "Empowerment is fundamentally an individual process that deepens with time if individual efforts are consciously embedded in more collective forms of solidary and mutual empowerment" (8).

How, then, can we apply these concepts in not only locating TOPA's political promise but also thinking through its future political promise?[8] In the remainder of the chapter I explore these concepts as they relate to three elements of the TOPA process—the right of first refusal, buyouts, and voluntary agreements.

The Right of First Refusal
The right of refusal is the linchpin of the TOPA statute. Refusing a contracted sale is what gives tenants control (i.e., agency) over their buildings and future decisions about them. They can choose a new owner or opt to own the building collectively. They can also decide what sort of tenure they want—rental, condo, or co-op. Finally, they can direct the type and scope of improvements made to their buildings.

The right of first refusal is often described as a right-to-buy program. In a technical sense this depiction is accurate. By refusing a sale, tenants notify the city that they will buy their building outright, or with assistance from a third party. However, the right of first refusal is no ordinary right-to-buy program.

Right-to-buy programs are usually thought of as encouraging neoliberal citizenship because they privilege ownership over renting and thus create a moral economy in which renting and, by extension, renters are deemed inferior, deviant, and/or pathological (Blomley 2005). Indeed, as a vehicle for expanding ownership in cities, condominiums are seen as cleansing the city

---

8. Although Edgar Pieterse's work has been exceptionally influential in the urban studies literature, most of the work has (rightly) focused on discussing his conceptual contributions in relation to cities in the global south (see Ernstson, Lawhon, and Duminy 2014; Ranganathan 2014). Thus, my efforts to tie his concepts back to the global north and issues specific to it are exploratory and ongoing.

of renters and their presumed pathologies and, in so doing, paving the way for enclosure of the urban commons (Kern and Wekerle 2008).

The right of refusal in the TOPA statute, however, does not automatically translate into home ownership. In fact, any shift in a building's tenure is decided by tenants themselves. The requirements of CRHCC also mean that a building can convert to condos only if a majority of residents (50 percent plus 1) vote to allow it. To me, one of the most surprising findings from my research was that what many observers construe as a right-to-buy program can, in fact, be used to maintain a building's rental tenure. In this regard, TOPA's right-to-buy provision represents an incremental yet radical shift in how a presumably neoliberal process functions, who drives it, and whose interests it serves.

Buyouts

Buyouts are a common part of the TOPA process. Tenants use them to attract developers who want as many units as possible for market-rate pricing. While there is no doubt that buyouts benefit developers, I was surprised to realize that they could also benefit tenants. Indeed, the suspicion I felt in my initial interview with Rick Eisen lessened when I spoke to tenants who had taken buyouts. Both of the tenants I interviewed at the Squire told me their buyouts were "liberating." Both used them to pay down heavy student-loan debt—a burden especially relevant for millennials, whose college costs have been much higher than in any prior generation. Unburdened of their debt, both men felt free to make life choices previously unavailable to them. Eric Rome also brought this point home for me in our interview:

> It [the buyout] just gives people a new chance in life. If you're weighted down by student-loan debt, or you're weighted off by credit-card debt, and you just lay awake at night going, "How am I ever going to do this?" Okay, you get out of it all at once, and maybe you pay a little more rent. But it's like a new lease on life.

Buyouts also flip the standard neoliberal script. A key criticism of neoliberalism is that urban-renewal schemes come at the expense of low-income and other working-class people. They are often dispossessed by such programs, kicked out of buildings undergoing conversion, forced out of homeless shelters slated for redevelopment, and harassed by police ordered to make new arrivals feel safe. Here, however, TOPA forces landlords and developers to share in the accumulation they claim in gentrifying contexts. As I note in Chapter 6, these shares can be significant. After following TOPA for so many years, I grew accustomed to hearing about buyout amounts in the

$50,000 range. These are extraordinary amounts when compared to those in other cities where tenants forced to move often consider themselves lucky to be reimbursed for moving expenses.

In this regard, buyouts can be seen as radical because they open up accumulation to tenants who had previously been locked out of such processes and in some cases were victims of them. They are also radical in that they do not require tenants to accumulate in prescribed ways. Indeed, a buyout gives tenants an opportunity to reject neoliberalism's preferred mechanism for wealth accumulation—home ownership.

We cannot, of course, declare buyouts wholly revolutionary. They come at a high cost for future tenants. In my sample, all bought-out units were brought up to market rates, meaning low- and moderate-income tenants who would have been able to afford them in the past will be excluded from them in the future. Unfortunately, Pieterse (2008) provides little guidance for how to define radical incrementalism in the particular context of neoliberalism. Indeed, there is great variation in the sorts of actions people can take within a neoliberal system. Some can be radical, upending neoliberal expectations; others can be neutral; still others can end up reproducing neoliberalism's worst tendencies. In some cases people can take actions that work at cross-purposes—limiting neoliberal excesses in one realm while exacerbating them in others. How, then, do we interpret a process like buyouts, which arguably has radical and complicit elements?

The first step is to realize that people living at the bottom of the urban social scale will not necessarily see the ties that bind them to others on the same rung. Although the left often wants members of oppressed groups (whether renters, minorities, or the homeless) to recognize and claim solidarity with their fellow group members as well as those in similarly stationed groups, they frequently do not. In the case of TOPA this means embracing the empowerment buyouts bring, even if that empowerment is for individuals rather than the tenant class at large. It also means not impugning those who embrace individual empowerment or eliminating avenues for it.

None of this is to suggest, of course, that individual empowerment should stand alone. Rather, it should be paired with efforts to protect the affordability of bought-out units. Additionally, support for buyouts does not mean progressive avenues for creating solidarities between categories of renters is impossible. In fact, the city could play a role in both arenas. It could, for example, purchase a portion of bought-out units and subsidize their prices for qualified low-income buyers. This approach is already similar to what the city does now with its First Right Purchase Program. The primary advantage here is that it would also provide a mechanism for building bridges between categories of tenants. That is, it would give tenants in TOPA buildings a way to address the negative fallout that often attends a decision to convert to condo. These ideas are, of course, merely starting suggestions. The larger, more important point is that a wholesale rejection of buyouts is not the answer.

Voluntary Agreements

In many ways the problems associated with voluntary agreements are no different from those associated with buyouts in the context of condo conversion. Just like TOPA buildings that convert to condo, those that sign voluntary agreements substantially increase housing costs. I argue, however, that voluntary agreements are insidious because they undermine both the TOPA and rent-control statutes. The city's rent-control ordinance should protect against exclusionary displacement in TOPA buildings staying rental. Instead, voluntary agreements hasten exclusionary displacement because vacancies (through buyout or later attrition) always result in an immediate, rather than gradual, increase to market rate.

Unlike buyouts, however, voluntary agreements contain no radical or empowering elements. I would classify them as extortionary inasmuch as developers often hold tenants hostage to them. Tenant leaders in the Squire and Harvard/Summit, for example, told me that third-party developers would agree to work with tenants only if tenants agreed to voluntary agreements. Moreover, tenants usually accept voluntary agreements in the abstract, before exact figures for new rents are determined. This was the case at the Harvard/Summit property. And once its tenant leaders saw the new rents, they had little leeway to challenge them because developers had tied completion of buildingwide improvements to the execution of the agreement.

In tenant-advocacy circles there is sometimes sharp disagreement about voluntary agreements. Eric Rome, who was the attorney for two of the tenants' associations in my sample (the Squire and Harvard/Summit), believes they are necessary because few developers will willingly invest in buildings without market-rate returns. However, as I discovered during my research, other individuals and groups working with tenants' associations vehemently disagree. One anonymous tenant advocate responded to that assertion by telling me, "That's a lie. That's an absolute lie. Or a disservice to the truth." This individual also noted that developers who rely on investors are more likely to require voluntary agreements than those who do not. An example is UIP, the company Harvard/Summit worked with and that I discuss in Chapter 6. The interviewee explained, "UIP's argument is that we live off of investor money, and investors expect a percentage return, and therefore, no matter what, we have to pay our investors off." Fortunately, not all for-profit developers rely on investor money to stay afloat, so returns can be spread over a longer period of time. This interview subject also noted that companies like UIP often use voluntary agreements as a backdoor way to empty more units after the TOPA process is complete. In particular, while they promise systemwide repairs (e.g., new plumbing), they refuse to do repairs until the voluntary agreement takes effect, usually about a year and a half after a TOPA process begins. During this period developers will offer tenants frustrated with slow repairs informal buyouts—a mechanism that ensures that even more units move to market rate.

I believe the policy response to voluntary agreements should be to eliminate them or significantly curtail them. There are a variety of ways this could be done. A soft approach would entail more regulatory oversight. The city's rent-control administrator, who must approve voluntary agreements before they take force, rarely makes radical changes to developers' proposed new rents in voluntary agreements. Though the city's rent-control administrator has told the press that she usually rejects most first-run voluntary agreements—see Lyda DePillis's (2012a) profile of UIP in the *Washington City Paper*—the final, approved agreements provide little solace for those hoping the city will step in to protect affordability. As I demonstrate in Chapter 6, *none* of the new rents listed in the Harvard/Summit's voluntary agreement are affordable for low-income tenants. Given these facts, it is perhaps not surprising that I rarely heard the rent-control administrator mentioned by name or office during my research on TOPA. It was as if the position did not exist as far as the TOPA process was concerned. This is not a necessary condition. Elected officials have the power to transform how city agencies regulate TOPA. The elimination of the 95/5 loophole happened only because a city councilmember—Jim Graham—publicized how DCRA handled requests for TOPA exemptions and in so doing garnered support for his bill to close the loophole. The city could also take a hard-line approach, rewriting the rent-control statute to eliminate voluntary agreements altogether or capping the increases at only slightly higher than currently allowed levels (e.g., from the current cap of 10 percent to 12 percent). At present, there is no ceiling for how much rents can be raised via voluntary agreement.

To work within the market system that governs the TOPA process in mixed-income buildings, it will also be necessary for city officials to take a greater role in grappling with the displacement occurring within its boundaries. At a discursive level, this will require the city to alter how it describes and explains the ongoing changes within its boundaries and to take some responsibility for them.

The necessity of discursive work was crystallized for me in the summer of 2013 when I read an article in the *Washington Post* about gentrification on 14th Street, a major thoroughfare that cuts through two of the city's current gentrification hotspots—the U Street corridor and Columbia Heights (Shin 2013). The author, Annys Shin, observed that gentrification on 14th Street went into "overdrive" after the 2008 recession. Leery of the stock market, nervous investors decided that real estate would be "a safe place to park hundreds of millions of dollars." According to Shin, twelve hundred new condos and apartments and nearly twenty-five new bars and restaurants opened on the street in a single nine-month period. Not surprisingly, the investment boom was mirrored in rents, which reached $2,700 per month.

My first reaction to Shin's article was alarm. If investors were looking for a place to temporarily park their cash, would they move it as soon as returns were higher elsewhere? I was also worried. How many low- and middle-income residents had been pushed out by the new luxury in their midst? Then, curiosity took over. Did new and old residents ignore one another or engage in battles over parking, smoking, yard ornaments, and the like?

In contrast, the reaction by city leaders was positive, even exultant. When Shin checked in with Harriet Tregoning, the city's director of the Office of Planning, to see what she thought about the area's rapid turnaround, she responded, "What is going on on 14th Street is fascinating, anomalous and wonderful for the city" (Shin 2013).

I was surprised but should not have been. A year earlier I had interviewed an anonymous, high-level city official about the approach the city had used to shape its revitalization efforts. I wanted to know if the individual thought the city had intentionally adopted the so-called adult strategy discussed in Chapter 2 to frame its efforts. Although the official answered with an emphatic no—"I think that's 100 percent the opposite of what we're doing"—the explanation that the official offered for the city's changing socioeconomic profile was as oblivious to gentrification's downsides as Tregoning's comments seemed to be. Instead of acknowledging the trade-offs any city would face in trying to rebuild itself, the individual suggested that gentrification was natural, the result of wider demographic shifts in the country.

> City official: So the demographics of the Western world are changing. Right? People are living longer. The population is getting older. You know, Japan is one very attenuated end of that spectrum, right?
> Gallaher: Mm-hm. Yeah.
> City official: Where they have a very, very large and growing population of elderly supported by an increasingly small population of young people. So in many ways, in urban America, in the growing cities of the U.S., we are seeing the population trends that the rest of the U.S. will see just a little bit earlier. So we have the population that the rest of the U.S. might see in around 2050 in terms of household size, in terms of the distribution of age in some ways, and in terms of diversity. So one of the enormous phenomena of the last several decades is the trend toward

smaller-sized households. At this point, only about 20 percent of DC households have school-aged children, and that's just part of a larger demographic trend. People have children later. Many more households decide not to have children. When they do have children, they typically have smaller families than they had before, and finally, of all the households in the city, there are just so many of them that are not composed of people who are of child-bearing age.

Although the demographics of the Western world are indeed changing, this individual's response seemed especially tone-deaf in a city radically altered by gentrification. As I note in Chapter 2, the city's changing racial and economic dynamics do not match those of the metro area as a whole. The changes in DC have also happened far too rapidly for longer-term demographic shifts to explain them.

The city also needs to be more involved in filling the gaps in the TOPA program. When I interviewed Eric Rome, however, he was not hopeful, suggesting the city was turning a blind eye to the wider problems that TOPA's limitations bring to light. I asked him, "So what could the city do to attain not just racial diversity but economic diversity that it's not already doing?" He replied:

> The answer—the simplest answer is more money, more dollars for affordable housing. You know, more of a commitment. You know, I don't have the answer. I'm not a policy person; I'm not a city planner; I don't have the answers. I'm an attorney who's been around a while, but what I keep saying to people is that the city—I don't know what the plan is, but the city needs a plan. The city doesn't have a plan.

To illustrate the city's approach, Rome mentioned a law that I had never heard of before our interview:

> The city has this District Opportunity to Purchase Act, something called DOPA, which the city has never used. If the tenants turn it down [i.e., fail to act on a TOPA notice], they [landlords] have to also send an offer to the city. So if the tenants fail to exercise their right, they have to send an offer to the city. So the city gets a right to purchase.

DOPA was designed to provide a safety net of sorts around the TOPA process. Of course, as Rome noted, DC cannot act as the landlord of last resort for all of its citizens, but if used sparingly, the statute could allow the city to save buildings where it could have the greatest impact. However, as Rome explained in our interview, "It's never been used. Never been used." The city could and should consider dusting off the statute and putting it to use.

In the Final Instance

I first learned about TOPA in a personal way, by going through the process in my building. It felt like a remarkable gift. I knew my life was about to change, and though I was terrified (of our developers, a sudden shift in the market, a shrinking bank account), I could not believe my luck. The idea of owning a tiny slice of my beloved neighborhood felt like an unexpected gift. Throughout the next decade, the potent combination of fear, excitement, even occasional giddiness never completely left me. With each new tenant leader I spoke to, I could remember each of these feelings individually and in combination.

However, it is also true that over time the charge was tempered by the contradictions TOPA presented. I was reminded that my fear was not an unreasonable reaction, that TOPA does not work for every tenants' association, and involves rounds and rounds of difficult decisions. As a result, my early feelings, that TOPA felt special, even a little revolutionary, seem somehow misplaced, both personally, as I initially felt them, and politically.

None of this means, however, that TOPA is not incrementally radical. It allows for surreptitious forms of radical change and provides venues for individual and local empowerment in a context usually marked by dispossession. Though it would be easy to dismiss TOPA because of its inconsistencies and limitations, options for building local autonomy outside market forces are few in number. City funds are too sparse to build a sizable base, and tenant-driven initiatives like LECs are themselves often dependent on the market for success. So trying to improve hybrid models like TOPA makes political sense. A safety net stitched from uniform cloth might be preferable, but a patchwork can suffice in the interim.

TOPA has real problems, of course, but by conceiving of radical change as something that can happen incrementally, we also acknowledge that imperfect policy interventions can be of pragmatic and political use. TOPA as a whole is not radical, but it can produce moments that feel and act radical, and that is a starting point for wider political empowerment of not just individual tenants but collectives of them.

Appendix 1

Glossary of Terms

Buyout: In the TOPA context, a sum of money a third-party developer gives to a tenant in exchange for the tenant agreeing to vacate the unit and relinquish any TOPA-related claim to it. Landlords may offer buyouts to tenants outside the TOPA context, but they are less common and do not come with stipulations related to the TOPA process.

Condominium: A multifamily residential structure in which individual units are privately owned; may also refer to a privately owned unit in a multifamily residential structure. A condo owner owns his or her unit outright as well as a share in the common elements of the multifamily structure, including stairways, elevators, hallways, shared plumbing, grounds, and so on.

Co-op: A multifamily residential structure in which residents own a share of the property; may also refer to an individual unit in a multifamily residential structure. When a person purchases a share in a co-op, he or she receives exclusive rights to a specific residential unit within the multifamily structure. He or she also owns a share in the common elements of the multifamily structure, including stairways, elevators, hallways, shared plumbing, grounds, and so on.

Direct displacement: A situation in which a tenant is forced to leave his or her rental property because the cost of the unit has become unaffordable (e.g., a steep rent hike) or the physical condition of the unit has become uninhabitable (e.g., crumbling ceilings, no or limited heat, etc.). Although tenants can be displaced from rental units at any time, incidents of direct displacement increase during periods of gentrification.

Exclusionary displacement: A situation in which a unit is voluntarily vacated but then made unavailable for a renter who could have afforded the unit at its most recent rate. Exclusion can be caused by a steep increase in rent, a tenure change (from rental apartment to condo), or a building's demolition, among other factors.

Housing Production Trust Fund: A District of Columbia trust fund established to encourage the building and/or preservation of affordable housing in the District. The fund finances city programs that help tenants going through the TOPA process. It also assists for- and nonprofit developers constructing and refurbishing affordable-housing units in the city.

Insider price: The price that tenants in a TOPA conversion pay for their apartment-cum-condominium. Insider prices are usually below the market price for similarly sized/apportioned units in the same neighborhood. Tenants negotiate for insider prices on their units by offering third-party developers the right to offer buyouts to incumbent tenants. Bought-out units are then sold at market rates.

Right of first refusal: A provision in the TOPA statute that gives tenants the right to refuse a contracted sale and to make the purchase instead for the contracted sale price.

Tenants' association: A small body of tenants elected by fellow tenants on a given property to represent tenant interests in informal and formal negotiations with landlords, city officials, developers, and so on. In the TOPA process, key rights, such as the right of first refusal, are awarded to tenants' associations rather than individual tenants.

TOPA notice: A provision of the RHCSA that requires landlords of residential properties to inform tenants when they plan to sell (or have already contracted to sell) their property. Once tenants receive a TOPA notice, they have thirty days to refuse the sale. A TOPA notice is formally known "an offer of sale notice."

Voluntary agreement: One of five ways a landlord can legally raise residential rents beyond existing caps on yearly rent increases established in the District of Columbia's rent-control statute. For a voluntary agreement to take effect, 70 percent of all tenants must agree to the higher rate of increase and sign the landlord's petition requesting it.

Appendix 2

A Short Primer on Condominiums

In the United States there are two types of ownership: individual and collective.[1] Under an individual form of ownership, a titleholder owns a given property (a dwelling and the land beneath it) and has exclusive rights to it. In collective ownership, at least some elements of a property are held in common by two or more individual owners. The three most common types of collective ownership today are townhouses, condominiums, and cooperatives (co-ops).

TYPES OF COLLECTIVE OWNERSHIP

Although townhouses, condominiums, and co-ops are all collectively owned, there are important differences in how collective ownership is organized in each. When a person purchases a townhouse, for example, he or she gains title to the home and the land underneath it. A townhouse owner also owns a share in common elements. Townhouses are usually built in rows, meaning that most share a wall with neighbors on one or both sides. Owners of townhouses also own a share of common areas, such as green space, recreational facilities, and community buildings.

When a person buys a condominium, he or she purchases exclusive ownership of a given unit as well as a share in common elements. Unlike townhouses, however, the

---

1. Types of ownership are distinct from types of purchase. In the United States, for example, property is purchased in one of four ways: fee simple, joint tenancy with right of survivorship, tenancy in common, and tenancy in entirety. These distinctions lay out how property is treated upon an owner's death and how it will be handled upon the dissolution of a marriage or partnership of owners. For a brief review, see "Types of Home Ownership" 2014.

land beneath a condo is owned in common. Moreover, because condominiums are often part of multiunit buildings, they tend to have more common elements than townhouses. Individual units in condos share not only walls with other units but also floors and ceilings (or more accurately, the supports between them). They also share ownership of the roofs, basements, hallways, lobbies, laundry facilities, and storage rooms in those buildings.

A person who purchases a unit in a cooperative does not own the individual unit he or she resides in or the land beneath it. Rather, he or she purchases a share in the entire property (which includes all units as well as common elements) and obtains exclusive rights to live in a given unit within it.

LEGAL BASIS FOR CONDOMINIUMS IN THE UNITED STATES

In the United States collective ownership of housing has existed since the late 1880s. According to Matthew Lasner (2015), the country's first collectively owned apartment building was in New York, in Manhattan, and was structured as a co-op. At the time, however, there was no legal structure in place to govern the formation of collectively owned housing, to mediate disputes between their owners, or to oversee their dissolution. Over time, cities and states began to craft such legislation, but laws remained a primarily local or state affair until the 1930s.

In response to the Great Depression, Franklin Roosevelt's administration sought to stimulate the supply of housing for low-income citizens and make mortgages more affordable for them. The 1934 National Housing Act, for example, allowed the government to underwrite loans for developers willing to build multifamily housing. It also allowed the apartments in these dwellings to be rented or sold. Until World War II, however, none of the loans secured through the program were used to build co-ops (Lasner 2009).

After World War II developers began applying for FHA loans to build co-ops and within a decade had built "tens of thousands" of them, first in New York City and later in southern California (Lasner 2009, 385). The housing shortage in the immediate aftermath of the war made co-ops a particularly attractive option for returning soldiers who wanted to set up new households but were stymied by limited supply (Jackson 1985).

The spread of co-ops beyond large coastal cities was limited, however, by private lenders, who were leery of loaning money to either developers or buyers of co-ops. Some of the wariness was due to government regulation. In an effort to limit speculation, for example, government regulations stipulated that co-op developers had to presell most of their units before they could break ground on construction (Lasner 2015). Restrictions inherent to the model of co-op governance also inhibited lenders. Specifically, many were put off by the right of co-op boards to veto potential buyers and, thus, to undo otherwise likely sales.

In the early 1960s, collective forms of ownership took off because of two concurrent trends. The first was spurred by developers. In the early 1960s multifamily housing developers began to abandon the cooperative model of ownership in favor of the condominium model, which had been previously rare in the United States (Lasner 2015). The second happened in 1961 when the National Housing Act was amended to allow the Federal Housing Administration to insure mortgages for properties inside multifamily dwellings. After these changes collective ownership became a national phenomenon, common not just in big cities like New York and Los Angeles but also in small cities and towns across the country (Harris 2011).

GOVERNANCE OF CONDOMINIUMS

Properties involving elements of collective ownership are often referred to as common interest developments (CIDs). CIDs are governed by home owners associations (HOAs). In condominiums HOAs are usually referred to as condominium associations (CAs).[2] In cooperatives they are usually called co-op boards.

HOAs have a number of powers and responsibilities. Most HOAs charge members a monthly association fee, which covers the cost of maintaining and repairing common elements. HOAs may also charge special assessments to finance major repairs, such as a new roof, or new amenities, such as a community pool. HOAs can also place restrictions on property owners. Some restrictions relate to appearance. Many HOAs limit exterior finishes to particular color palettes and styles. Other restrictions govern the use of outdoor space, including yards, decks, patios, and balconies. Some HOAs prohibit swing sets, clotheslines, sheds, and yard ornaments.

In the United States collective ownership has both advantages and disadvantages. Condominium ownership can be ideal for those who are physically unable to do yard work or maintain the exterior elements of a house. The elderly, for example, often find yard work physically taxing. Likewise, people who are disabled frequently lack the mobility required for outdoor maintenance. Even for those with the capacity to do yard work, condo living can be appealing. People who work long hours often do not want to spend their limited free time raking leaves or mowing the grass. Condominiums built around particular lifestyles—for example, for childless people, the elderly, pet owners—can also provide an "automatic" community for people in similar stages of life or with shared interests. Condominium developments for retirees can be attractive to people who want to ensure social interactions continue after work ends and children leave the nest.

However, collective ownership can also entail any number of potential headaches. Because HOAs can set limits on how exteriors are painted and yards or patios are used, bitter fights sometimes erupt over them. In 2012, for example, an HOA in Fairfax County, Virginia, a suburb of DC, went bankrupt after a four-year legal battle with one of its members. The dispute began in 2008 when a couple in the townhouse community put a campaign sign in their yard. The sign was a few inches bigger than the HOA's rules permitted, and the HOA board contacted the offending neighbors to tell them to take it down. The couple responded by cutting the sign in half, ensuring both pieces complied with the HOA's regulations. The HOA was not amused and fined the couple $900. The couple then took the HOA to court, arguing that levying a fine was beyond the scope of the HOA's powers. After four years and multiple lawsuits, the couple ultimately prevailed. During the fight, however, association dues increased fivefold, and at its end the HOA was put into receivership (Jouvenal 2013).

---

2. In some states HOAs and CAs are governed by the same legal statutes. In other states, such as Florida, they are not. For a summary of differences between HOAs and CAs in Florida, see Direktor 2011.

While the Fairfax HOA's bankruptcy was the result of a lawsuit, delinquent fees are a more common cause of HOA bankruptcy. After the 2008 recession, fee delinquency became an acute problem for HOAs. At the height of the recession, HOAs tended to see unpaid dues from two types of people. The first were owners who lost jobs or saw their incomes decline as a result of the recession. Although some people in this situation dipped into savings to make their HOA payments, others stopped paying association dues in order to cover the mortgage or other bills. Over time, some of these owners defaulted, and their properties went into foreclosure. The second were property speculators who purchased homes and condos with the hope of flipping them for quick profit. When housing values began to decline, investors who had yet to flip were caught flat-footed. As with owner-occupied units, responses varied. Some speculators sold their units at a loss. Others held on to them but delayed or stopped paying association fees. Eventually, many of these properties went into foreclosure. A 2010 survey conducted by the Community Associations Institute, an HOA trade group, found that 32 percent of respondents had delinquency rates at 20 percent and greater. In the group's 2005 survey, by contrast, only 5 percent of respondents had delinquency rates over 10 percent (Community Associations Institute 2011, 14–15).

Even though foreclosed properties automatically transfer to banks holding the mortgages in default, banks were less-than-ideal owners during the recession. Some banks, for example, retained foreclosed properties rather than sell them. In areas hard hit by the 2008 recession, banks often had excessive inventories of foreclosed properties and insufficient staff to bring them quickly back to market. Others were simply loath to sell because of the dismal state of the market. Regardless of the banks' reasons for avoiding resale, HOAs across the country found banks were reluctant dues payers (Leposky 2012; Owers 2012; Kass 2010).

Other banks took a different, albeit equally harmful approach—they delayed foreclosing on properties in HOAs. The logic was simple. Even if a bank was no longer receiving mortgage payments on a given property, the owner, not the bank, retained ultimate responsibility for maintenance and upkeep, real estate taxes, property insurance, and association fees. Letting such properties sit until a market rebound made sense for some banks because they were able to avoid incurring extra costs on already-overvalued properties. However, it also meant that delinquent properties were not brought back to health with a new owner able to pay dues (see Kass 2010).

Unpaid fees can be devastating to HOAs, most of which use fees for maintenance and repair work as well as everyday operations. Older condos in DC, for example, often have buildingwide (rather than unit-based) heating and cooling systems. In these buildings association fees cover the cost of everyone's heating and cooling. When fees are not paid, associations can find themselves in a situation similar to that of individual home owners who lose their jobs—choosing which bills to pay and hoping unpaid ones do not result in the shutoff of key services.

Even a few foreclosures can have a negative effect on an HOA, triggering conditions that can lead to a downward spiral. When a person purchases a condo unit, for example, he or she is usually advised to review the CA's financial statements to ensure it is in good economic standing. Potential buyers are advised to avoid buying properties in buildings with poor finances. In the Fairfax HOA dispute described earlier, local real estate agents reported that buyers were leery of the complex because of its legal battles

(Jouvenal 2013). Poor HOA financials can also make it difficult for owners without economic problems to sell their properties.

FUTURE TRENDS IN CONDOMINIUMS

Condos are increasingly seen as vehicles for investment rather than as homes to live in. Many condo developers, for example, market condos to young professionals as a stepping-stone to adulthood (Kern 2010), an investment they can cash out when they are ready to buy "real" homes. In the extreme, developers and real estate brokers drop the pretense of *home* ownership altogether. Condos are not even described as temporary homes; instead, they are sold as an investment opportunity with a high rate of return.[3]

The fact that U.S. law also allows Limited Liability Corporations (LLCs) to purchase and own property also means that real estate is an ideal place to invest and simultaneously launder illicit cash. LLCs established to purchase property do not have to be registered in the name of the actual purchaser (accountants, family members, or other associates can be listed instead), so it can be difficult to ascertain who the actual owners of such properties are (Story and Saul 2015).

Although LLCs can be established for legitimate reasons, a recent *New York Times* exposé uncovered several cases of wealthy foreigners purchasing real estate in the United States with presumably stolen money (Story and Xanic von Bertrab 2015). The case of José Murat Casab, the former governor of Oaxaca, a poor state in southern Mexico, is an example. Murat Casab first began buying property in the United States in 2004 while he was still governor of Oaxaca. Although his annual salary was just over $11,500, he was able to purchase, through LLCs, several luxury condominiums in the United States, including two condos at a ski resort in Utah, one in a luxury tower in Manhattan, and still another in a beach town in South Texas. The condo in Manhattan was purchased for $1.18 million by a trust named Herrera. Given his salary and the modest means of his parents, Murat Casab is widely presumed to have made his money through the corruption that defines political life in Mexico (Story and Xanic von Bertrab 2015).

To be sure, not all condos are created equal. Global investors do not park their money in condo developments in small towns like Lynchburg, Virginia, or even bigger ones like Lexington, Kentucky. However, in the cities where they do invest in condos—New York, San Francisco, Boston, and DC, among others—the effects on the housing market are chilling. As Matthew Lasner notes in a *New York Times* op-ed responding to the exposé:

> In Manhattan, the trend is so pronounced that a whole new category of real estate has emerged around the southern edges of Central Park: supertall,

---

3. Condos can be a profitable form of investment in several ways. A person who incurs a mortgage for a condo investment can rent out the unit to cover the cost of mortgage and association fees. If the rent charged on the unit is higher than total costs, the investor can also make a small monthly profit. If a condo is purchased outright with cash, rents can create a steady stream of income. An owner who purchases a condo outright may also hold the unit in reserve for personal use. In a booming real estate market, an idle condo can still be seen as a good investment because if the owner decides to sell it, he or she can sell it for substantially more than the original purchase price.

ultraluxury buildings, with more than half of the homes being sold to anonymous buyers (some perhaps looking to stash ill-gotten gains) who rarely, if ever occupy them. The city meanwhile, struggles to produce sufficient housing for those who do live there. (2015, A23)

Without significant government intervention, condos will continue, at least in some cities, to shape the housing market in negative ways. The transformation of condos into investment vehicles not only drives up real estate prices; it also discourages actual home construction in the few open spaces that remain in such cities.

Appendix 3

Interviews

Anonymous city official	November 5, 2012
Anonymous tenant advocate	December 24, 2013
Blake Biles	August 12, 2011; December 24, 2013
Rick Eisen	September 5, 2010
Stephen Goewey	November 9, 2009
Lawrence Green*	June 11, 2012
Steve Jones*	April 18, 2012
Afifa Klouj	October 5, 2010
David Laichena	September 24, 2010
Shirley Lawson	September 17, 2010
Genevieve Moreland	May 30, 2013; December 13, 2013
Cajia Owens	October 1, 2010
Jenny Reed	November 5, 2014
Eric Rome	June 27, 2013
George Rothman	August 13, 2009
John Samuels*	October 16, 2014
Cathy Schneider	May 7, 2013
Dan Silverman	February 15, 2013
Matthew Tibbs	November 9, 2009
Juan Pablo Vacatello	June 26, 2013
Clinton Yates	October 19, 2012

---

* Pseudonym

References

Abramovitz, Mimi. 2010. "Women, Social Reproduction and the Neo-liberal Assault on the US Welfare State." In *The Legal Tender of Gender: Law, Welfare and the Regulation of Women's Poverty*, edited by Shelley Gavigan and Dorothy Chunn, 15–46. Portland, OR: Hart.

Abramowitz, Michael, and Marcia Slacum Greene. 1989. "City Faces Struggle over Budget Drained by Social Costs Series." *Washington Post*, January 8, p. A1.

Advisory Neighborhood Commission 4B. 2011. "21-25 Kennedy St. NW: Project Summary." Available at http://www.anc4b.info/21_Kennedy_Summary.pdf.

Agarwal, Sumit, Yongheng Deng, Chenxi Luo, and Wenlan Qian. 2014. "The Hidden Peril: The Role of the Condo Loan Market in the Recent Financial Crisis." Social Science Research Network working paper, March. Available at http://ssrn.com/abstract=2171751.

Arrighi, Giovanni. 1978. "Towards a Theory of Capitalist Crisis." *New Left Review* 3 (1): 3–24.

Austermuhle, Martin. 2013. "Cool Disco Donut Changes Name after Being Criticized for Co-opting Identity of Legendary D.C. Tagger." *DCist*, January 31. Available at http://dcist.com/2013/01/cool_disco_donut_changes_name_after.php.

Baer, Kathryn. 2012. "Next Round in DC's Affordable Housing Battle." *Poverty and Policy* (blog), October 29. Available at http://povertyandpolicy.wordpress.com/2012/10/29/next-round-in-dcs-affordable-housing-battle.

Barras, Jonetta Rose. 1998. *Last of the Black Emperors: The Hollow Comeback of Marion Barry and the New Age of Black Leaders*. Baltimore: Bancroft Press.

"Barry Signs Emergency Bill on Condominiums." 1979. *Washington Post*, November 24, p. B12.

Baschuk, Bryce. 2010. "Four Takes on Tenant Rights in DC." *Urban Turf*, August 25. Available at http://dc.urbanturf.com/articles/blog/four_takes_on_tenant_rights_in_dc/2421.

Beitel, Karl. 2013. *Local Protests, Global Movements: Capital, Community, and State in San Francisco*. Philadelphia: Temple University Press.

Belton, Danielle. 2010. "The Power of the Black Woman Vote and DC's Adrian Fenty." *Black Snob* (blog), August 26. Available at http://blacksnob.squarespace.com/snob_blog/2010/8/26/the-power-of-the-black-woman-vote-and-dcs-adrian-fenty.html.

Benfield, Kaid. 2013. "The Secret to D.C.'s Stunning Population Growth? Old People." *CityLab*, August 12. Available at http://www.citylab.com/housing/2013/08/how-dc-saved-its-central-city/6499.

Bennett, Larry. 2010. *The Third City: Chicago and American Urbanism*. Chicago: University of Chicago Press.

Biegler, Caitlin. 2012. "A Big Gap: Income Inequality in the District Remains One of the Highest in the Nation." DC Fiscal Policy Institute, March 8. Available at http://www.dcfpi.org/wp-content/uploads/2012/03/03-08-12incomeinequality1.pdf.

Blomley, Nicholas. 2005. "Remember Property?" *Progress in Human Geography* 29 (2): 125–127.

———. 2008. "Enclosure, Common Right and the Property of the Poor." *Social and Legal Studies* 17 (3): 311–331.

Bonnette, Robert. 2003. "Housing Costs of Renters: 2000." *Census 2000 Brief*, May. Available at http://www.census.gov/prod/2003pubs/c2kbr-21.pdf.

Boyd, Michelle. 2005. "The Downside of Racial Uplift: The Meaning of Gentrification in an African-American Neighborhood." *City and Society* 17 (2): 265–288.

Brenner, Neil, Jamie Peck, and Nik Theodore. 2010. "Variegated Neoliberalization: Geographies, Modalities, Pathways." *Global Networks* 10 (2): 182–222.

Brenner, Neil, and Nik Theodore. 2002. "Cities and the Geographies of 'Actually Existing Neoliberalism.'" *Antipode* 34 (3): 349–379.

Broadwater, Luke. 2011. "Urban 'Pioneers' Risk Much for Their 'Hoods." *Baltimore Sun*, October 19. Available at http://articles.baltimoresun.com/2011-10-19/entertainment/bs-b-urban-pioneers-20111009_1_vacant-house-number-of-vacant-homes-pigtown.

Brown, Emma. 2013. "15 D.C. Public Schools to Close." *Washington Post*, January 18, p. A1.

Brown, Emma, and Marc Fisher. 2014. "Key Details from Thompson's Plea Agreement." *Washington Post*, March 11, p. A10.

Bureau of Labor Statistics. 2015. "Unemployment in the Washington Area by County, March 2015." May 12. Available at http://www.bls.gov/regions/mid-atlantic/news-release/2015/unemployment_washingtondc_20150512.htm.

Butler, Tim, Chris Hamnett, and Mark Ramsden. 2008. "Inward and Upward? Marking Out Social Class Change in London, 1981–2001." *Urban Studies* 45 (2): 67–88.

Byrne, J. Peter. 2003. "Two Cheers for Gentrification." *Howard Law Journal* 46 (3): 405–432.

Cenziper, Debbie, and Sarah Cohen. 2008. "The Profit in Decay: Landlords Who Empty Buildings of Tenants Reap Extra Benefit under Law." *Washington Post*, March 9, p. A1.

Cenziper, Debbie, Michael Sallah, and Steven Rich. 2013. "Faulty Addresses Keep Delinquent D.C. Taxpayers in Dark." *Washington Post*, October 11, p. A1.

REFERENCES

Chabot, Douglas. 2008. "Casting New Light on a Continuing Problem: Re-considering the Scope and Protections Offered by Massachusetts's Condominium Conversion Regulations." *Suffolk University Law Review* 42 (1): 101–128.

Chang, Elizabeth, Neely Tucker, Jessica Goldstein, Clinton Yates, and Marcia Davis. 2013. "The March of the Millennials." *Washington Post Magazine*, October 20, pp. 12–21.

Cherkis, Jason. 2013. "D.C. General Holds 600 Homeless Children, Often without Heat, Hot Water, Cribs." *Huffington Post*, February 13. Available at http://www.huffingtonpost.com/2013/02/13/dc-general-homeless_n_2677266.html.

Clinton, William J. 1997. "Address before a Joint Session of the Congress on the State of the Union, January 23, 1996." In *Public Papers of the Presidents of the United States: William J. Clinton, 1996*, vol. 1, *January 1 to June 30, 1996*, 79–87. Washington, DC: Government Printing Office.

Comeau, Sarah. 2012. "Judicial Sponsored Gentrification of the District of Columbia: The Tenant Opportunity to Purchase Act." *Journal of Gender, Social Policy, and Law* 19 (1): 401–423.

Community Associations Institute. 2011. "Credit Risk Retention—Docket No. R-1411." Available at http://www.federalreserve.gov/SECRS/2011/December/20111220/R-1411/R-1411_080111_87569_417744798016_1.pdf.

Consumer Financial Protection Bureau. 2013. "Consumer Financial Protection Bureau Issues Rule to Protect Consumers from Irresponsible Mortgage Lending." January 10. Available at http://www.consumerfinance.gov/newsroom/consumer-financial-protection-bureau-issues-rule-to-protect-consumers-from-irresponsible-mortgage-lending/.

Corn, David. 2012. "Secret Video: Romney Tells Millionaire Donors What He *Really* Thinks of Obama Voters." *Mother Jones*, September 17. Available at http://www.motherjones.com/politics/2012/09/secret-video-romney-private-fundraiser.

Craig, Tim. 2009. "Recreation Funds Flow Freely in D.C.; Fenty Promotes New Pools and Playgrounds, but Can City Afford Them?" *Washington Post*, August 29, p. A1.

———. 2010. "Fliers Urge Voters to 'Slap' Fenty." *Washington Post*, June 15. Available at http://washingtonpost.com/dc/2010/06/fliers_urge_voters_to_slap_fen.html.

Crockett, Stephen A., Jr. 2012a. "The Brixton: It's New, Happening and Another Example of African-American Historical 'Swagger-Jacking.'" *Washington Post*, August 3. Available at http://www.washingtonpost.com/blogs/therootdc/post/the-brixton-its-new-happening-and-another-example-of-african-american-historical-swagger-jacking/2012/08/03/b189b254-dcee-11e1-a894-af35ab98c616_blog.html.

———. 2012b. "'Swagger-Jacking' U Street: The Conversation Continues." *Washington Post*, August 7. Available at http://www.washingtonpost.com/blogs/therootdc/post/swagger-jacking-u-street-the-conversation-continues/2012/08/07/55c46762-e0ad-11e1-a421-8bf0f0e5aa11_blog.html.

Crutcher, Michael. 2010. *Treme: Race and Place in a New Orleans Neighborhood*. Athens: University of Georgia Press.

Dardick, Hal, and Kristen Mack. 2011. "Chicago's Ward Remap Begins with Everyone on Alert." *Chicago Tribune*, July 14. Available at http://articles.chicagotribune.com/2011-07-14/news/ct-met-city-council-redraw-wards-20110714_1_ward-remap-ward-boundaries-aldermen.

Davidson, Mark, and Elvin Wyly. 2012. "Classifying London: Social Division and Space Claims in the Post-industrial City." *City* 16 (4): 395–421.

———. 2013. "Class Analysis for Whom? An Alien-ated View of London." *City* 17 (3): 299–311.

Davis, Mike. 2006. *Planet of Slums*. London: Verso.

Day, Christian, and Mark Fogel. 1981. "The Condominium Crisis: A Problem Unresolved." *Journal of Urban and Contemporary Law* 21:3–85.

DC Appleseed Center. 1997. "Criteria for Analyzing Proposals for Financial Assistance to the District of Columbia." May 29. Available at http://www.dcappleseed.com/wp-content/uploads/2013/09/finassistcomp.pdf.

DeBonis, Mike. 2012a. "Census: D.C. Added 30,000 Residents in 27 Months." *Washington Post*, December 20. Available at http://www.washingtonpost.com/blogs/mike-debonis/wp/2012/12/20/census-d-c-added-30000-residents-in-27-months.

———. 2012b. "Chartered Health Plan on Cusp of Sale to AmeriHealth Mercy." *Washington Post*, December 3. Available at http://www.washingtonpost.com/blogs/mike-debonis/wp/2012/12/03/chartered-health-plan-on-cusp-of-sale-to-amerihealth-mercy/.

———. 2012c. "The Rise and Fall of Jeffrey Thompson's Health Care Profits." *Washington Post*, March 27. Available at http://www.washingtonpost.com/blogs/mike-debonis/post/the-rise-and-fall-of-jeffrey-thompsons-health-care-profits/2012/03/27/gIQAvYN2eS_blog.html.

———. 2013. "D.C. Public Housing Waiting List to Close April 12." *Washington Post*, April 4, p. B3.

DeBonis, Mike, Michael Sallah, and Debbie Cenziper. 2013. "District to Cancel Dozens of Tax Liens." *Washington Post*, September 14, p. A1.

DeFilippis, James. 2004. *Unmaking Goliath: Community Control in the Face of Global Capital*. New York: Routledge.

Department of Housing and Community Development. 2013. "What You Should Know about Rent Control in the District of Columbia." Available at http://dhcd.dc.gov/sites/default/files/dc/sites/dhcd/publication/attachments/RentControlFactSheet.pdf.

———. 2014. "Home Purchase Assistance Program (HPAP)." Available at http://dhcd.dc.gov/service/home-purchase-assistance-program.

DePillis, Lydia. 2010a. "American Dream Gone Awry: Tenants in Columbia Heights Thought Buying Their Apartments Would Be Easy. They Were Wrong." *Washington City Paper*, July 8. Available at http://www.washingtoncitypaper.com/blogs/housingcomplex/2010/07/08/american-dream-gone-awry-tenants-in-columbia-heights-thought-buying-their-apartments-would-be-easy-they-were-wrong.

———. 2010b. "Another City-Supported Tenant Purchase Goes Under." *Washington City Paper*, August 31. Available at http://www.washingtoncitypaper.com/blogs/housingcomplex/2010/08/31/another-city-supported-tenant-purchase-goes-under.

———. 2010c. "The Housing Production Trust Fund Is the New Social Security." *Washington City Paper*, May 10. Available at http://www.washingtoncitypaper.com/blogs/housingcomplex/2010/05/10/the-housing-production-trust-fund-is-the-new-social-security.

REFERENCES

———. 2011a. "Evans: The NCRC Was Wack, Don't Bring It Back." *Washington City Paper*, January 6. Available at http://www.washingtoncitypaper.com/blogs/housingcomplex/2011/01/06/evans-the-ncrc-was-wack-dont-bring-it-back.

———. 2011b. "Ruling on Case That Changed Tenant Rules Is Bittersweet." *Washington City Paper*, April 25. Available at http://www.washingtoncitypaper.com/blogs/housingcomplex/2011/04/25/ruling-on-case-that-changed-tenant-rules-is-bittersweet.

———. 2012a. "Column Outtakes: Who Should Rent Control Protect?" *Washington City Paper*, April 19. Available at http://www.washingtoncitypaper.com/blogs/housingcomplex/2012/04/19/column-outtakes-who-should-rent-control-protect.

———. 2012b. "Does Sustainable D.C. Have a Race Problem?" *Washington City Paper*, April 25. Available at http://www.washingtoncitypaper.com/blogs/housingcomplex/2012/04/25/does-sustainable-d-c-have-a-race-problem.

———. 2012c. "UIP Rising." *Washington City Paper*, April 18. Available at http://www.washingtoncitypaper.com/blogs/housingcomplex/2012/04/18/uip-rising.

DeSena, Judith. 2009. *Gentrification and Inequality in Brooklyn: New Kids on the Block*. Lanham, MD: Lexington Books.

Diamond, Michael. 2013. "Shared Equity Housing: Cultural Understandings and the Meaning of Ownership." In *The Public Nature of Private Property*, edited by Michael Diamond and Robin Paul Mallo, 37–64. London: Ashgate.

Dietsch, Deborah. 2013. "It's a Renovation for One." *Washington Post*, January 26, p. E1.

Direktor, Ken. 2011. "Differences between Condo and HOA Laws." *Condos and HOAs: Living with Rules* (blog), March 4. Available at http://blogs.sun-sentinel.com/condoblog/2011/03/differences-between-condo-and-hoa-laws.html.

District of Columbia Bar Association. 1995. "Small Housing Providers and Their Tenants: Practical Advice on Laws and Regulations Governing Rental Real Estate in the District of Columbia." Available at http://gradlife.gwu.edu/merlin-cgi/p/downloadFile/d/8177/n/off/other/1/name/DCSmallHousingInfopdf.

District of Columbia Department of Insurance, Securities and Banking. 2008. "Report on Examination: DC Chartered Health Plan, Inc. as of December 31, 2007." Available at http://disb.dc.gov/sites/default/files/dc/sites/disb/publication/attachments/dc_chartered_2007_final_exam_report.pdf.

———. 2012. "Department of Insurance, Securities and Banking Puts Chartered Health Plan in Receivership." October 19. Available at http://disb.dc.gov/release/department-insurance-securities-and-banking-puts-chartered-health-plan-receivership.

District of Columbia Office of Planning. 2012. "Washington D.C. Housing and Neighborhoods: Setting the Context 2000 to 2012." April 17. Available at http://www.taskforce2012.org/Portals/1/docs/Presentation-by-Office-of-Planning-CHSTF-Housing-Context.pdf.

Dreier, Peter. 2011. "Reagan's Real Legacy." *The Nation*, February 4. Available at http://www.thenation.com/article/158321/reagans-real-legacy#.

Duany, Andres. 2001. "Three Cheers for Gentrification: It Helps Revive Cities and Doesn't Hurt the Poor." *American Enterprise* 12 (3): 38–39.

Dutra, Jeremy W. 2002. "You Can't Tear It Down: The Origins of the D.C. Historic Preservation Act." Georgetown Law Historic Preservation Papers Series, Paper 1. Available at http://scholarship.law.georgetown.edu/cgi/viewcontent.cgi?article=1000&context=hpps_papers.

Eisen, J. 1979. "9 on Council Back Bill for Tough Condo Law." *Washington Post*, November 14, p. C6.

Eisen, Richard C. 1993. "Rental Housing Conversion and Sale Act: A Practitioner's Roadmap to Tenant Ownership." *District of Columbia Law Review* 2 (1): 91–112.

Eisinger, Peter. 1988. *The Rise of the Entrepreneurial State*. Madison: University of Wisconsin Press.

Ernstson, Henrik, Mary Lawhon, and James Duminy. 2014. "Conceptual Vectors of African Urbanism: 'Engaged Theory-Making' and 'Platforms of Engagement.'" *Regional Studies* 48 (9): 1563–1577.

Falcon, Elizabeth. 2012. "Cuts Threaten Successful Homeownership Program." *Greater Greater Washington* (blog), May 9. Available at http://greatergreaterwashington.org/efalcon/page/2.

Feagin, Joe, and Robert Parker. 2002. *Building American Cities: The Urban Real Estate Game*. Washington, DC: Beard Books.

Filardo, Mary, Marni Allen, Nancy Huvendick, Ping Sung, Margery Turner, Jennifer Comey, Barika Williams, and Elizabeth Guernsey. 2008. *Quality Schools and Healthy Neighborhoods: A Research Report*. Washington, DC: 21st Century School Fund, Brookings Institution, and the Urban Institute.

Financial Status: District of Columbia Finances; Testimony Before the Committee on the District of Columbia, House of Representatives (statement of John W. Hill Jr.). 1994. 103rd Cong. Available at http://www.gao.gov/assets/110/105642.pdf.

Fine, David. 1980. "The Condominium Conversion Problem: Causes and Solutions." *Duke Law Journal* 29 (2–3): 306–335.

Fisher, Marc. 2008. "Rethinking the Amazing Shrinking Shelter." *Washington Post*, September 18, p. B1.

———. 2011. "Scandals Are Taking D.C. Back to the Bad Old Days, Some Say." *Washington Post*, June 7, p. B1.

Fitzpatrick, Sandra, and Maria Goodwin. 2001. *The Guide to Black Washington*. New York: Hippocrene.

Fletcher, Michael. 2015. "A Shattered Foundation: African Americans Who Bought Homes in Prince George's Have Watched Their Wealth Vanish." *Washington Post*, January 24, p. A1.

Flores, Christopher. 2001. "Down Market." *Washington City Paper*, March 2. Available at http://www.washingtoncitypaper.com/articles/21343/down-market.

Florida, Richard. 2002. *The Rise of the Creative Class*. New York: Basic Books.

Foster, Carl. 2012. "Gentrification in Black and White." *Washington Post*, February 5, p. C6.

Franke-Ruta, Garance. 2012. "Facts and Fictions of D.C.'s Gentrification." *CityLab*, August 10. Available at http://www.citylab.com/politics/2012/08/facts-and-fictions-gentrification-dc/2914.

Freedman, Robert. 2012. "FHA Eases Some Key Condo Financing Limits." *Speaking of Real Estate* (blog), September 13. Available at http://speakingofrealestate.blogs.realtor.org/2012/09/13/fha-eases-some-key-condo-financing-limits.

Freeman, Lance. 2011. *There Goes the 'Hood: Views of Gentrification from the Ground Up*. Philadelphia: Temple University Press.

Fujitsuka, Yoshihiro. 2005. "Gentrification and Neighborhood Dynamics in Japan: The Case of Kyoto." In *Gentrification in a Global Context: The New Urban Colonialism*, edited by Rowland Atkinson and Gary Bridge, 139–154. New York: Routledge.

REFERENCES

Furman Center for Real Estate and Urban Policy. 2010. "Mortgage Lending during the Great Recession: HMDA 2009." *Furman Center Data Brief*, November. Available at http://furmancenter.org/files/publications/HMDA_2009_databrief.pdf.

Garreau, Joel. 1995. "Rx for D.C.: Radical Surgery; How Fast, Drastic Remedies Can Save the Nation's Capital." *Washington Post*, March 5, p. C1.

Gelman, Jeffrey H. 2010. "The TOPA Effect: TOPA Law Keeps Investors Away." *Pipeline*, August–September, pp. 7, 12. Available at http://www.dcbia.org/pipeline/Piplne_AugSep10_web.pdf.

Gibson, Campbell. 1998. "Population of the 100 Largest Cities and Other Urban Places in the United States: 1790 to 1990." U.S. Census Bureau, Population Division Working Paper No. 27. Available at http://www.census.gov/population/www/documentation/twps0027/twps0027.html.

Gibson, Campbell, and Kay Jung. 2005. "Historical Census Statistics on Population Totals by Race, 1790 to 1990, and by Hispanic Origin, 1970 to 1990, for Large Cities and Other Urban Places in the United States." U.S. Census Bureau, Population Division Working Paper No. 76. Available at http://www.census.gov/population/www/documentation/twps0076/twps0076.html.

Gillette, Howard. 2006. *Between Justice and Beauty: Race, Planning, and the Failure of Urban Policy in Washington, D.C.* Philadelphia: University of Pennsylvania Press.

Glass, Ruth. 1964. "Introduction." In *London: Aspects of Change*, edited by Centre for Urban Studies, xiii–xlii. London: MacGibbon and Kee.

Glassman, J. 2006. "Primitive Accumulation, Accumulation by Dispossession, Accumulation by 'Extra-economic' Means." *Progress in Human Geography* 3 (5): 608–625.

Gose, Joe. 2004. "Condo Conversion Craze." *National Real Estate Investor*, June 1. Available at http://nreionline.com/condo_conversion/real_estate_condo_conversion_craze.

Gotham, Kevin Fox. 2005. "Tourism Gentrification: The Case of New Orleans' Vieux Carre (French Quarter)." *Urban Studies* 42 (7): 1099–1121.

Gowen, Annie. 2011. "Homelessness Increases in D.C. Area." *Washington Post*, April 14, p. B1.

———. 2013. "Homeless Advocates Call D.C. Role Inadequate." *Washington Post*, February 12, p. A1.

Gramlich, Edward. 2008. *Subprime Mortgages: America's Latest Boom and Bust*. Washington, DC: Urban Institute Press.

Gratz, Roberta Brandes. 2010. "O Urban Pioneers!" *New York Times*, September 1. Available at http://opinionator.blogs.nytimes.com/2010/09/01/o-urban-pioneers.

Gray, Vincent. 2012. "A Vision for a Sustainable DC." Available at http://sustainable.dc.gov/sites/default/files/dc/sites/sustainable/publication/attachments/sustainable%20DC%20Vision%20Plan%202.2.pdf.

Greenwood, Arin. 2011. "'Free Franklin' Protesters Propose Reopening Franklin School Homeless Shelter." *Huffington Post*, November 23. Available at http://www.huffingtonpost.com/2011/11/22/free-franklin-protesters-occupy-dc_n_1108435.html.

Grim, Ryan. 2006a. "DCRA: Defending the City's Ruling Aristocracy." *Washington City Paper*, June 30. Available at http://www.washingtoncitypaper.com/cover/2006/cover0630.html.

———. 2006b. "The Painmaker: The D.C. Council Closed Richard Luchs' Favorite Loophole. So the Real-Estate Attorney Found Another." *Washington City Paper*, January 13. Available at http://www.washingtoncitypaper.com/cover/2006/cover0113.html.

Hackworth, Jason. 2002. "Postrecession Gentrification in New York City." *Urban Affairs Review* 37:815–843.

Hackworth, Jason, and Neil Smith. 2001. "The Changing State of Gentrification." *Tijdschrift voor Economische en Sociale Geografie* [Journal of Economic and Social Geography] 92 (4): 464–477.

Hamnett, Chris. 2004. "Flat Break-Ups: the British Condominium Conversion Experience." In *World Minds: Geographical Perspectives on 100 Problems*, edited by Donald Janelle, Barney Warf, and Kathy Hansen, 157–161. Boston: Kluwer Academic.

Hamnett, Chris, and Tim Butler. 2013. "Re-classifying London: A Growing Middle Class and Increasing Inequality; A Response to Davidson and Wyly." *City* 17 (2): 197–208.

Hamnett, Chris, and Bill Randolph. 1984. "The Role of Landlord Disinvestments in Housing Market Transformation: An Analysis of the Flat Break-Up Market in Central London." *Transactions of the Institute of British Geographers* 9:259–279.

———. 1988. *Cities, Housing and Profits: Flat Break-Up and the Decline of Private Renting*. London: Hutchinson.

Hamnett, Chris, and Drew Whitelegg. 2007. "Loft Conversion and Gentrification in London: From Industrial to Postindustrial Land Use." *Environment and Planning A* 39 (1): 106–124.

Harding, Amber. 2012. "What Can DC Do to Stop the Dramatic Rise in Family Homelessness?" *District's Dime* (blog), March 14. Available at http://www.dcfpi.org/what-can-dc-do-to-stop-the-dramatic-rise-in-family-homelessness.

Harney, Kenneth. 2008. "Loan Underwriting Guidelines Cut into Condo Market." *Post and Courier*, April 19. Available at http://www.postandcourier.com/article/20080419/PC0504/304199975.

———. 2012. "FHA Eases Rules for Certifying Condos." *Washington Post*, September 22, p. E3.

Harris, Douglas. 2011. "Condominium and the City: The Rise of Property in Vancouver." *Law and Social Inquiry* 36 (3): 694–726.

Harrison, Bennett, and Paul Osterman. 1974. "Public Employment and Urban Poverty: Some New Facts and a Policy Analysis." *Urban Affairs* 9 (3): 303–336.

Harrison Institute for Public Law. 2006. "An Analysis of the Strengths and Deficiencies of Washington, D.C.'s Tenant Opportunity to Purchase Act." Available at http://content.knowledgeplex.org/kp2/cache/documents/1834/183436.pdf.

Hartman, Chester. 1984. "The Right to Stay Put." In *Land Reform, American Style*, edited by Charles Geisler and Frank Popper, 302–318. Totowa, NJ: Rowman and Allanheld.

Harvey, David. 1989. "From Managerialism to Entrepreneurialism: The Transformation of Urban Governance in Late Capitalism." *Geografisker Annaler* 71:3–17.

———. 2000. *Spaces of Hope*. Berkeley: University of California Press.

———. 2005. *A Brief History of Neoliberalism*. Oxford: Oxford University Press.

———. 2008. "The Right to the City." *New Left Review* 53:23–40.

Hayek, Friedrich. 1944. *The Road to Serfdom*. Chicago: University of Chicago Press.

Hendey, Leah, Rebecca Grace, Zach McDade, and Peter A. Tatian. 2011. *Washington, D.C. Metropolitan Area Foreclosure Monitor, Winter 2011*. Washington, DC: Urban Institute.

Hilton, Shani O. 2011. "Confessions of a Black Gentrifier." *Washington City Paper*, March 18. Available at http://www.washingtoncitypaper.com/articles/40564/confessions-of-a-black-dc-gentrifier.

REFERENCES

Holt, Jeff. 2009. "A Summary of the Primary Causes of the Housing Bubble and the Resulting Credit Crisis: A Non-technical Paper." *Journal of Business Inquiry* 8 (1): 120–129.

Hopkins, Christopher Dean. 2010. "Peebles Rips Fenty on Refusal to Meet with Angelou, Height." *Washington Post*, January 28. Available at http://www.washingtonpost.com/blogs/dc-wire/post/peebles-rips-fenty-on-refusal-to-meet-with-angelou-height/2010/12/20/ABTOsEG_blog.html.

Hopkinson, Natalie. 2012. *Go-Go Live: The Musical Life and Death of a Chocolate City*. Durham, NC: Duke University Press.

Horwitz, Sari. 1995. "Panel Revisiting Schools Finds Little Progress." *Washington Post*, January 19, p. B1.

Howell, Kathryn Leigh. 2013. "Transforming Neighborhoods, Changing Communities: Collective Agency and Rights in a New Era of Urban Redevelopment in Washington, DC." Ph.D. diss., University of Texas at Austin.

Huron, Amanda. 2012. "The Work of the Urban Commons: Limited-Equity Cooperatives in Washington, D.C." Ph.D. diss., City University of New York.

Hyra, Derek S. 2008. *The New Urban Renewal: The Economic Transformation of Harlem and Bronzeville*. Chicago: University of Chicago Press.

IMGoph. 2012. "Urban Pioneers." *District Curmudgeon* (blog), November 26. Available at http://distcurm.blogspot.com/2012/11/urban-pioneers.html.

Jackson, Kenneth. 1985. *Crabgrass Frontier: The Suburbanization of the United States*. New York: Oxford University Press.

Jaffe, Harry. 2010. "So Called 'Plan' for White Supremacy Lives on in DC." *Washington Examiner*, August 30. Available at http://www.freerepublic.com/focus/f-news/2580444/posts.

Jenkins, Anthony. 1999. "Black Enough? Some People Wonder Whether D.C.'s Mayor Really Is. Here Is One of Them." *Washington Post*, January 17, p. B1.

Jones, Steven T. 2013. "Supervisors Approve Condo Legislation with Veto-Proof Majority." *San Francisco Bay Guardian*, June 11. Available at http://www.sfbg.com/politics/2013/06/11/supervisors-approve-condo-legislation-veto-proof-majority.

Jouvenal, Justin. 2013. "The Spat That Laid Low Olde Belhaven." *Washington Post*, February 10, p. A1.

Judkis, Maura. 2013. "Frosted Reception." *Washington Post*, February 1, p. C1.

Kahan, Marcel, Shmuel Leshem, and Raghu Sundaram. 2012. "First-Purchase Rights: Rights of First Refusal and Rights of First Offer." New York University Law and Economics Working Papers, Paper 110. Available at http://lsr.nellco.org/cgi/viewcontent.cgi?article=1114&context=nyu_lewp.

Kass, Benny L. 2004. "D.C. Landlords Must Give Tenants a Chance to Buy Property." *Washington Post*, July 17, p. F3.

———. 2010. "Condo Groups Facing Unpaid Dues Push for Foreclosures." *Washington Post*, November 20, p. E3.

Keenan, Bernard. 1987. "Condominium Conversion of Residential Rental Units: A Proposal for State Regulation and a Model Act." *University of Michigan Journal of Law Reform* 20 (3): 639–725.

Kellogg, Alex. 2011. "D.C., Long 'Chocolate City,' Becoming More Vanilla." *National Public Radio*, February 15. Available at http://www.npr.org/2011/02/15/133754531/d-c-long-chocolate-city-becoming-more-vanilla.

Kern, Leslie. 2010. *Sex and the Revitalized City: Gender, Condominium Development, and Urban Citizenship.* Vancouver: University of British Columbia Press.

Kern, Leslie, and Gerda Wekerle. 2008. "Gendered Spaces of Redevelopment: Gendered Politics of City Building." In *Gender in an Urban World: Research in Urban Sociology,* vol. 9, edited by Judith DeSensa, 233–262. Bingley, UK: JAI Press.

King, Colbert I. 2010. "D.C. Mayoral Campaign Has Echoes of 1994." *Washington Post,* August 7, p. A13.

Klopott, Freeman. 2010. "Fenty, Gray Both Lay Claim to Rec Center." *Washington Examiner,* August 26. Available at http://washingtonexaminer.com/fenty-gray-both-lay-claim-to-rec-center/article/89924.

Labbé, Theola, and David Nakamura. 2008. "DC School Closings List Is Revised." *Washington Post,* February 2, p. B1.

LaFraniere, Sharon. 1990. "Barry Arrested on Cocaine Charges in Undercover FBI, Police Operation." *Washington Post,* January 19, sec. A1.

Lasner, Matthew G. 2009. "Own-Your-Owns, Co-ops, Town Houses: Hybrid Housing Types and the New Urban Form in Postwar Southern California." *Journal of the Society of Architectural Historians* 68 (3): 378–403.

———. 2012. *High Life: Condo Living in the Suburban Century.* New Haven, CT: Yale University Press.

———. 2015. "Reform the Condominium." *New York Times,* February 17, p. A23.

Lauber, Daniel. 1984. "Condominium Conversions: A Reform in Need of Reform." In *Land Reform American Style,* edited by Charles Geisler and Frank J Popper, 273–301. Totowa, NJ: Rowman and Allanheld.

Lazere, Ed. 2013. "Testimony of Ed Lazere, Executive Director." DC Fiscal Policy Institute, October 28. Available at http://www.dcfpi.org/wp-content/uploads/2013/10/10.28.13-lazere-minimum-wage-testimony.pdf.

Lazere, Ed, and Robert Pohlman. 2008. "Affordable Housing in the District Depends on a Stable Housing Production Trust Fund." DC Fiscal Policy Institute, October 20. Available at http://dcfpi.org/wp-content/uploads/2008/10/10-20-08stablehptfreport.pdf.

Lee, Shin, and Chris Webster. 2006. "Gated Communities: An Emerging Global Urban Landscape." *GeoJournal* 66 (1–2): 27–42.

Lees, Loretta, Tom Slater, and Elvin Wyly. 2008. *Gentrification.* New York: Routledge.

Lehrer, Ute, and Andrea Winkler. 2006. "Public or Private? The Pope Squat and Housing Struggles in Toronto." *Social Justice* 33 (3): 142–157.

Leposky, George. 2012. "When Owners Don't Pay: HOA Boards Struggle to Make Ends Meet." *New Jersey Cooperator,* October. Available at http://njcooperator.com/articles/932/1/When-Owners-Don039t-Pay/Page1.html.

Lesko, Kathleen, Valerie Babb, and Carroll Gibbs. 1991. *Black Georgetown Remembered: A History of Its Black Community from the Founding of "the Town of George" in 1751 to the Present Day.* Washington, DC: Georgetown University Press.

Leslie, Deborah, and John Paul Catungal. 2012. "Social Justice and the Creative City: Class, Gender, and Racial Inequalities." *Geography Compass* 6 (3): 111–122.

Lipietz, Alain. 1992. *Towards a New Economic Order: Postfordism, Ecology, and Democracy.* Oxford: Oxford University Press.

REFERENCES

Locy, Toni. 1995. "Federal Court Seizes Control of D.C. Child Welfare System." *Washington Post*, May 23, p. A1.

Loeb, Vernon. 1995a. "Barry Asks Court to Overturn Receivership for Public Housing." *Washington Post*, January 11, p. B3.

———. 1995b. "In an Ailing City, Vital Services Cease to Function: Dozens of Departments Failing DC Residents." *Washington Post*, January 29, p. A1.

———. 1998. "Barry Brings Halt to Turbulent D.C. Saga." *Washington Post*, May 22, p. A1.

Lusane, Clarence. 1999. *Pipe Dream Blues: Racism and the War on Drugs*. Boston: South End Press.

Maciag, Mike. 2015. "Gentrification in America Report." *Governing: The State and Localities* 28 (5): 28–35.

MacLeod, Gordon. 2002. "From Urban Entrepreneurialism to a 'Revanchist City'? On the Spatial Injustices of Glasgow's Renaissance." *Antipode* 34 (3): 602–624.

Marcuse, Peter. 1985. "Gentrification, Abandonment, and Displacement: Connections, Causes, and Policy Responses in New York City." *Journal of Urban and Contemporary Law* 28 (1): 195–240.

Martin, Deborah, and Joseph Pierce. 2013. "Reconceptualizing Resistance: Residuals of the State and Democratic Radical Pluralism." *Antipode* 45:61–79.

Masur, Kate. 2010. *An Example for All the Land: Emancipation and the Struggle over Equality in Washington, D.C*. Chapel Hill: University of North Carolina Press.

McCarthy, James. 2005. "Commons as Counterhegemonic Projects." *Capitalism, Nature, Socialism* 16 (1): 9–24.

McGrory, Mary. 1987. "City of the White Flag." *Washington Post*, January 27, p. A2.

Mencimer, Stephanie. 2001. "Rich Man, Spore Man: If the Elite Want to Survive Bioterrorism, They'll Have to Make Sure the Poor Do Too." *Washington Monthly*, December. Available at http://www.washingtonmonthly.com/features/2001/0112.mencimer.html.

Metropolitan Police Department. 2013. *Annual Report*. Washington, DC: Metropolitan Police Department.

Meyer, Eugene L. 2013. "Real Estate Changes Abound in DC." *Capitol File*, Summer, pp. 88–93.

Meyer, Jack, Randall Bovbjerg, Barbara Ormond, and Gina Lagomarsino. 2010. *Expanding Health Coverage in the District of Columbia: D.C.'s Shift from Providing Services to Subsidizing Individuals and Its Continuing Challenges in Promoting Health, 1999–2009*. Washington, DC: Brookings Institution.

Miles, Steven. 2012. "The Neoliberal City and the Pro-active Complicity of the Citizen Consumer." *Journal of Consumer Culture* 12 (2): 216–230.

Milloy, Courtland. 2010. "D.C. Election Didn't Just Unseat Abrasive Mayor Fenty: It Was a Populist Revolt." *Washington Post*, September 16, p. B1.

———. 2012. "For Ivy City, 'The Plan' Isn't Paranoia." *Washington Post*, December 11, p. B1.

Mitchell, Don. 2001. "Postmodern Geographical Praxis? Postmodern Impulse and the War against Homeless People in the 'Post-justice' City." In *Postmodern Geography: Theory and Praxis*, edited by Claudio Minca, 57–92. Oxford: Blackwell.

———. 2003. *The Right to the City: Social Justice and the Fight for Public Space*. New York: Guilford.

Montgomery, David. 1999. "D.C.'s Bureaucracy: A Day in the Maze." *Washington Post*, February 7, p. A1.

Morello, Carol, and Dan Keating. 2010. "D.C. Population Soars Past 600,000." *Washington Post*, December 22, p. A4.

Morrissey, Aaron. 2011. "We're Game If You Are, Mr. Milloy." *DCist* (blog), September 27. Available at http://dcist.com/2011/09/were_game_if_you_are_mr_milloy.php.

Nakamura, David. 2007. "Fenty's School Takeover Approved." *Washington Post*, April 20, p. B1.

———. 2008. "Remaining Homeless Moved out of Shelter: Activists Say Other Spaces Are Needed." *Washington Post*, September 27, p. B2.

National Low Income Housing Coalition. 2012. *Out of Reach 2012: America's Forgotten Housing Crisis*. Washington, DC: National Low Income Housing Coalition.

Negi, Rohit, and Marc Auerbach. 2009. "The Contemporary Significance of Primitive Accumulation: Introductory Comments." *Human Geography* 2 (3): 89–90.

Neibauer, Michael. 2013. "Bernstein Cos.' Southwest D.C. Project Shrinks in Wake of Historic Designation." *Washington Business Journal*, October 1. Available at http://www.bizjournals.com/washington/breaking_ground/2013/10/bernsteins-southwest-dc-project.html.

Neighborhood Info DC. 2015. "DC 2010 Tract Profile—Population: Tract 44." Available at http://www.neighborhoodinfodc.org/censustract10/nbr_prof_trct64.html.

O'Cleireacain, Carol, and Alice Rivlin. 2001. "Envisioning a Future Washington." *Brookings Institution Research Brief*, June. Available at http://www.brookings.edu/~/media/research/files/reports/2001/6/cities%20ocleireacain/dcfuture.pdf.

O'Connell, Jonathan. 2009. "D.C. Wants to Redevelop Franklin School." *Washington Business Journal*, September 28. Available at http://www.bizjournals.com/washington/stories/2009/09/28/daily20.html.

Orvetti, P. J. 2010. "Gray Stuns Fenty on Home Turf: Challenger Easily Wins Ward 4 Straw Poll." *NBC Washington*, August 5. Available at http://www.nbcwashington.com/news/local/Gray-Stuns-Fenty-on-Home-Turf-100024544.html.

Osman, Suleiman. 2012. *The Invention of Brownstone Brooklyn: Gentrification and the Search for Authenticity in Postwar New York*. Oxford: Oxford University Press.

Owers, Paul. 2012. "HOAs Foreclose on Big Banks." *Sun Sentinel*, August 12. Available at http://articles.sun-sentinel.com/2012-08-12/features/fl-hoa-foreclose-banks-20120810_1_maintenance-fees-deutsche-bank-foreclosure-filings.

Page, Clarence. 1989. "D.C.'s Black Muslim Dopebusters." *Chicago Tribune*, April 23. Available at http://articles.chicagotribune.com/1989-04-23/news/8904060551_1_black-muslims-muslim-representative-rough-justice.

Park, Robert, Ernest W. Burgess, and Roderick D. McKenzie. 1925. *The City*. Chicago: University of Chicago Press.

Patterson, Orlando. 2010. "For African-Americans, a Virtual Depression—Why?" *The Nation*, June 30. Available at http://www.thenation.com/article/36882/african-americans-virtual-depression#.

Peck, Jamie. 2005. "Struggling with the Creative Class." *International Journal of Urban and Regional Research* 29 (4): 740–770.

Peck, Jamie, Nik Theodore, and Neil Brenner. 2009. "Neoliberal Urbanism: Models, Moments, Mutations." *SAIS Review* 29 (1): 49–66.

REFERENCES

Pérez, Gina. 2002. "The Other 'Real World' Gentrification and the Social Construction of Place in Chicago." *Urban Anthropology* 31 (1): 37–68.
Phillips, Joy, Robert Beasley, and Art Rodgers. 2005. "District of Columbia Population and Housing Trends." District of Columbia Office of Planning, Fall. Available at http://www.neighborhoodinfodc.org/pdfs/demographic_trends05.pdf.
Phillips-Fein, Kim. 2013. "The Legacy of the 1970s Fiscal Crisis." *The Nation*, April 16. Available at http://www.thenation.com/article/173873/legacy-1970s-fiscal-crisis.
Pierre, Robert E. 2007. "Trust Fund Makes Headway, Report Says." *Washington Post*, April 20, p. B2.
Pieterse, Edgar. 2008. *City Futures: Confronting the Crisis of Urban Development*. London: Zed Books.
Prince, Sabiyha. 2014. *African Americans and Gentrification in Washington, D.C.: Race, Class and Social Justice in the Nation's Capital*. Burlington, VT: Ashgate.
Proscio, Tony. 2012. *Becoming What We Can Be: Stories of Community Development in Washington, DC*. Washington, DC: Local Initiatives Support Corporation.
Purcell, Mark. 2003. "Citizenship and the Right to the Global City: Reimagining the Capitalist World Order." *International Journal of Urban and Regional Research* 27 (3): 564–590.
Ranganathan, Malini. 2014. "Emancipatory Urban Politics and the Everyday State: Improvisation and Translation at the Frontlines." Paper presented at Radical Incrementalism: Theories/Practices of Emancipatory Change, African Center for Cities, University of Cape Town, October 23–24.
Reed, Jenny. 2010. "Poverty on the Rise in the District: The Impact of Unemployment in 2009 and 2010." DC Fiscal Policy Institute, March 24. Available at http://www.dcfpi.org/wp-content/uploads/2010/03/3-24-10EstimatingPoverty2009.pdf.
———. 2012. "Disappearing Act: Affordable Housing in DC Is Vanishing amid Sharply Rising Housing Costs." DC Fiscal Policy Institute, May 7. Available at http://www.dcfpi.org/wp-content/uploads/2012/05/5-7-12-Housing-and-Income-Trends-FINAL.pdf.
———. 2013a. "DC's First Right Purchase Program Helps to Preserve Affordable Housing and Is One of DC's Key Anti-displacement Tools." DC Fiscal Policy Institute, September 24. Available at http://www.dcfpi.org/wp-content/uploads/2013/09/9-24-13-First_Right_Purchase_Paper-Final.pdf.
———. 2013b. "Testimony of Jenny Reed, Policy Director." DC Fiscal Policy Institute, February 22. Available at http://www.dcfpi.org/wp-content/uploads/2013/03/2-22-13-DHCD-Oversight.pdf.
Rental Housing Conversion and Sale (Council Act 3-204): Oversight Hearing and Markup before the Committee on the District of Columbia, House of Representatives. 1980. 96th Cong. September 4.
"Rent Control: A Good Move. . . ." 1980. *Washington Post*, November 29, p. A22.
Richburg, Keith. 1980. "City Council in Final-Day Spurt Approves Restrictions on Condominium Conversions." *Washington Post*, July 30, p. C1.
Robinson, Eugene. 1981. "Study Shows D.C. Work Force Is Comparable to Other Cities'." *Washington Post*, June 26, p. B3.
Rosiak, Luke. 2011. "D.C.'s 'Chocolate City' Moniker Melting." *Washington Times*, August 18. Available at http://www.washingtontimes.com/news/2011/aug/18/chocolate-city-moniker-melting.

Ruble, Blair A. 2012. *U Street: A Biography*. Baltimore: Johns Hopkins University Press.

Saegert, Susan. 2006. "Building Civic Capacity in Urban Neighborhoods: An Empirically Grounded Anatomy." *Journal of Urban Affairs* 28 (3): 275–294.

Sallah, Michael, and Debbie Cenziper. 2013. "Mystery Firm Buys Liens 'like a Machine.'" *Washington Post*, December 9, p. A1.

Sallah, Michael, Debbie Cenziper, and Steven Rich. 2013. "Homes for the Taking: How a Small Tax Debt Can Become a Big Problem in the District." *Washington Post*, September 8, p. A1.

Samuels, Robert. 2014. "D.C.'s Plan to End Homeless Crisis Prompts a Different Struggle." *Washington Post*, August 30, p. B1.

Schaffer, Michael. 2011. "Best of D.C. 2011: Best New Political Label." *Washington City Paper*, December 22. Available at http://www.washingtoncitypaper.com/bestofdc/peopleandplaces/2011/best-new-political-label.

———. 2012. "A Guide for the Responsible Gentrifier." *Washington City Paper*, April 27. Available at http://www.washingtoncitypaper.com/articles/42565/handbook-for-the-responsible-gentrifier.

Shaun. 2010. "Mayfair Mansions: Condos No More." *DCMud* (blog), March 2. Available at http://dcmud.blogspot.com/2010/03/mayfair-mansions-condos-no-more.html.

Shiller, Robert. 2008. *The Subprime Solution: How Today's Global Financial Crisis Happened, and What to Do about It*. Princeton, NJ: Princeton University Press.

Shin, Annys. 2001. "Ten Things to Do before Closing a Prison." *Washington City Paper*, March 9. Available at http://www.washingtoncitypaper.com/articles/21385/ten-things-to-do-before-closing-a-prison.

———. 2013. "An Unlikely Catalyst in D.C." *Washington Post*, July 21, p. A1.

Simmons, Beth, Frank Dobbin, and Geoffrey Garrett. 2007. "Introduction: The Diffusion of Liberalization." In *The Global Diffusion of Markets and Democracy*, edited by Beth Simmons, Frank Dobbin, and Geoffrey Garrett, 1–63. Cambridge: Cambridge University Press.

Sinclair, Timothy J. 1994. "Passing Judgment: Credit Rating Processes as Regulatory Mechanisms of Governance in the Emerging World Order." *Review of International Political Economy* 1:133–159.

Sinzinger, Kathryn. 2005. "DCRA in Disarray; Graham: Agency Has Lost Sight of Mission." *Common Denominator*, March 7. Available at http://www.thecommondenominator.com/030705_news1.html.

Slater, Tom. 2006. "The Eviction of Critical Perspectives from Gentrification Research." *International Journal of Urban and Regional Research* 30 (4): 737–757.

———. 2009. "Missing Marcuse: On Gentrification and Displacement." *City* 13 (2–3): 292–311.

———. 2010. "On Gentrification Still Missing Marcuse: Hamnett's Foggy Analysis of London Town." *City* 14 (1–2): 170–186.

Smith, Neil. 1979. "Towards a Theory of Gentrification." *Journal of the American Planning Association* 45:538–548.

———. 1986. "Gentrification, the Frontier, and the Restructuring of Urban Space." In *Gentrification of the City*, edited by Neil Smith and Peter Williams, 15–34. Boston: Allen and Unwin.

REFERENCES

———. 1996. *The New Urban Frontier: Gentrification and the Revanchist City.* New York: Routledge.

Smith, Rend. 2010. "What's Tweeting Courtland Milloy?" *Washington City Paper,* November 26. Available at http://www.washingtoncitypaper.com/articles/40086/whats-tweeting-courtland-milloy/full.

———. 2011. "Myopic Twits: Older, Blinder and Wise-Asser." *Washington City Paper,* September 26. Available at http://www.washingtoncitypaper.com/blogs/citydesk/2011/09/26/myopic-twits-older-blinder-and-wise-asser.

Springer, Simon. 2012. "Anarchism! What Geography Still Ought to Be." *Antipode* 44 (5): 1605–1624.

Starr, Paul. 1988. "The Meaning of Privatization." *Yale Law and Policy Review* 6:6–41.

Stein, Perry. 2014. "Four Ways of the Condo." *Washington City Paper,* May 16. Available at http://www.washingtoncitypaper.com/blogs/citydesk/2014/05/16/four-ways-of-the-condo.

Sternbergh, Adam. 2009. "What's Wrong with Gentrification? The Displacement Myth." *New York,* December 11. Available at http://nymag.com/news/intelligencer/62675.

Stewart, Nikita. 2013. "Jeffrey E. Thompson: The Rise and Fall of D.C.'s 'Governor.'" *Washington Post,* July 14, p. A1.

Stewart, Nikita, and Jeff Mays. 2010. "A Tale of Two Post-racial Mayors," *The Root,* September 14. Available at http://www.theroot.com/articles/politics/2010/09/how_adrian_fenty_lost_the_black_vote_how_cory_booker_may_lose_the_black_vote.html.

Stiglitz, Joseph. 2003. *Globalization and Its Discontents.* New York: W. W. Norton.

Story, Louise, and Stephanie Saul. 2015. "Hidden Wealth Flows to Elite New York Condos." *New York Times,* February 8, p. A1.

Story, Louise, and Alejandra Xanic von Bertrab. 2015. "Political Clout in Mexico, Homes in the U.S." *New York Times,* February 11, p. A1.

Stray-Gundersen, Kay. 1981. "Regulatory Responses to the Condominium Conversion Process." *Washington University Law Review* 59 (1): 513–534.

Suderman, Alan. 2010. "Is Adrian Fenty a Jerk?" *Washington City Paper,* August 20. Available at http://www.washingtoncitypaper.com/articles/39616/is-adrian-fenty-a-jerk-politicians-say-he-is-but.

———. 2011. "Medicaid Malpractice." *Washington City Paper,* June 1. Available at http://www.washingtoncitypaper.com/blogs/looselips/2011/06/01/medicaid-malpractice.

Tavernise, Sabrina. 2011. "A Population Changes, Uneasily." *New York Times,* July 17. Available at http://www.nytimes.com/2011/07/18/us/18dc.html.

Tenacity Group. 2008. "Tenacity Tenant Conversions." Available at http://www.tenacitygroup.com/ttc/index.htm.

Thabit, Walter. 2003. *How East New York Became a Ghetto.* New York: New York University Press.

Thomas, Michelle. 2014. "Listing We Love: A Sleek, Modern Condo in Logan Circle." *Washingtonian,* September 22. Available at http://www.washingtonian.com/blogs/openhouse/listing-we-love/listing-we-love-a-sleek-modern-condo-in-logan-circle.php.

Tong, Zhong Yi. 2005. *Washington, D.C.'s First-Time Home-Buyer Tax Credit: An Assessment of the Program.* Washington, DC: Fannie Mae Foundation.

Turner, Lark. 2014. "Why Larger Condo Units Aren't Being Built in D.C." *UrbanTurf*, July 18. Available at http://dc.urbanturf.com/articles/blog/if_the_district_needs_them_why_arent_developers_building_bigger_condos/8755.

Turque, Bill. 2012. "DCPS Enrollment: Missing the Mark by $18 Million." *Washington Post*, February 16. Available at http://www.washingtonpost.com/blogs/dc-schools-insider/post/dcps-enrollment-missing-the-mark-by-18-million/2012/02/16/gIQAnu2RIR_blog.html.

21st Century School Fund, Urban Institute, and Brookings Institution. 2009. "Analysis of the Impact of DCPS School Closings for SY2008–2009." March 17. Available at http://www.21csf.org/csf-home/publications/MemoImpactSchoolClosingsMarch2009.pdf.

"Types of Home Ownership." 2014. FindLaw. Available at http://realestate.findlaw.com/buying-a-home/types-of-home-ownership.html.

U.S. Census Bureau. 2001. *Profiles of General Demographic Characteristics: 2000 Census of Population and Housing, United States*. Washington, DC: U.S. Census Bureau. Available at https://www.census.gov/prod/cen2000/dp1/2khus.pdf.

———. 2010. *State and Metropolitan Area Data Book: 2010*. Washington, DC: U.S. Government Printing Office. Available at http://www.census.gov/prod/2010pubs/10smadb/2010smadb.pdf.

———. 2012. *Statistical Abstract of the United States: 2012*. Washington, DC: U.S. Census Bureau. Available at http://www.census.gov/compendia/statab/2012edition.html.

———. 2013. "Small Area Health Insurance Estimates (SAHIE): 2011 Highlights." Available at http://www.census.gov/did/www/sahie/data/2011/SAHIE_Highlights_2011.pdf.

van Weesep, Jan. 1984. "Condominium Conversion in Amsterdam: Boon or Burden?" *Urban Geography* 5 (2): 165–177.

———. 2005. "Condominium." In *Encyclopedia of the City*, edited by Roger W. Caves, 94–95. New York: Routledge.

Vigdor, Jacob, Douglas Massey, and Alice Rivlin. 2002. "Does Gentrification Harm the Poor?" In *Brookings-Wharton Papers on Urban Affairs, 2002*, edited by William Gale and Janet Rothenberg Pack, 133–182. Washington, DC: Brookings Institution.

Walker, David M. 2008. "Gentrification Moves to the Global South: An Analysis of the Programa de Rescate, a Neoliberal Urban Policy in Mexico City's Centro Historico." Ph.D. diss., University of Kentucky. Available at http://uknowledge.uky.edu/cgi/viewcontent.cgi?article=1657&context=gradschool_diss.

Waller, James. 2000. *Prejudice across America*. Jackson: University Press of Mississippi.

Walsh, Mary Williams. 2009. "Muni Bonds May Face Downgrade." *New York Times*, April 7. Available at http://www.nytimes.com/2009/04/08/business/economy/08muni.html.

Walters, Jonathan. 2002. "Capital Gains: The District of Columbia, Once the Nation's Poster Child for Managerial Incompetence, Is Staging a Comeback." *Governing*, August. Available at http://www.governing.com/topics/politics/Capital-Gains.html.

Weil, Martin, and Gabriel Escobar. 1991. "D.C. Sets Homicide Record." *Washington Post*, December 25, p. A1.

Weinberger, Jerry. 2011. "Gentrifying Washington, D.C.: The Nation's Capital Is Becoming Friendlier and More Diverse." *City Journal*, November 4. Available at http://www.city-journal.org/2011/eon1104jw.html.

REFERENCES

Weiner, Aaron. 2013. "Gray Pledges One-Time $100 Million Investment in Affordable Housing." *Washington City Paper*, February 5. Available at http://www.washingtoncitypaper.com/blogs/housingcomplex/2013/02/05/gray-pledges-one-time-100-million-investment-in-affordable-housing.
———. 2014. "Losing Control." *Washington City Paper*, December 12. Available at http://www.washingtoncitypaper.com/articles/46608/losing-control-dcs-rent-control-laws-are-supposed-to-keep.
Weiss, Eric M. 2005a. "Clash over Real Estate Law Ends Up before Panel." *Washington Post*, March 13, p. C4.
———. 2005b. "D.C. Agency Suspends Role in Property Sales." *Washington Post*, March 5, p. B5.
Welch, Matt. 2010. "Loathsome Columnist of the Month: Courtland Milloy." *Hit and Run Blog*, September 17. Available at http://reason.com/blog/2010/09/17/loathsome-columnist-of-the-mo.
"'Welfare Queen' Becomes Issue in Reagan Campaign." 1976. *New York Times*, February 15, p. 51.
Whitaker, Joseph, and Patrice Camp. 1979. "City's Emergency Condominium Law Overturned." *Washington Post*, October 20, p. B1.
Williams, Brett. 2009. "Deadly Inequalities: Race, Illness, and Poverty in Washington, D.C., since 1945." In *African American Urban History since World War II*, edited by Kenneth L. Kusmer and Joe W. Trotter, 142–159. Chicago: University of Chicago Press.
Willoughby, Charles J. 2012. "Audit of the District's Condominium Conversion Fees." District of Columbia Office of the Inspector General, February 17. Available at http://app.oig.dc.gov/news/PDF/release10/OIG%20No%2008-1-18CR%20-%20Condo%20Conversion%20Fees.pdf.
———. 2013. "District of Columbia Housing Authority, Client Placement Division: Report of Special Evaluation." District of Columbia Office of the Inspector General, March. Available at http://app.oig.dc.gov/news/PDF/release10/DCHA%20Final%20Report%20Mar%2015%202013.pdf.
Wyly, Elvin, and Daniel Hammel. 2001. "Gentrification, Housing Policy, and the New Context of Urban Redevelopment." In *Critical Perspectives on Urban Redevelopment*, edited by Kevin Fox Gotham, 211–276. Bingley, UK: Emerald Group.
Yates, Clinton. 2013. "Why Cool 'Disco' Dan Matters." *Washington Post*, February 15, p. C2.
Yglesias, Matthew. 2012. "The Plan Is Real and It's Called Population Growth." *Slate*, December 13. Available at http://www.slate.com/blogs/moneybox/2012/12/13/the_plan_is_real_there_is_a_plan_to_eradicate_dc_s_black_majority_and_it.html.
Zukin, Sharon. 1987. "Gentrification: Culture and Capital in the Urban Core." *Annual Review of Sociology* 13:129–147.

CITED LEGISLATION

Condominium Act of 1976, D.C. Code §§42-1901–42-1904.
Condominium and Cooperative Conversion Stabilization Act of 1979, D.C. Law 3-53.
District of Columbia Financial Responsibility and Management Assistance Act of 1995, Public Law 104-8, 109 Stat. 142.

Dodd-Frank Wall Street Reform and Consumer Protection Act of 2010, Public Law 111-203.
Home Rule Act of 1973, D.C. Code §1-201, Public Law 93-198, 87 Stat. 777.
Horizontal Property Act of 1963, D.C. Code §42-2002(2).
National Housing Act of 1934, Public Law 84-345, 48 Stat. 847.
National Housing Act of 1961, Public Law 87-70, 75 Stat. 149.
Rental Housing Act of 1977, D.C. Law 2-54.
Rental Housing Conversion and Sale Act of 1980, D.C. Law 3-86, D.C. Code §§42-3401–42-3405.
Rental Housing Conversion and Sale Act of 1980, District Opportunity to Purchase Act of 2001, D.C. Code §§42-3404.31–42-3404.37.
Rental Housing Conversion and Sale Act of 1980, Tenant Opportunity to Purchase Act, D.C. Code §42-3404.02.
Taxpayer Relief Act of 1997, Public Law 105-34, 111 Stat. 787.

Index

Page numbers in italics indicate material in figures or tables.

"Accumulation by dispossession," 215
Adams Bank, 176
Adams Morgan, 112
Adjustable-rate mortgage (ARM), 128
Adult strategy, 51–56, 227
Advisory Neighborhood Commission (ANC), 89, 178
Aldridge, James, 186, 188
Ambrose, Sharon, 185, 189
Anacostia neighborhood, 82
Anacostia River, 52, 58, 60, 109, 113, 123
Anarchism, 214, 219
Anchor institution, 53
Angelou, Maya, 78, 79
Anonymous city official, 227–228
Anonymous tenant advocate, 225–226
Arnold and Porter, 193–196, 200–201, 206
Atlas District, 70
Attrition, 56, 113, 139, 171, 177, 182, 194, 212n, 225
"The authority," 4. *See also* Control board

Barclay Apartments, 191–193, 195, 200, 202n14, 203–208. *See also* Schneider, Cathy
Barras, Jonetta Rose, 68
Barry, Marion, 5, 18, 50, 68, 72, 78, 83, 98, 184, 189

Bear Stearns, 176
Benjamin Franklin School, 58, 61–64
Bernstein family, 114, 119, 190–192, 195–197, 200, 208, 212, 218. *See also* 95/5 transfer
Bernstein Group, 131–133
Biles, Blake: and Bernstein sale case, 190–191, 192–193, 196–197, 201–202; and Jim Graham, 193; and 95/5 transfers, 190–191, 196–197; and pro bono work, 193–194; and RHCSA, 109; on tenants and tenants' associations, 194–195; and the TOPA process, 87, 125n, 158, 182–183, 201–202, 203. *See also* Bernstein family; Schneider, Cathy
"Black Broadway," 75
Black culture, 75
"Black politics," 68
B lending, 128
Brookings Institution, 51, 59
Brown, Chuck, 9
Bush, George H. W., 16
Business improvement districts (BIDs), 50
Buyouts: and affordability of rental housing, 148, 150, 155–156, 215, 219–220; and Cathedral Court, 126, 139, 142, *143*, *144*; and displacement, 31, 115, 117, 155–156, 179, 211; Eric Rome on, 109, 223; and Garden Towers, 142, *143*, *144*; and Harvard/Summit, 141–142, *143*, *144*, 156; and

Buyouts (*continued*)
    Kennedy Street, 143, *144*, 179; and Mayfair Mansions, 123, *143*, *144*, 170–171, 174, 179; and middle- versus low-income residents, 159–160; and the Squire, 140–141, *143*, *144*, 145–146, 223; tenant-reported numbers on, 115; under TOPA, 19, *93*, 95, 119, 138–146, 202, 217, 223–225; and Town Center, 142, *143*, *144*. *See also* Voluntary agreements

Calloway, Cab, 8
"Can you top this?" strategy, 124–125, 132, 136, 139
Capital accumulation, 45, 103, 218, 224
Capitalism, 15, 23, 43–44, 216–218
Capital mobility, 27
Capitals (NHL team), 63
Carmel Partners, 191, 195–197, 202–204, 205n, 218
Cathedral Court, *108*, *109*, *110*, 113: affordable housing at, *151*; and buyouts, 126, 139, 142, *143*, *144*; insider prices and condo conversion at, 125–134; tenants who stayed put at, *122*; and TOPA process, 135–136; and urban (dis)investment, 134; and voluntary agreements, 147, 150, *151*. *See also* Goewey, Stephen; Tibbs, Matthew
Census Bureau, 5, 42n7
Chocolate City (Parliament album), 18
"Chocolate City" moniker, 9n, 39, 75, 77
Civil rights era, 9, 18, 166
Civil War, 49, 68
Cleveland Park, 82
Clinton, Bill, 16, 47
Coalition for Nonprofit Housing and Economic Development, 56
Coleman, Pamela, 123
Collective bargaining, 43
Collective ownership, 28
Columbia Heights, 6, 11, *14*, 21, 33, 67, 88, 109, 112, 117, 190, 226
Columbia Road, 194
Comeau, Sarah, 21
Community land trusts, 27
Community Preservation and Development Corporation (CPDC), 170
Condo associations, 161–162
Condo conversion: and Chris Hammett, 25–26; and condominium regulations, 2–3, 161–163; in DC, 35, *36*, 106, 114; and DC condominium legislation history, 97–98; and developers, 102, 122, 162–163, 169–170, 210, 213; and displacement, 1–3, 26, 90, 101, 210–211, 212n; and Garden Towers, 109; and gentrification, 2–3, 22–26, 36; and Harvard/Summit, 112; and housing costs, 154–155; and Jim Graham, 188–189; and Kennedy Street, 174–176; and local autonomy, 29, 118; and Mayfair Mansions, 109, 169–170, 172; and neoliberalism, 103–104, 214–215; and race, 169; and RHCSA, 18, 90–96; and the Squire, 140, 162; and "tenant capitalism," 216; and TOPA, 1, 18–19, 21, 29, 156, 165, 182, 219, 223; and urban revanchism, 105; and voluntary agreements, 147, 225
Condominium Act of 1976, 97
Condominium and Cooperative Conversion Stabilization Act of 1979, 97
Conforming loans, 161–163
Congress Heights, 82
Consumer Financial Protection Bureau, 160
Control board, 4–5, 27, 34, 50–51, 58–59, 61, 64, 86, 108n2, 117, 208
Conversion of Rental Housing to Condominium or Cooperative (CRHCC), 18, 91–92, 96, 120, 210, 219, 223
Cool Disco Dan, 75–76
Cooperatives (co-ops), 2, 18, 21, 24, 28, 91–95, 97, 118, *122*, 175–179, 219, 222; limited equity cooperatives, 21, 27–29, 175, 219, 229; Unity Co-op, 175–179
Creative class, 16, 77, 79. *See also* Urban pioneers
Crisis of accumulation, 44
Crockett, Stephen A., 75–77, 81, 83–85
"Cultural vulturalism," 75

Davis, Mike, 221
DC Chartered Health Plan, 59–60
DC Fiscal Policy Institute (DCFPI), 28, 41, 180, 220
DC General, 58–61, 63–65
D.C. Healthcare Systems, 60
Deanwood, 78
DeFilippis, James, 15, 27–28, 29, 118, 137
Deindustrialization, 26, 49
Department of Consumer and Regulatory Affairs (DCRA), 35, 165, 182, 185–186, 188–192, 208, 212, 226
Department of Housing and Community Development (DHCD), 2n, *93*, 94, 165–166, 171–173, 212, 220
Department of Insurance Securities and Banking, 60–61
Department of Parks and Recreation, 78
Dependency, 15, 24, 45, 214

INDEX

DePillis, Lydia, 103, 147–148, 150, 173–174, 180, 226. *See also* Urban Investment Partners (UIP)
Desegregation, 81
Diplomats (rap group), 75
Direct displacement, 30–31, 65, 115–117, 121, 154, 157, 211; mitigation of, 121–124
Disinvestment. *See* Urban disinvestment
Displacement: and condo conversion, 1–3, 26, 90, 101, 210–211, 212n; and empowerment, 214, 218; and family strategy and adult strategy, 53, 55–56; and gentrification, 13, 17–18, 29–31, 115–117, 120–121, 157; and Housing Production Trust Fund, 55–56; and local autonomy, 26; measurement of, 22, 29–31, 106, 114–117, 156–157; mitigation of, 121–124; and race, 18, 83–85, 89; regulation of, 64–65, 208, 212; and RHSCA, 90, 96–97, 101; and TOPA, 1, 19, 22, 30–31, 65, 115, 117, 120–157, 179–180, 208, 210–212, 214, 219–221; and urban (re)investment, 17, 101, 103; and voluntary agreements, 225–226. *See also* Adult strategy; Family strategy; Gentrification
Displacement-free gentrification, 29–30
Displacement pressure, 30, 116
District Inspector General's Office, 165
District of Columbia Bar Association, 147
District of Columbia Court of Appeals, 197
District of Columbia Financial Responsibility and Management Assistance Act, 4, 49, 59n
District of Columbia Horizontal Property Act (1963), 97n6
District of Columbia Public School System (DCPS), 56–58, 77, 80
District Opportunity to Purchase Act (DOPA), 228–229
Dodd-Frank Wall Street Reform and Consumer Protection Act (2010), 160
"Dodge City" moniker, 33, 75. *See also* Murder capital, DC as
"Doggedreader," 74
Dorsey, Darney, 186
Dupont Circle, 6, 190

Eisen, Rick: and buyouts, 223; and "Can you top this?" strategy, 132; on empowerment, 214; and Marshall Heights, 169, 172–174; and Mayfair Mansions, 169–170, 172, 173–174; and Mercy Housing, 177–178; and Town Center, 131–132. *See also* Laichena, David; Rome, Eric
Eisen and Rome, 188–189

Ellington, Duke, 8, 87
Emergency-room-as-primary-care model, 61, 64
Empowerment, 179, 214–215, 217, 221–222, 224, 229; recursive political empowerment, 221–222
Exclusionary displacement, 30–31, 65, 116–117, 121, 138, 154–155, 157, 179, 211–212, 221, 225

Factory-to-loft conversion, 25–26, 30
Family strategy, 51–57
Fannie Mae and Freddie Mac, 160–163
Fannie Mae Foundation, 54;
Farm Service Agency (FSA), 161
Federal Housing Administration (FHA), 23, 135, 161, 162n9
Fenty, Adrian, 27, 50, 54, 56, 61–63, 77–80, 188
FIRE (Finance, Insurance, and Real Estate) sector, 15
First Right Purchase Program, 28, 93, 94, 159n2, 220, 224
Florida, Richard, 16, 77
Forrester Construction, 174
Fort Totten Metro, 111, 175
Foster, Carl, 67
14th Street, *8–10*, *12*, 226–227
Franke-Ruta, Garance, 81, 83–85
Franklin School, 58, 61–65, *62*

Garden Towers, *108*, *109*, *110*, 113; affordable housing at, 150, *151*; and buyouts, 142, *143*, *144*, 147; and developers, 135; tenants who stayed put at, *122*; and TOPA process, 136–137, 157; and voluntary agreements, 148, 150, *151*
Gentrification, 13; and condo conversion, 2–3, 22–26, *36*; in DC, 34–42; and displacement, 13, 17–18, 29–31, 115–117, 120–121, 157; Garden Towers and, 113; Harvard/Summit and, 113; Kennedy Street and, 111, 113; and local autonomy, 26–29, 156; and low-income residences, 159, 179–180, 182–183; Mayfair Mansions and, 113; and 95/5 transfers, 190; and political economy, 15–16, 42–43; and politics of staying put, 18, 211; and race, 34, 38–40, 67–89, 169; and RHSCA, 101, 219; stages of, 43; and TOPA, 21–22, 26, 28, 87–89, 101, 105, 119–121, 123, 156–157, 159, 179–180, 202, 215, 218–219; Town Center and, 113; and urban investment, 2–4, *108*–109; and urban pioneers, 16, 70–71, 85; and voluntary agreements, 157

INDEX

Georgetown, 6, 49, 86n
Georgetown University Medical Center, 60
Ghandi, Natwar, 59
Goewey, Stephen, 126–130, 134, 139, 145. *See also* Cathedral Court
Go-go music, 9
Graham, Jim, 185–190, 192–193, 226
Gray, Vincent, 27, 50, 56, 61, 73, 80
Great Depression, 43
Great Migration, 68
Great recession. *See* 2008 recession
Green, Lawrence, 139–141, 145–146, 148–150, 162. *See also* The Squire
Griffin, Mark, 181
Grim, Ryan, 182, 184, 189
"Guaranteed financing," 159–160

Hackworth, Jason, 108
Hamnett, Chris, 25–26, 30, 157. *See also* Condo conversion
Harding, Amber, 65
Harried, Linda, 186–189
Hartman, Chester, 18
Harvard Street, 112, 141–142
Harvard/Summit, *108*, 112, *112*; affordable housing at, 150–155; and buyouts, 141–142, *143*, *144*, 156; and "Can you top this?" strategy, 124; and developers, 124, 141–142, 163–165, 225–226; insider prices and condo conversion at, 163–165; tenants who stayed put at, *122*; and TOPA process, 124, 156; and urban (dis)investment, 134–136; and voluntary agreements, 147–155, 156, 225–226. *See also* Rome, Eric
Harvey, David, 16
Height, Dorothy, 78–79
Hilton, Shani, 82–83
Hogg, Dan, 75–76
Home Purchase Assistance Program, 159n2, 173
Home Rule Act of 1973, 49, 68, 97–98, 100
Horse trading, 19, 94, 119, 124–125, 202
House Concurrent Resolution 420, 98
Housing bubble, 34, 40, 102, 128, 173
Housing Production Trust Fund, 55–56, 64, 96, 159n2, 213
Howard University, 77, 82
Howell, Kathryn, 21
H Street, 70
Huron, Amanda, 21, 28. *See also* Limited equity cooperatives (LECs)

"Indirect displacement," 30

Inflation, 44
Ivy City, 72–74

Jaffe, Harry, 71–72, 74. *See also* "The Plan"
Jim Crow era, 8
Johnson, Lyndon B., 9
Jones, Steve, 145–146

Kass, Benny, 101, 216
Keenan, Bernard, 2
Kelly, Sharon Pratt, 5
Kennedy Street, *108*, 110–111, 113; and buyouts, 138, *143*, *144*, 150n21, 156; and developers, 166; and displacement, 156, 212n; low-income residences at, 158; tenants who stayed put at, *122*; and TOPA process, 158, 174–180; and urban (dis)investment, 134; and voluntary agreements, 147, 148n, 156
Kern, Leslie, 23–24
Key Bridge, 51
Keynesianism, 15, 43–47, 64, 209, 215
King, Colbert I., 78
King, Martin Luther, Jr., 9, *11*, 166. *See also* Riots
Klouj, Afifa, 104, 130–134, 139, 142. *See also* Town Center

Laichena, David, 134, 174–179. *See also* Kennedy Street
Latin American Youth Center, 179
Lawson, Shirley, 1, 123, 134, 137, 166–174. *See also* Mayfair Mansions
Limited equity cooperatives (LECs), 21, 27–29, 175, 219, 229
Local autonomy, 22, 26–29, 90–91, 106, 117–119, 156–157, 180, 208, 218, 229
Logan Circle, 117
Luchs, Richard, 181, 186, 188, 191, 195n8
Luxurification, 14, 27, 119, 122, 211

Macaluso, Judith N., 73
"Majority transfer," 184
Manna Inc., 109. *See also* Rothman, George
Marcus and Millichap, 190–191
Marcuse, Peter, 30, 116–117, 138. *See also* Exclusionary displacement
Marshall Heights Community Development Organization, 167–174, 213
Marxism, 215
Mass displacement, 156
Mayfair Mansions, *108*, 109–110, *111*, 113; and buyouts, 138, *143*, *144*, 150n21, 156; and developers, 166, 172, 216; and displacement,

INDEX

123, 175, 210; and Housing Production Trust Fund, 213; low-income residences at, 158, 174, 213, 216; and Rick Eisen, 169; tenants' association at, 168; tenants who stayed put at, *122*; and TOPA process, 137, 156–158, 166–174, 180, 216; and urban (dis)investment, 134; and voluntary agreements, 147, 148n
McKinney, Stuart, 100–101
Mercy Housing, 176–178
Mercy Loan Fund, 176
Meridian Hill Park, 109
Mi Casa, 176, 178–179, 212n
Middle-class flight, 4, 166
Millennials, 16–17, 33, 223
Milloy, Courtland, 71–74, 79
Moreland, Genevieve, 134–136, 141–142, 149–151, 164–165. *See also* Harvard/Summit
Mount Pleasant, 190
Murder capital, DC as, 5–6, 33, 51, 75
Mutual housing associations, 27

Nathan, Robert, 100–101
National Capital Redevelopment Corporation (NCRC), 133
National Cathedral, 20n, 109
National Guard, 9, *11*
National Housing Act of 1934, 234
National Housing Act of 1961, 97n6
National Labor Relations Board, 44
National Low Income Housing Coalition, 17
Nationals stadium, 81
Nation of Islam, 166
Neo-Keynesianism, 215
Neoliberalism, 45–50; and condos, 22–24, 103–104, 156; in DC, 33, 48–50, 61, 64, 72, 91; and empowerment, 214–215; and gentrification, 15; and local autonomy, 26–27; and TOPA, 209–210, 215–219, 221–224
Neoliberal urbanism, 218
New Hampshire Avenue, 174
New York Avenue, 54
95/5 transfer, 114, 181–208, 209, 212, 226
Nonconforming loans, 163
North Capital Street, 174
Northeast quadrant, 72, 78
North of Massachusetts (NOMA), 54
Northwest quadrant, 88

O'Cleireacain, Carol, 51–54, 57. *See also* Adult strategy; Family strategy
Office of the Deputy Mayor for Planning and Economic Development, 133n11

"One-drop rule," 77
100 percent transfer, 114, 181, 184
Orange, Vincent, 80
Owens, Cajia, 135–136, 142. *See also* Garden Towers

Parliament (band), 18
Penn Quarter, 63
Persistent poverty, 35, 38, 47
Petworth, 117
Pieterse, Edgar, 221–222, 224
"The Plan," 71–74
Plotkin, Mark, 77
PN Hoffman, 182
Politics of staying put, 32, 209–210
Portfolio lenders, 163
Potomac River, 49, 52
Prince, Sabiyha, 74n5
Prince of Petworth, 84–85
Private mortgage insurance (PMI), 151
Privatization, 48, 61, 216
P Street, 6, *8*, *9*, *12*, *13*, 14, 116
Public benefit corporation (PBC), 59
Public goods, 47, 215
public-private partnerships, 48, 133

Quarry Enterprises, 191, 198

Race: and Adrian Fenty, 77–80; and community and collectivity, 104, 118; and condo conversion, 169; and DC history, 4, 21; and DC population demographics, 38–39; and displacement, 18, 83–85, 89; and gentrification, 34, 38–39, *40*, 67–89, 169; and "The Plan," 74; and TOPA, 87–89, 104, 118, 130–131, 228. *See also* Displacement; "The Plan"
"Race war," 74
Radical incrementalism, 221–222, 224
Randolph, William, 25–26
Reagan, Ronald, 15, 46
"Realization crises," 44n12
Reconstruction period, 68
Reed, Jenny, 220
Reinvestment, 2–3, 15–17, 22, 27, 137
Rental Housing Act of 1977, 97
Rental Housing Conversion and Sale Act (1980; RHCSA), 18–19, 31, 90–91, 95–103, 105, 109, 120, 124, 127, 138, 184, 210, 219
Revanchism, 23, 101, 103–105
Revitalization, 29, 65, 227
Rhee, Michelle, 54, 57–58, 78–79
Right of first refusal, 18–19, 90–92, 94, 97, 100–104, 118, 124, 126, 131, 133, 158–159,

Right of first refusal (*continued*) 168, 185, 192, 195, 203, 217, 222–223; refusal to accept buyouts, 123; right to offer buyouts, 19, 95; right to purchase, 18, 91, 96, 104, 156, 192, 199, 201, 212, 214, 216–217, 222–223, 228
Riots, 9, *11*, 84, 166
Rivlin, Alice, 51–54, 57
Rock Creek Park, 6, 58, 113, 126, 147
Rome, Eric: on affordable housing, 216; and buyouts, 109, 138, 141–143, 150, 223; and "Can you top this?" strategy, 124, 132; on condos, 29n, 94n, 163–164; and Harvard/Summit, 124, 141, 149–150, 164n, 225; and 95/5 transfers, 188–189; and the Squire, 149n, 162n7, 225; and TOPA process, 29n, 109, 124, 162n7, 217, 228–229; and voluntary agreements, 109, 149, 150, 225. *See also* Eisen, Rick; Moreland, Genevieve
Rothman, George, 109, 159–160
Rural Housing Service (RHS), 161

Samuels, John, 191–193, 202–208
San Francisco City Council, 3
Schaffer, Michael, 88–89
Schneider, Cathy, 191–194, 197, 200–204, 206–208
Segregation, 81, 166
Shin, Annys, 226–227
Silverman, Dan, 84–85
Single Purchase and Sale Agreement, 191, 197
Smith, Neil, 2, 16, 23, 24, 70, 108
Social determinants of health, 60
Social justice, 28, 90, 118, 156, 180, 209–210, 214–215, 219
Southwest quadrant, 111
The Squire, *108*, 112, 113; and buyouts, 139–146, 150, 223; and developers, 162–163, 223, 225–226; and hybrid condo conversion, 162–163; and landlord bullying, 139; tentants who stayed put at, *122*; and voluntary agreements, 146, 148–150, 225–226. *See also* Rome, Eric
Steptoe and Johnson, 195
Stray-Gundersen, Kay, 95
Subprime mortgages, 128, 160–162
Suburbanization, 15, 23, 44, 47, 49
Summit Street, 112, 141, 142
Superior Court of the District of Columbia, 61, 97–98, 195
Surplus value, 44n12
Swagger jacking, 74–77, 81, 83–85, 87

Tax Payer Relief Act (1997), 54
Tenacity Group, 103, 126, 128–133, 135, 193
"Tenant capitalism," 216
Tenant lawsuits, 190, 194–200, 218
Tenleytown, 55, 78
Third-wave gentrification, 108–109
Thompson, Jeffery, 60–61
Tibbs, Matthew, 126–130, 134, 139. *See also* Cathedral Court
Tivoli Theatre, 11, 13
TOPA (Tenant Opportunity to Purchase Act), 1–2; and displacement, 1–2, 19, 22, 30–31, 65, 115, 117, 120–157, 179–180, 208, 210–212, 214, 219–221; and gentrification, 21–22, 26, 28, 87–89, 101, 105, 119–121, 123, 156–157, 159, 179–180, 202, 215, 218–219; and race, 87–89, 104, 118, 130–131, 228; and RHCSA, 18–19, 90–105, 120, 124, 138, 184. *See also* Displacement; Gentrification; Race; Rental Housing Conversion and Sale Act (1980; RHCSA); TOPA notice
TOPA notice, 2, 91, 114, 166, 168, 181–183, 185, 203–204, 228
Town Center, *108*, 111–112, 113; affordable housing at, 150, *151*, 154, 156; and buyouts, 139, 142, *143*, *144*; and developers, 159; and displacement, 210; insider prices and condo conversion at, 125, 130–134, 159; and landlord bullying, 139; tenants who stayed put at, *122*; and urban (dis)investment, 134; and voluntary agreements, 147, 150, *151*. *See also* Klouj, Afifa
Tregoning, Harriet, 227
2008 recession: and DC finances, 5; and homelessness in DC, 63, 65; and housing market in DC, 56, 94, 109, 140, 146, 155, 160, 162–163, 165–166, 173, 176, 178–179; and persistent poverty in DC, 38

UnitedHealthcare, 59
Unity Co-op, 175–179
University Legal Services for the District of Columbia (ULS-DC), 138n
Urban commons, 215, 223
Urban disinvestment, 4, 15, 17, 23, 27, 30, 44, 49, 119, 134–135, 137–138, 148, 159
"Urban entrepreneurialism," 16
Urban Investment Partners (UIP), 102–103, 134, 149–150, 155, 225–226
Urban pioneers, 16, 69–71. *See also* Creative class
Urban reinvestment, 2–3, 15–17, 22, 27, 137
Urban rental stock, 19, 41, 96, 102

INDEX

Urban revitalization, 29, 65, 227
U.S. Government Accountability Office (GAO), 5
U Street, 6, 9, 11, 33, 75, 82–84, 109, 117, 226

Vacatello, Juan Pablo, 179
Verizon Center, 63
Veterans Administration (VA), 161
"Virtuous circle," 43
Voluntary agreements, 109, 138, 146–157, 211–212, 219–222, 225–226. *See also* Buyouts

Wall Street, 160, 176
Warehousing model, 62–63, 65
Washington Home Ownership Council, 97
Washington Legal Clinic for the Homeless, 65
Wekerle, Gerda, 23–24

White House, 47, 63
Whitelegg, Drew, 25–26, 30, 157. *See also* Condo conversion
Wiggins, Lillian, 71–72
Williams, Anthony, 50, 54–55, 59, 77
Wilson, Charles, 98–101
Wilson Building, 61, 165
Wisconsin Avenue, 6
Wizards (NBA team), 63
World War II, 15, 40, 43, 109, 110, 124, 234

Yards Park, 81
Yates, Clinton, 71–72, 74
Yglesias, Matthew, 73. *See also* "The Plan"

Zapata, Raenelle, 182, 186–187, 189
Zone in transition, 8

Carolyn Gallaher is Associate Professor in the School of International Service at American University. She is the author of *On the Fault Line: Race, Class, and the American Patriot Movement* and *After the Peace: Loyalist Paramilitaries in Post-accord Northern Ireland*.